THE FUTURE OF EDUCATION

THE FUTURE OF EDUCATION
Perspectives on National Standards in America

NINA COBB, editor

With an introduction by Robert Orrill

College Entrance Examination Board, New York

The College Board is a national nonprofit association that champions educational excellence for all students through the ongoing collaboration of more than 2,900 member schools, colleges, universities, education systems, and associations. The Board promotes—by means of responsive forums, research, programs, and policy development—universal access to high standards of learning, equity of opportunity, and sufficient financial support so that every student is prepared for success in college and work.

"Curriculum Ferment in the 1890s" by Dr. Herbert M. Kliebard originally appeared in the *The Struggle for the American Curriculum, 1893–1958* and is used by permission of the author.

"The Politics of National Standards" originally appeared in the October 6, 1993 issue of *Education Week* and is used by permission of the author.

"The Threat to Freedom in Goals 2000" orginally appeared in the April 16, 1994 issue of *Education Week* and is used by permission of the author.

"Policy and Practice: The Relations between Governance and Instruction" originally appeared in *Review of Research in Education 18.* Copyright 1992 by the American Educational Research Association. Reprinted by permission of the publisher.

"Problems and Issues Facing the National Standards Project in English" originally appeared in *Education and Urban Society* 26:2 (February 1994) and is reprinted by permission of Corwin Press, Inc.

In all of its publishing activities, the College Board endeavors to present the works of authors who are well qualified to write with authority on the subject at hand and to present accurate and timely information. However, the opinions, interpretations, and conclusions of the authors are their own and do not necessarily represent those of the College Board; nothing contained herein should be assumed to represent an official position of the College Board or any of its members.

Copies of this publication can be ordered from College Board Publications, Box 886, New York, NY 10101-0886. The price is $16.95.

Library of Congress Catalog Number: 94-068877
International Standard Book Number: 0-87447-530-9

Printed in the United States of America

CONTENTS

I. INTRODUCTION

II. CURRICULUM, HISTORY, AND STANDARDS

III. PERSPECTIVES ON NATIONAL STANDARDS

IV. STANDARDS AND EDUCATIONAL POLICY

PART I

INTRODUCTION

1

Titanic Structure or Human Scale: School Reform at the Close of the Twentieth Century

ROBERT ORRILL

Robert Orrill is executive director, Office of Academic Affairs, The College Board

It is a given in most current writing about education that our schools need reforming. This belief derives from many sources, but observers frequently cite the publication of *A Nation At Risk* in 1983 as its most seminal point. Employing unusually militant language, this report of the National Commission on Excellence in Education sought to substantiate that something had gone seriously wrong with our educational system and argued that, in consequence, the nation itself was in dire peril. In one among a number of much quoted statements, the commissioners warned that "the educational foundations of our society are presently being eroded by a rising tide of mediocrity that threatens our very future as a nation and a people" (National Commission on Excellence in Education 1983). While sometimes questioned, this grave view still casts a long shadow over debates about the future of our public schools (Angus and Mirel 1993). More than a decade later, for example, one hears the current chairman of IBM saying that the schools are failing and, in so doing, are pushing the country into "a deeply dangerous situation." By failure, he means that the schools are not producing "a labor force that is prepared to solve problems and compete on a global level." The only solution that will save the economy, he claims, is to arrive at "a national strategy for resurgence that reaches every school in the country" (Gerstner 1994).

Doubtless, our schools do face serious challenges and an uncertain future. We would be the victims of a harmful complacency to think otherwise. Nonetheless, it may be useful to pause as we near the threshold of a new century and ask if we have matters in proportion. Why is it that reformers think all of our problems as a nation should be handed to schools to solve? Often, as John Goodlad says, this leads to "an orgy of unrealistic expectations for our schools" (Goodlad and Keating 1994). Never mind education for thoughtful citizenship. We also enjoin schools to do everything from curing social injustice to propelling the nation to the forefront of global economic competition. Indeed, schools get the blame when we as a people seem to falter in almost any fundamental respect. It is telling, of course, that they get none of the credit at present when the economy appears once again to be on the upswing after the "crisis" of a few years ago. Far too often, schools serve as scapegoats for the failure of other institutions and for social ills that they had no part in making. The resulting "bashing" of schools and teachers helps nothing and hinders constructive action.

One difficulty with crisis rhetoric is that it tends to suppress or devalue modest initiatives. In a "national emergency" how can small measures count for much? Moreover, such rhetoric seeks to persuade that the times we find ourselves in are unique, when a clear understanding probably depends much more on our seeing the extent to which current problems are continuations of older ones. A Nation At Risk, for example, warns that our "society and its educational institutions seem to have lost sight of the basic purposes of schooling, and of the high expectations and disciplined effort needed to attain them" (National Commission on Excellence in Education 1983, 5–6). In fact, in this century we have never had a genuinely stable consensus about either the purpose of the public schools or the kind and level of performance that we want from students when they graduate from them.[1] It does not help, therefore, to misconstrue the current situation as one in which certainty has given way to confusion. In many important respects, we are not currently experiencing such a sharp departure from previous conditions. Rather, we are closer to the mark if we see how long unresolved rivalries and deep instabilities have always made a shared conception of schooling difficult to achieve.

School reform, in fact, must be regarded as a contested tradition, not one in which agreement has been the rule. Therefore this collection of

[1]See any history of public schools and curriculum such as Kliebard, Herbert M., *The Struggle for the American Curriculum, 1893–1958*. New York and London: Routledge, 1986; Krug, Edward A., *The Shaping of the American High School*. New York, Evanston, and London: Harper & Row, 1964; Tanner, Daniel and Laurel Tanner, *History of the School Curriculum*. New York: Macmillan Publishing Company, London: Collier Macmillan Publishers, 1990.

essays and commentaries about the future of public education begins with an excerpt from Herbert Kliebard's historical prologue to this century's curriculum debates. In this selection, the terms that Kliebard employs to describe our experience are not ones of consensus but of continuing "struggle." If our schools ever worked well or knew what they were about, there were always reformers who urged that they had it wrong. Moreover, reformers argued most fiercely among themselves and against one another. As Kliebard points out, "there was not one but several reform movements in education during the twentieth century each with a distinct agenda for action" (Kliebard 1986, 29). Over time, these agendas did not supersede one another, though sometimes one or the other may appear to have gained the upper hand. Rather, they persistently clashed in their ideas about what schools should be as well as in their definitions of what kind of learning is most worthwhile. Moreover, no settled outcome has yet been reached. Instead, Kliebard writes, "what became the American curriculum was not the result of any decisive victory of any of the contending parties, but a loose, largely unarticulated, and not very tidy compromise."

National Standards

Unquestionably, it would be all to the good if we as a nation had a more settled and commonly shared understanding of what public schools should reasonably be expected to do. Now, some reformers believe that we have taken a giant step toward this resolution with the recent passage of the Goals 2000: Educate America Act. This law is the springboard for a reform strategy with the national scope wanted by the chair of IBM and others. Advocates of this legislation explain that its intent is to bring about an "unprecedented shift in educational practice in the country" by opening the way for the establishment of "voluntary national education standards, or explicit expectations of what students should know and be able to do" (Smith, Fuhrman, and O'Day 1994). These advocates often point to the Curriculum Standards issued in March 1989, by the National Council of Teachers of Mathematics (NCTM) as a model for the kind of guidance needed in other "core" subject areas.[2] It is important to note, however, that NCTM undertook this standards work on its own initiative in the early 1980s because of a growing sense among professionals that new developments in the field called for a redefinition of school mathematics. In this case, then, the impetus came from a need to take account of substantial

[2]The designated subject areas are English, arts, foreign languages, geography, history, civics, mathematics, and science.

intellectual change within the discipline. The mathematics community was pursuing fresh vision, not reacting to a government mandate.

In this regard, contributor Diane Massell points out that the situation is significantly different in the case of professional organizations now beginning to develop standards in other subject areas. Here, federal agencies have played a large role in funding and launching the initiatives, acting under a political imperative to fill out the full standards framework envisioned in Goals 2000. Unlike the case of mathematics, it is not at all clear that professionals in many of these other subject areas share the view that a consensus about standards is either desirable or necessary in their fields at the present moment. Many, in fact, believe that intellectual developments in their subject areas are moving too rapidly to warrant constraining definitional moves. They worry that something quite inert, and not animating, will result if government reformers continue to insist on a "single set of standards" to govern their work. Indeed, in his section Myron Atkin points out that it is this need to take account of current disciplinary complexity and flux that is leading many countries in Europe and Asia to take a more flexible stance toward standards. With some exceptions, the keynote abroad appears to be on opening the curriculum to a wider range of viewpoints rather than settling on fixed answers. Reformers should bear this in mind when they speak of our need for "world class standards."

From a variety of perspectives, many of the selections in this book explore the serious tensions that may develop when government policies conflict with the judgment of professionals in a field. Such tensions are already apparent. In a controversial case, the federal Department of Education recently withdrew its financial support for the standards project in the English Language Arts because, in its estimation, the professional groups undertaking it were not making "substantial progress." This action, of course, involved clear differences between the agency and professionals about both the form and substance of appropriate standards. According to B. David Pearson, the dean of education at the University of Illinois, and director of the Language Arts project, it also sought to make clear who was in charge. Indeed, his reaction to the news of the government's action may signal the end of innocence among professionals regarding who, in fact, is really managing the national standards enterprise. "I thought we were developing these standards for kids, their parents, and their teachers," Pearson said. "Apparently, the federal government was the real audience all along" (Pearson 1994).

Most probably, the nation's teachers will not be encouraged by these recent events in English Language Arts or otherwise be inspired by standards that they have little role in shaping. In a later section, Massell points out that the experience of many teachers "is that government is an intrusive entity, that it has steadily eroded their professional autonomy, and that they must protect themselves from it as much as possible." How then will they respond to the heightened government activism envisioned in the Goals 2000 legislation? Much hangs on the answer to this question. It is, after all, only teachers who can transform standards into real, concrete experiences for students; and they are not likely to do this with enthusiasm if new expectations fail to reflect sound professional judgment about teaching and learning or do not emanate from a credible source. This means that standards must reflect best practice, not what is deemed politically acceptable at a given moment in time or what is dictated by governmental fiat.

We will return to the question of the role of teachers in standards setting again in this introduction. It may be useful, however, to say something briefly about an overarching criticism that has been made about all of the subject area standards, to the extent that they are intelligible from the drafts that have appeared to date. Simply stated, the problem is how they all hang together. Following the lead of government, each subject area has set about its task separately, in splendid isolation from all the others, and without any prior deliberation regarding basic assumptions or arrangement for ongoing consultation about work in progress. Not surprisingly, then, the draft documents now emerging vary significantly in format, terminology, and even understanding of the definition and purpose of standards. In consequence, critics rightly point out that both practitioners and the public will experience much confusion when they try to comprehend the standards and relate them one to another. This, of course, poses a major problem for their ultimate acceptance and use.

Moreover, critics charge that the standards documents exhibit a crushing weight when taken either separately or together. There are "too many" subjects and "too much" in each of them. Speakers at conferences now vie for laughs by projecting the age of a high school graduate who would in fact "know and be able to do" all that the subject areas are proclaiming as necessary (so far, I've heard "28," "44," and "the time of eligibility for Social Security"). Indeed, some have questioned the motives of the subject areas, asserting that what is involved in the standards projects is more a grab for resources and time in the school day than a genuine concern about student learning. This does not seem warranted. The subject areas did not ask for things to be done this way. It is true, however, that the sheer quantity of the standards threatens to produce a situation in which the standards will "collide" and "compete" with one another in actual school settings rather than make a coherent whole. Thus, the standards in their current form do not appear to offer a genuine cure for the frag-

mentation and congestion from which the school curriculum has long suffered. Indeed, they could exacerbate these problems.

Taken together, these criticisms have resulted in a call from some
quarters for a second and more defining stage in the standards development process—one in which the standards are "cut down to size" and
"rationalized" across subject areas. This is sometimes referred to as
"standardizing the standards." Doubtless, serious and sustained attention
to connections across subject areas is vitally important, but this again
raises serious questions for educators. Who will do this and through what
structure and process? Will federal and state governments seek to control
any such efforts, even though they have little expertise to bring to bear
on disciplinary issues? In sum, will it be done on a genuinely substantive
basis; or will it be nothing more than a politically negotiated "cut and
paste" job with decisions brought forth once again on the basis of so
many hours of this or that? We must hope not. Such a course of action
would tend only to encourage subject area professionals to compete for
time and resources rather than to cooperate and work in concert. This is
a failed path that political conditions have forced upon curriculum decision making many times in the past; and it is not one that serves the
needs of students or supports the development of a shared educational
vision.

The Goals 2000: Educate America Act

The idea, of course, is not that the "national standards" should exist in
some disembodied state. Instead, they are to be nested in a structure of
newly conceived political and governmental interactions. This introduction can touch only on a few of the many complex issues raised by the
full Goals 2000 reform plan. A host of others have been raised by the
contributors to this volume. Indeed, this book is intended as an invitation
to educators to enter into conversation about these questions, to pose
others, and to participate actively in shaping answers that currently are
in short supply. One of the contributors, Tom Loveless, alerts us that this
chance is rapidly slipping away if it has not already been lost. The reform
aspirations of the 1980s, he argues, may in fact represent "a missed opportunity to debate and resolve what our schools are about, a lost opportunity to sharpen the purpose of schooling in America."

The reason, Loveless says, is the nature of the Goals 2000: Educate
America Act. Like David Pearson, he finds that the intent of this legislation
is not to speak directly to, or elicit the judgment of, teachers and professional educators. "School personnel," he writes, "are not the audience for

this legislation; more than anything else, Goals 2000 consists of a conversation among governments—federal, state, and local." Loveless summarizes the "intergovernmental thrust" of the bill in this way:

> The legislation relies upon the elaborate machinery of governmental bureaucracies to operate as a catalyst for school reform. The federal government will tell state governments that they need to do better, state governments will tell local districts that they need to do better, and principals will tell teachers that they need to do better—trickle down school reform.

Loveless concludes by saying that "the bill proclaims to layers of government that education needs fundamental reform, ignoring the teachers, students, and parents who sit at the center of educational efforts."

It is unlikely that advocates of Goals 2000 would agree with this characterization of how the legislation will work, but few, if any, would deny that its intent is indeed to strengthen the hand of government in school reform. This strengthening is to take place mostly at state and federal levels. Implicit in the act is the aim of further diminishing, even extinguishing, our long tradition of local control in U.S. schools. Indeed, Elmore and Fuhrman, two policy analysts writing in support of Goals 2000, predict that its "unfolding processes will almost certainly mean that traditional conceptions of local control will become increasingly unworkable in the future" (Fuhrman and Elmore 1944, 211).

Fuhrman and Elmore further tell us that, in future, the "first, most basic political reality is that curriculum decisions will be made in state and national arenas, rather than exclusively in local and school-level arenas." The Goals 2000 legislation helps curriculum making along toward "a more national focus" by creating two new quasi-governmental agencies: an expanded National Education Goals Panel (NEGP) and a National Educational Standards and Improvement Council (NESIC). Much is unclear about the operation of these two agencies, but we do know that the membership of the first will consist entirely of political officeholders and that of the second of political appointees. An explicit aim, then, is to politicize many important aspects of educational decision making with the intention of gaining broad political and public support for reform measures. A primary responsibility of NESIC will be to "certify" national standards for K through 12 education in eight designated subject areas. In a related function, it will determine how education reform plans developed by states conform to or reflect these national standards. In time, NESIC may also judge whether assessments are aligned with these standards; but how it will do any of these things is as yet largely undetermined.

Advocates of Goals 2000 are quick to defend these moves against charges of increasing federal intervention in educational matters. Elmore and Fuhrman strongly assert that to "say . . . curriculum is increasingly a subject for national policy debate is *not* equivalent to saying that the federal government will get into the business of making curriculum policy any more than it has in the past." This, of course, is more than a little disingenuous. What is it when federal legislation designates some subject areas as part of the "core curriculum" while remaining silent about others? Or when it privileges work in subject areas over interdisciplinary learning? Or when it does not recognize a long-standing organizing principle for the curriculum, such as "social studies," which is prominent in most schools? All of these things are curriculum making writ very large.

Fuhrman and Elmore, however, do fully acknowledge that the intent of Goals 2000 is to politicize school reform and the "governance of curriculum." In their view, this only makes explicit and potentially more manageable what has always been implicit but only haphazardly understood. "The political nature of curriculum," they write, "is deeply knit into the history of education in the United States." It follows for them, therefore, that if "we can't keep politics out of curriculum, then perhaps we should think about how to harness basic political processes to the improvement of curriculum." The publication they have edited, in fact, is presented as a kind of "how to" book (they call it a "short course") for educational professionals in "the politics of curriculum reform and governance."

Being perceptive policy analysts, Fuhrman and Elmore recognize that their urgings may not be consistent with values educators hold very deeply. Teachers, especially, are likely to believe that expert judgment should count for much more than political weight in making decisions about student learning. In addition, they are also likely to think that judgments about curriculum are better arrived at collegially than by the actions of governments and politicians. Politics may be involved in both processes, but it is of very different kinds. In collegial activities, authority is arrived at *between* professionals—not handed down from above as in the case of governmental processes. Moreover, as Michael Polanyi has explained, collegial authority is "essentially mutual," something created and shared in common among a community of professionals (Polanyi 1969). When you intervene in such communities from without, on the authority of some higher or central agency, the result is to constrain, even paralyze, cooperation among colleagues.

It may also be important to bear in mind that, while politicians disagree mightily among themselves, they are unlikely to tolerate much disagreement among academics about educational standards. This could be very damaging to the standards movement, because disagreement is, in fact, essential to the "living" nature of standards. Standards must always be open to further discussion and revision. If this is not the case, standards fall short of being standards. They become only regulations. Polanyi pointed out that, when standards are taken seriously in a professional community, they inherently have in them an always present "internal tension" between orthodoxy and dissent. Without dissent, there can be no change and no growth. Inherent in serious standards, then, is a "dual function." On one hand, they press for conformity to a consensus viewpoint; but, on the other, they encourage an originality that is critical of consensus positions. If standards are to be generative in the work of teachers, not sterile prescriptions, they must have in them this dynamic capacity to cut both ways, both to create consensus and to provoke disagreement with the same consensus.

It is not at all clear, however, that Goals 2000 reformers care about collegiality among teachers or think that it matters very much in bringing about needed change. Their first and foremost concern is with transformation on the largest possible scale, not on a teacher-to-teacher or teacher-to-student basis. They are intent that everyone, at all levels of education, becomes more accountable to a larger national "system." As they see it, this system should have its locus in state governments that operate under the influence of an "increasing consensus on national purposes" for education. How this influence will be exercised remains a somewhat murky matter, but in their chapter, Kirst and Guthrie provide a valuable analysis of how federal funding programs may be employed to effect educational decisions at state and local levels. In any case, the intention to constrain local automony is clear enough. If Fuhrman and Elmore are correct, increasing "interdependencies" among levels of government—national, state, and local—will make it "increasingly difficult to argue that schools or districts should be allowed to operate as if they were not part of a broader system" (212).

Unsurprisingly, it is not anticipated that this "systematizing" trend will make educational decision making any simpler or more straightforward. Instead, Fuhrman and Elmore expect that these complicated interactions among levels of government will "increase the complexity of decisions about what gets taught to whom, and with what effect" (212). As they see it, it will be necessary for teachers and educators to develop a much greater degree of "political sophistication" if they are to enter and influence this "conversation among governments." This should give us serious pause. Is this really how we want teachers to be spending their time? Do we want them engaging in time-consuming political processes or to be in the classroom with their students? Should they give as much attention to the acquisition of political skills and systems analyses as to gaining command of their subject areas? Somehow reform appears to have gotten its priorities a curious way round. It seems now that teachers must first learn the "system" before they can effectively work with students.

This appears to be where the reform impulse of the 1980s has brought us. In the minds of some influential reformers, the size of the perceived crisis dictates the large scale of the needed intervention. More than a decade ago, the reform movement helped place the twin goals of equity and excellence at the forefront of the education agenda. The acknowledged need was to provide a more challenging education for all, not just some, of our students. This goal remains, but some reform leaders are now convinced that it can be attained only through a combination of political maneuver and systems engineering on the largest possible scale. Small deeds and everyday victories do not seem to count for much. Teachers, it seems, will just have to figure out how their work with students fits into a complex, very large, essentially political structure. This evokes an image, called to mind by George Santayana, of the great buildings of the world that are fronted by great doors. These great doors, he observed, were heavy to swing in their immensity and, if left open, let in too much cold or glare. So a much smaller door had to be cut in the larger one "for more convenient entrance and exit." This he characterized eloquently as "the modest human scale reasserting itself in the midst of titanic structure (Santayana 1968)." If Goals 2000 moves forward as some envision it, we may find that the future of education in this country will depend upon the cutting of many such small doors.

Acknowledgments

The contributions to this volume provide a variety of perspectives on national standards and school reform. If anything unites them all, it is a willingness to take up questions raised by the national standards movement and to search into them from an inquiring rather than a polemical stance. The authors of these essays and commentaries often do take strong positions, but they never do so at the expense of simplifying the complexity of the issues they are addressing. This is a volume, therefore, that is characterized more by sharp questions than by a uniform point of view. Its great value, we believe, is in how much the contributions, taken together, increase our own capacity to think critically about the Goals 2000 school reform initiative.

Several of the papers in this book were originally commissioned as resources for a conference on standards and school reform sponsored by the Forum on Standards and Learning. Others were added as a result of continuing discussions among participants at that conference. The Forum is cosponsored by the College Board and six national subject-matter organizations—the National Council of Teachers of Mathematics, the National Council of Teachers of English, the National Science Teachers Association, the National Council for the Social Studies, the Music Educators National Conference, and the American Council on the Teaching of Foreign Languages. Together, these associations represent more than 280,000 teachers and educators nationwide, as well as several thousand secondary and postsecondary institutions across the country.

As a result of the conference, the sponsoring associations set in motion a plan to create an operational alliance that will enable educators to address issues that cut across, and extend beyond, the standards work now underway in many specific subject areas. The purposes of the alliance are:

- to address questions of overall purpose and coherence in elementary and secondary education;
- to sustain the integrity of academic standards produced by subject area professionals, including providing assistance for ongoing evaluation and revision;
- to illuminate common and connecting principles of learning that should be fostered across subject areas;
- to promote the generative, rather than prescriptive, nature of standards in contributing to the professional growth of teachers and other educational practitioners.

As an offspring of the Forum, this book is the result of a collegial effort. Along the way to completion, many hands joined in its making. We are grateful to all who contributed and apologize that lack of space makes it impossible to recognize each individually. Special thanks go to the authors and to the editor, Nina Cobb. Finally, but not least, the book could not have entered the world without the careful attention given to it by Hannah Selby, Madelyn Roesch, Dorothy Downie, Peter Nelson, and Geoffrey Kirshner.

References

Angus, David, and Jeffrey Mirel. Nov. 17, 1993. "High School Course-Taking and Educational Reform." *Education Week.*

Fuhrman, Susan, H., and Richard F. Elmore. 1994. "Education Professionals and Curriculum Governance," *The Governance of Curriculum*, Yearbook. Alexandria, Va.: Association for Supervision and Curriculum Development.

Gerstner, Louis V., Jr. May 27, 1994. "Our Schools Are Failing. Do We Care?" *The New York Times.*

Goodlad, John I., and Pamela Keating. 1994. *Access to Knowledge*. New York: The College
  Board.
Kliebard, Herbert M. 1986. *The Struggle for the American Curriculum, 1893–1958*. New York
  and London: Routledge.
National Commission on Excellence in Education. 1983. *A Nation at Risk*. Washington, D.C.:
  U.S. Department of Education.
Pearson, B. David. March 30, 1994. Quoted by Karen Diegmueller in "English Group Loses
  Funding for Standards." *Education Week*.
Polanyi, Michael. 1969. "The Republic of Science: Its Political and Economic Theory." In
  Knowing and Being. Chicago: University of Chicago Press.
Santayana, George. 1968. "The Human Scale." In *Selected Critical Writings of George San-
  tayana, Volume 2*. Cambridge, England: Cambridge University Press.
Smith, Marshall S., Susan H. Fuhrman, and Jennifer O'Day. 1994. "National Curriculum Stan-
  dards: Are They Desirable and Feasible?" *The Governance of Curriculum*, Yearbook. Al-
  exandria, Va.: Association for Supervision and Curriculum Development.

**PART
II**

CURRICULUM, HISTORY, AND STANDARDS

2

Curriculum Ferment
in the 1890s

HERBERT M. KLIEBARD

Herbert M. Kliebard is a professor in the department of Educational Policy Studies at the University of Wisconsin–Madison.

At the heart of America's education system in the nineteenth century was the teacher. It was the teacher, ill-trained, harassed and underpaid, often immature, who was expected to embody the standard virtues and community values and, at the same time, to mete out stern discipline to the unruly and dull-witted. But, by the 1890s, nineteenth-century society with its reliance on the face-to-face community was clearly in decline, and with the recognition of social change came a radically altered vision of the role of schooling. As cities grew, the schools were no longer the direct instruments of a visible and unified community. Rather, they became an ever-more critical mediating institution between the family and a puzzling and impersonal social order, an institution through which the norms and ways of surviving in the new industrial society would be conveyed. Traditional family life was not only in decline; even when it remained stable, it was no longer deemed sufficient to initiate the young into a complex and technological world.

With the change in the social role of the school came a change in the educational center of gravity; it shifted from the tangible presence of the teacher to the remote knowledge and values incarnate in the curriculum. By the 1890s, the forces that were to struggle for control of the American curriculum were in place, and the early part of the twentieth century became the battleground for that struggle.

Preoccupation with the curriculum did not, of course, appear suddenly full-blown. There had been signs earlier in the nineteenth century of a growing attention to what had become the course of study in American schools. From about 1800 to 1830, the monitorial method, an English export, had enjoyed a short-lived favor in cities like New York and Philadelphia, and the Lancastrian system, as it was sometimes called, required a careful breakdown of the course of study into standard units of work (Kaestle 1973). Perhaps the most profound standardizing influence on the curriculum of nineteenth-century schools was the widespread use of popular textbooks such as the McGuffey reading series and the famous blueback spellers. Insofar as poorly educated teachers had to rely on such textbooks as the standard for what to teach, these books contributed to a growing nationalization of the curriculum. In Chicago, between 1856 and 1864, the superintendent of schools, William Harvey Wells, divided all students in the city into grades and established a distinct course of study for each subject at each grade level (Tyack 1974, 45–6). This early attention to curriculum was a portent of what, in the twentieth century, became a national preoccupation.

Public Awareness of Social Change

Although changes in American society were being wrought throughout most of the nineteenth century, public awareness of those changes seemed to reach crisis proportions in the 1890s. An acute public awareness of the social changes that had been taking place for some time was tied to such developments as a tremendous growth in popular journalism in the late nineteenth century, including both magazines and newspapers, and also the powerful influence created by the rapid advance of railroads as a means of relatively cheap and reliable transportation. Both these developments, in addition to the continued growth of cities, were significant factors in the transformation of American society from one characterized by relatively isolated self-contained communities into an urban, industrial nation. The decade of the 1870s, for example, was a period in which the sheer number of newspapers in America doubled, and by 1880 the *New York Graphic* published the first photographic reproduction in a newspaper, portending a dramatic rise in readership. Between 1882 and 1886 alone, the price of daily newspapers dropped from four cents per copy to one cent, due largely to the success enjoyed by Joseph Pulitzer's *New York World* (Mott 1941, 508), and the introduction in 1890 of the first successful Linotype machine promised even further growth. In 1872, only two American daily newspapers could claim a circulation of over 100,000, but, by 1892, seven more newspapers exceeded that figure (507). A world beyond the immediate community was rapidly becoming visible.

But it was not newspapers alone that were bringing this new consciousness to Americans in the late nineteenth century. Magazines as we know them today began publication around 1882, and, in fact, the circulation of weekly magazines in America exceeded that of newspapers in the period that followed. By 1892, for example, the circulation of *Ladies Home Journal* had reached an astounding 700,000 (507). Neither should book readership be ignored. Edward Bellamy's utopian and socialist-leaning novel *Looking Backward* sold over a million copies in 1888, giving rise to the growth of organizations dedicated to the realization of Bellamy's ideas. The printed word, unquestionably, was intruding on the insulation that had characterized American society in an earlier period.

Of at least equal importance to mass circulation journalism was the effect on American social life of the growth of railroads in the late nineteenth century. By 1880, the East and the Midwest had adopted four feet eight inches as the standard track gauge, but the overwhelming majority of the southern track lines were five feet, and the western states had laid very narrow track lines in the early 1880s. By 1883, however, leaders of the railroad industry had created the system of standardized time zones that we use today, and, by the end of that decade, most railroad track in the United States had become standardized.

In 1889, the United States already had 125,000 miles of railroad in operation, whereas Great Britain had only about 20,000 miles and Russia 19,000. As Robert Wiebe (1967) has pointed out, "The primary significance of America's new railroad complex lay not in the dramatic connections between New York and San Francisco but in the access a Kewanee, Illinois, or an Aberdeen, South Dakota, enjoyed to the rest of the nation, and the nation to it" (47). Like mass journalism, railroads were penetrating the towns and villages across the United States, creating not only new industries and new markets, but changing social attitudes and remaking our sense of what kind of world we were living in.

For a time, that social transformation seemed almost unacknowledged, or, in some cases, attributable to radical influences or other visible enemies. By the 1890s, however, the signs of change were unmistakable, although these signs were sometimes viewed with alarm and sometimes with approval. The population of the United States doubled in the last four decades of the nineteenth century due in large measure to the arrival of 14 million immigrants. Cities like Chicago grew enormously over that period, with that city reaching a million in population by 1900, a growth of about tenfold in 40 years. Psychologically, the impending arrival of the twentieth century must itself have been one source of reflection and national soul-searching. Underneath the gaiety that, in popular terms, is supposed to have permeated the 1890s, there lay a profound psychic tension that made people wonder what kind of America was in the making.

Surely, the panic of 1893 and the severe economic depression that followed were also occasions for deep concern and reflection. With the society in such a rapid state of flux, it should not be surprising that the matter of what we teach our children in school should also come under scrutiny.

Mental Discipline As Curriculum Theory

The curriculum status quo in the 1890s was represented by the doctrine of mental discipline and its adherents. Although the roots of mental discipline as a curriculum theory go back at least as far as Plato's notion that the study of geometry was a way to improve general intelligence, its nineteenth-century version was derived most directly from the eighteenth-century German psychologist, Christian Wolff (1740), who laid out a carefully detailed hierarchy of faculties that was presumed to comprise the human mind. Mental disciplinarians built on that psychological theory by alleging that certain subjects had the power to strengthen faculties such as memory, reasoning, will, and imagination. Moreover, mental disciplinarians argued, certain ways of teaching these subjects could further invigorate the mind and develop these powers. Just as the muscles of the body could be strengthened through vigorous exercise, so the mental muscles, the faculties, could be trained through properly conceived mental gymnastics. Thus, they were able to elaborate a rather coherent and seemingly plausible way of addressing the persistent problems that had perplexed educators and philosophers for centuries. Such puzzling questions as what we should teach, what rules we should apply to the teaching of subjects, and even questions of balance and integration in the curriculum could be addressed simply, but effectively, through the analogy of mind and body. There was even assumed to be a natural order for the emergence of faculties, and if this order were followed, a defensible sequence in the curriculum could be enunciated. Moreover, the range of faculties presented a basis for defining the scope of the curriculum. Since neglect of any faculty meant atrophy, it became incumbent on educators to see to it that no imbalances were created in the curriculum by emphasizing subjects that developed some faculties and not others. An ideal education meant all-round mental fitness, not just the development of one or two mental muscles.

The most famous document of nineteenth-century mental disciplinarianism was the report of the Yale faculty in 1828, essentially an impassioned defense of traditional education and humanistic values in the face of possible intrusions by the natural sciences and practical subjects. The report recognized two main functions of education, "the *discipline* and the *furniture* of the mind" ("Original Papers" 1829, 300), that is, strengthening the powers of the mind (what we would today call developing the ability to think) and filling the mind with content (what we would today call the acquisition of knowledge and skills). The authors of the report, Yale President Jeremiah Day and Professor James K. Kingsley, a leading classical scholar, had no doubt that the former was by far the more significant function of education (as we would probably assert today), and, to them, this meant a reaffirmation of the curriculum they had been teaching all along ("Original Papers"). Greek, Latin, and mathematics as well as belles lettres had, after all, in their experience, established their value, whereas some of the newer subjects, such as modern foreign languages, were unproven quantities. Thus, there was firm resistance to any tinkering with what appeared to be a sound and proven program of studies. By the end of the nineteenth century, the textbooks being written for the growing number of normal schools in the United States overwhelmingly adopted the mind-as-a-muscle metaphor as the basis for explaining to future teachers what they ought to teach and how they ought to go about it. As that metaphor became firmly established, the implicit injunction to think of the mind *as if* it were a muscle, began to lose its "as if" quality, and, to many teachers, the mind became quite literally a muscle (Turbayne 1962).

To a large extent, the belief that the mind was in fact, or at least like, a muscle provided the backdrop for a regime in school of monotonous drill, harsh discipline, and mindless verbatim recitation. This may very well have gone on anyway, since the poorly trained and often very young teachers undoubtedly were at a loss to do anything else, but mental discipline provided them with an authoritative justification for continuing to do it. Anecdotal accounts of school life in the nineteenth and early twentieth centuries attest to the fact that, with few exceptions, schools were joyless and dreary places. In 1913, for example, a factory inspector, Helen M. Todd, decided to find out from the child laborers themselves whether they would prefer to go back to school rather than remain in the squalor of the factories. Todd systematically asked 500 children in these factories whether they would choose to work or go to school if their families were reasonably well-off and they did not have to work. Of the 500, 412 told her, sometimes in graphic terms, that they preferred factory labor to the monotony, humiliation, and even sheer cruelty that they experienced in school. These children, it would seem, did not choose the sweatshops of Chicago strictly out of economic necessity. To some extent, the schools around the turn of the century drove them there. With a reevaluation of America's social institutions in the air, it was no wonder that the doctrine that had become identified with existing conditions in the public schools should come under critical scrutiny.

By the 1890s, visible cracks were becoming apparent in the walls of mental discipline. As a theory of curriculum, after all, it represented a curious and not very stable compromise. If, indeed, the mind were really like a muscle and could be strengthened by exercise, why could not we exercise it on a wide variety of different subjects rather than the restricted set that was customarily prescribed? Why even could not a faculty like memory be developed through exercise with nonsense syllables? The theory of faculty psychology had merged with the nineteenth-century version of the liberal arts, forming a shaky coalition that served to perpetuate a time-honored literary curriculum. The question emerging in many people's minds was whether a curriculum that has its origins in the courtly life of Renaissance Europe was appropriate to the demands of the new industrial society. Although the demise of mental discipline is often associated with its failure to survive the test of empirical verification, first by William James (1890, 666–7) and later by several experiments conducted by Edward L. Thorndike (Thorndike and Woodworth 1901; Thorndike 1924), the collapse of mental discipline and the effort to restructure the schooling that was associated with it was most directly a consequence of a changing social order which brought with it a different conception of what knowledge is of most worth.

Although lags between what knowledge a society values and what knowledge gets embodied in the curriculum of its schools are not uncommon, it is hard to imagine a culture in which the knowledge deemed to be valuable for whatever reason does not find its way into what is taught deliberately to the young of that society. This holds true whether it be knowledge of how to hunt in a society sustained by hunting animals or the study of Latin as a rite of initiation into a special class or sex education in a society where unwanted pregnancies have become a source of national concern. The route between the knowledge a society values and its incorporation into the curriculum becomes infinitely more tortuous, however, where we take into account the fact that different segments in any society will emphasize different forms of knowledge as most valuable for that society. Rarely is there universal agreement as to which resources of a culture are the most worthwhile. The practical knowledge of how to hunt animals must somehow be reconciled with a knowledge of the myths of the tribe; a knowledge of Latin declensions must be weighed against linguistic competence and literary traditions indigenous to the culture; and sex education must be seen against a backdrop of conflicting moral and religious values. Hence, at any given time, we do not find a monolithic supremacy exercised by one interest group; rather we find different interest groups competing for dominance over the curriculum and, at different times, achieving some measure of control depending on local as well as general social conditions. Each of these interest groups, then, represents a force for a different selection of knowledge and values from the culture and hence a kind of lobby for a different curriculum.

Reactions to Changing Conditions

In the 1890s, not only do we see the theory of mental discipline starting to unravel as a consequence of increased awareness of a social transformation, but we see beginning to gel the interest groups that were to become the controlling factors in the struggle for the American curriculum in the twentieth century. One immediate impetus for change came as a consequence of a massive new influx of students into secondary schools beginning around 1890. In 1890, only between 6 and 7 percent of the population of youth 14 to 17 years old was attending secondary school. By 1900, it was already over 11 percent, and in 1920, about a third of that age-group was enrolled in secondary schools. By 1930, the number had reached almost four and a half million, over 51 percent of that population. It is difficult to establish precisely what created this sudden interest in secondary education on the part of American youth. To some extent, it may have been related to the growth of the American common school in the three or four decades preceding 1890 which created a new population whose children were ready to enter upon a secondary education. In addition, technological changes, such as the use of the telephone, affected the ability of early adolescents to find employment. (A ready source of jobs, for example, had been as a messenger.) A technological unemployment among teenagers, in a sense, left them with nothing better to do than to go to high school (Troen 1976). To a large extent, also, clerical jobs requiring higher levels of training were consistently better paying than manual labor in this period, making attendance in high school a worthwhile investment. In addition, the clustering of a larger segment of the American population into cities made attendance in high schools simply more convenient. Evidently, the social changes that were becoming increasingly visible in the 1890s were serving to focus new attention on the institution of schooling. Certainly, the dramatic rise in secondary school enrollments could not long go unnoticed. In particular, it raised the question as to whether the curriculum that had been so ardently defended in the Yale report and had remained essentially intact ever since could continue to serve a new population of students and, for all intents and purposes, a new society.

Although the National Education Association's Committee of Ten was appointed in 1892 originally to deal with another issue, the rather mundane problem of uniform college entrance requirements, their work and their recommendations were inevitably affected by the curricular implications of the growing demand by adolescents and their parents for a secondary school education. The immediate impetus for creating the committee in the first place was that high school principals had been bewailing the fact that different colleges were prescribing different entrance requirements and, since about half of the high school graduating classes went on to college (Krug 1962), it became exceedingly difficult to prepare so many students differently depending on their choice of college. While this in itself was a problem of considerable practical importance, almost inevitably it became imbedded in broader matters of principle, such as the extent to which a single curriculum, or type of curriculum, would be feasible or desirable in the face, not only of larger numbers of students, but, more importantly, of what was often perceived to be a different type of student.

When Charles W. Eliot, the patrician president of Harvard University, was appointed chairman of the National Education Association's Committee of Ten, it was recognition of the great influence he had exercised not only in higher education but in elementary and secondary schools as well. Eliot had been active in the National Education Association and was in demand as a speaker for local and regional teacher associations. His appointment also symbolically indicated his leadership, at least for this period, of one of four major interest groups that were to vie for control of the American curriculum in the twentieth century. Eliot, for a time at least, was in the forefront of the *humanist* interest group which, though largely unseen by professional educators in later periods, continued to exercise a strong measure of control over the American curriculum.

Eliot, a humanist in his general orientation, was also a mental disciplinarian, but, although this commitment affected his thinking on curriculum matters to a large extent, Eliot was not exactly a defender of the status quo in curriculum matters. His reputation as an education reformer extended beyond his espousal of the elective system at Harvard to his recommendations for reform at the elementary and secondary levels. In an article written in the same year that he was appointed to head the Committee of Ten, for example, Eliot (1892b) argued that "there has been too much reliance on the principle of authority, too little on the progressive and persistent appeal to reason" (425–26) and that "no amount of *memoriter* study of languages or of the natural sciences and no attainments in arithmetic will protect a man or woman ... from succumbing to the first plausible delusion or sophism he or she may encounter" (423).

Eliot, essentially, was the champion of the systematic development of reasoning power as the central function of the schools, and he recognized that much of what transpired in schools was simply unrelated to that function. Undoubtedly drawing on his own background as a scientist, Eliot saw reasoning power as a process of observing accurately, making correct records of the observations, classification, and categorization, and, finally, making correct inferences from these mental operations. It was with respect to these mental habits that Eliot thought the curriculum should be directed, adding, however, that the power to express one's thoughts "clearly, concisely, and cogently" (419) is also a critical task of schooling.

Eliot differed from most mental disciplinarians in that he thought that any subject, so long as it were capable of being studied over a sustained period, was potentially a disciplinary subject. This meant that he was not nearly as restrictive as other mental disciplinarians in curriculum matters and was consistent, of course, with his strong commitment to the elective principle at Harvard. That commitment represented a sharp break with a tradition in higher education of rigidly prescribed curricula as exemplified in the Yale curriculum. Eliot's support for electivism in curriculum matters extended as far down as the later elementary grades. In a sense, although Eliot did not emphasize education for the purpose of direct social reform, he remained an optimist with respect to human capabilities. The right selection of subjects along with the right way of teaching them could develop citizens of all classes endowed in accordance with the humanist ideal—with the power of reason, sensitivity to beauty, and high moral character. To those skeptics who pointed to great individual variation in native endowment, Eliot's response, essentially, was that "we Americans habitually underestimate the capacity of pupils at almost every stage of education from the primary school through the university" and that, for example, "the proportion of grammar school children incapable of pursuing geometry, algebra, and a foreign language would turn out to be much smaller than we now imagine" (Eliot 1892a, 620–21).

When the Committee of Ten published its report early in 1893, it bore Eliot's unmistakable stamp, although, here and there, some compromise was evident. Eliot, for example, had to settle for a choice of four different courses of study in the high school rather than the system of electives that he would undoubtedly have preferred. Here was the measure of uniformity in the high school curriculum that the school administrators had been seeking. Colleges were expected to accept any of the four as a basis of admission. But on the question of dividing the school population according to the criterion of who was going to college and who was not, the committee was firm and unanimous. There would be no curricular distinction between those students who were preparing for college and those who were preparing for "life," a position entirely consistent with the doctrine of mental discipline, as was the stand taken by the committee that the subjects should not be taught differently to different population groups. All students, the committee reasoned, regardless of destination, were entitled to the best ways of teaching the various subjects. What is more, education for life, they maintained, *is* education for college, and the colleges should accept a good education for life as the proper preparation for the rigors of college studies (National Education Association 1893).

Eliot's report was greeted with much approbation, but also some sharp criticism, mainly on the ground that the committee had not attuned itself sufficiently to the changing nature of the school population. Undoubtedly, the most powerful of the critics and surely one of the most vocal was the person who had early on assumed unquestioned leadership of the child-study movement in the United States, G. Stanley Hall. Hall is the pivotal figure in the second of the four interest groups seeking to influence the curriculum at the turn of the century, the *developmentalists*, who proceeded basically from the assumption that the natural order of development in the child was the most significant and scientifically defensible basis for determining what should be taught. The child-study movement was one outgrowth of the new status accorded science in the latter part of the nineteenth century and consisted, to a large extent, of research that involved the careful observation and recording of children's behavior at various stages of development.

Coincidentally, it was Eliot who had invited Hall to deliver lectures on pedagogy at Harvard in 1880, and that appointment led eventually to Hall's first major research in child-study, an article entitled "The Contents of Children's Minds" (1883). As the title indicates, Hall's study consisted essentially of an inventory of the contents of children's minds. Presumably, if we knew what was already in there, we could proceed much more systematically in determining what ought to be taught in school. Reflecting his own distinctly mystical reverence for rural life (he once claimed that he liked to take off his clothes and roll naked in the fields of his native Massachusetts), Hall tried to discover what children really knew about animals and plants. Did they know what a plough was? Or a spade? Or a hoe? Did a city child really have any notion of what a pond was or the distinction between a river and a brook? Did they know the parts and organs of their own bodies? Could they identify a square or a circle? Hall concluded on the basis of his investigation that teachers assumed too much about the contents of children's minds—that a lot of Boston's schoolchildren did not know what a cow was or a hill or an island. Although Hall himself often enlivened these cold data with his distinctive penchant for myth and mysticism, his criticism of the position of the Committee of Ten was perceived by many as the voice of science and progress directed against an entrenched establishment barely courageous enough to put forward moderate reforms in the face of a monumental challenge to the efficacy of the existing curriculum.

Hall attributed to various National Education Association committees the growing tendency to count and measure everything educational. "Everything must count and so much, for herein lies its educational value," he complained. "There is no more wild, free, vigorous growth of the forest, but everything is in pots or rows like a rococo garden" (Hall 1904b, 509). Such uniformity, according to Hall, was at variance with the natural spontaneity that adolescents presumably exude: "The pupil is in the age of spontaneous variation which at no period of life is so great. He does not want a standardized, overpeptonized mental diet. It palls on his appetite" (509).

When Hall focused specifically on the recommendations of the Committee of Ten, he asserted what he referred to as their "three extraordinary fallacies." The first was that all pupils should be taught in the same way and to the same extent, regardless of "probable destination." His charge that this was a "masterpiece of college policy" became the conventional wisdom about the Committee of Ten in the twentieth century. It was here that Hall referred to the "great army of incapables, shading down to those who should be in schools for the dullards or subnormal children" (Hall 1904b, 510). The school population, presumably, was so variable as to native endowment that a common curriculum was simply unworkable. Hall's second objection was to the assertion that all subjects were of equal educational value if taught equally well. He could "recall no fallacy that so completely evicts content and enthrones form" (512). For mental disciplinarians, such as those that comprised the committee, the form of the subject was what conveyed its disciplinary value; the content was, after all, only the "furniture." Here, Hall was rejecting that fundamental assumption. Finally, Hall saw "only mischief" in the doctrine that "fitting for college is essentially the same as fitting for life" (512). In this last charge, Hall was subtly turning the committee's recommendation on its head. They had argued that fitting for life was the same as fitting for college. They felt they had designed an appropriate curriculum for life and were asking colleges to accept that curriculum as the basis for admission. To Hall, however, this was just part of the strategy that the committee had used to impose college domination on the high school curriculum. In responding to these charges, Eliot reiterated his optimism in the power of human intelligence and reason. He rejected, for example, the notion that there was a "great army of incapables" invading the schools of the

1890s, contending instead that the actual number of "incapables" was "but an insignificant proportion" of the school population. Also, in a statement that has a peculiarly modern ring, Eliot foresaw the possibility that a differentiated curriculum could have the effect of determining the social and occupational destinies of students, rather than reflecting their native propensities and capacities: "Thoughtful students of . . . *psychology of adolescence* will refuse to believe that the American public intends to have its children sorted before their teens into clerks, watchmakers, lithographers, telegraph operators, masons, teamsters, farm laborers, and so forth, and treated differently in their schools according to those prophecies of their appropriate life careers. Who are to make these prophecies?" (Eliot 1905, 330–31). Here again, however, Hall proved to be more prescient in terms of emerging education policy than was Eliot. Predicting future destination as the basis for adapting the curriculum to different segments of the school population became a major feature of curriculum planning in the decades ahead.

Conflict between Interest Groups

As the twentieth century progressed, the Committee of Ten became a kind of symbol of the failure of the schools to react sufficiently to social change and the changing school population and to the crass domination exercised by the college over the high school. The academic subjects that the committee saw as appropriate for the general education of all students were seen by many later reformers as appropriate only for that segment of the high school population that was destined to go on to college. In fact, subjects like French and algebra came to be called college-entrance subjects, a term practically unknown in the nineteenth century. Even subjects like English became differentiated with standard literary works prescribed for those destined for college, while popular works and "practical" English were provided for the majority. Many of these curriculum changes reflected Hall's perception that the new population of high school students simply were incapable of pursuing the kind of curriculum that the Committee of Ten advocated.

Actually, however, the recommendations of the Committee of Ten represented a moderate departure from the traditional curriculum of the nineteenth century. The study of Greek was restricted to the Classical course and, even there, the amount of Greek was reduced from the traditional three years to two, and two of the four courses of study, the Modern Languages and English, had no Latin requirement at all. While the committee expressed the view that the Classical and the Latin–Scientific curricula were in some sense superior to the Modern Languages and the English, this was because the two former programs were better developed and had more experienced teachers, not because they were intrinsically better. The committee hoped that the effect of their doctrine of the equivalence of school studies would eventually put modern academic subjects on a par with classical ones, at least in principle if not in actual practice. Where the committee refused to compromise was in terms of the humanist ideal of a liberal education for all.

In its time the Report of the Committee of Ten engendered so much lively controversy that, by 1895, another committee, unimaginatively called the Committee of Fifteen, was ready to report on the elementary school curriculum. Wearing the mantle of the humanist position this time was America's leading Hegelian, the powerful and articulate United States Commissioner of Education, William Torrey Harris. (Superintendent of Schools William H. Maxwell of Brooklyn, New York, the chairman of the committee, divided the 15 members into 3 subcommittees of 5, each dealing with a different aspect of elementary education. As head of the subcommittee that was to deal with the correlation of studies, Harris was responsible for the curriculum portion of the report.) As a highly regarded Superintendent of Schools in St. Louis between 1869 and 1880, Harris had the practical experience that lent one sort of credence to his pronouncements; but he also was the editor of the *Journal of Speculative Philosophy*, the leading organ of American Hegelianism, and his scholarly reputation was considerable as well. Although he had been a member of the Committee of Ten, Harris took pains in his subcommittee report to disassociate himself from the mental discipline position, then beginning to decline (National Education Association 1895). Instead, Harris tried to articulate a new rationale for a humanistic curriculum, not only in the report itself, but in his many articles and speeches at National Education Association conferences. Harris, perhaps more than Eliot, was sensitive to the social changes that were occurring all around him, but he maintained that a curriculum constructed around the finest resources of Western civilization was still the most appropriate and desirable for America's schools. Whatever may have been the magnitude of the transformation in America's social institutions or the alleged changes in character of the school population, his five "windows of the soul," as he liked to call them— grammar, literature and art, mathematics, geography, and history—would remain the means by which the culture of the race would be transmitted to the vast majority of Americans. Somewhat suspicious of the rise of the natural sciences, Harris emerged as the great defender of humanistic studies in the curriculum. Although he embraced certain reform causes such as women's access to higher education, Harris earned a reputation as a conservative in education policy through his lukewarm reaction to manual training (a cause that was meeting with almost universal approbation among leaders in education), his deep reservations about the virtues of child-study as a basis for determining what to teach (once referring to it as "so much froth"), and as an outright opponent of specialized vocational training. In his view, the intrusion of new values by industrial society made it even more imperative that the school become a haven for the tried and true virtues he so deeply cherished. The common school for Harris was a specialized institution with a very distinct function to perform: the passing on of the great Western cultural heritage, leaving other institutions, the family, church, and industry to perform theirs.

But, by 1895, the forces of opposition to the traditional humanist curriculum had grown in numbers and organization. At the same National Education Association meeting in Saratoga Springs, New York, in 1892, where the Committee of Ten was appointed, a group of American education leaders, many of whom had studied in Germany and who thought of themselves as scientific in outlook, formed the National Herbart Society. Among them was a shy, 33-year-old faculty member from the University of Michigan, John Dewey. Despite the fact that, like Hall, Dewey disagreed with the American Herbartian position on a number of fundamental matters (although for different reasons), Dewey probably saw the group as the most promising in terms of effecting change in what had become a stagnant, often repressive, American school system. Three years after its formation, at the 1895 meeting of the National Education Association in Cleveland, Ohio, the Herbartians felt ready for direct confrontation with the person they saw as the embodiment of conservatism and reaction, the United States Commissioner of Education. Although Herbartianism as a movement with a specific identification in American education had a rather short-lived heyday, beginning to decline as early as 1905, Herbartian ideas and reactions to their ideas continued to exercise a profound influence on the American curriculum long after the movement itself faded from existence as a distinct entity.

Leading the attack on Harris was the president of the National Herbart Society, Charles DeGarmo. The details of the rather convoluted criticism of the Committee of Fifteen Report are not as important as the daring and the symbolism of the confrontation. Actually, much of the controversy revolved around the fact that Harris, in making his subcommittee report on the Correlation of Studies in Elementary Education, had used key Herbartian terms, such as correlation and concentration, but not in the prescribed Herbartian manner. When reporting on the five major branches of study, for example, Harris, although he avoided this time using his own standard term for these branches, "the windows of the soul," clearly was making the case for each separately as an important study and not in their interrelationship to one another, a pivotal point in Herbartian curriculum theory. Harris used the term "correlation" to mean "correlating the pupil with his spiritual and natural environment" (National Education Association 1895, 40–41), but not to mean the interrelationship among the subjects themselves. When he used the Herbartian concept "concentration," he used it only in the everyday sense that the work of the elementary school should be "concentrated" around the five coordinate groups of study that Harris had been advocating for years. Although there were some differences among themselves in their own use of the term, Herbartians usually used "concentration" to refer to the practice of using a particular subject, such as history or literature, as a focal point for all subjects, thereby achieving the unity in the curriculum they sought. Here and there, Harris seemed to go out of his way to attack Herbartian practice, such as their frequent use of *Robinson Crusoe* as a way of unifying all the studies in the third grade, Harris referring to it as "a shallow and uninteresting kind of correlation" (84).

The reaction to Harris's report on the part of his battle-ready opponents was fierce. The first to plunge into the fray was Frank McMurry who, along with his brother Charles, were central figures in the Herbartian movement. McMurry used the example of "Egypt" as a way of showing how the various branches of the elementary school curriculum could be correlated around such a concept. Colonel Francis Parker, who had by this time earned a national reputation as an educational reformer, was only a fringe member of the Herbartian group, but he unequivocally made his sympathies clear, comparing Harris's report to "the play of *Hamlet* with Hamlet left out" ("Discussion" 1895, 165). When DeGarmo took the floor, his criticism was also sweeping. He suggested that, contrary to the charge of the committee, the committee had not actually dealt with the correlation of studies. Harris, a skilled platform performer, defended himself vigorously, and, in the months that followed the confrontation, the debate continued with almost the same intensity in professional journals. The meeting in Cleveland became, in a sense, the Fort Sumter of a war that was to rage for most of the twentieth century. Whatever may have been the merits of the Herbartian criticism, the clash between Harris and the Herbartians marked the beginning of a realignment of the forces that were to battle for control of the American curriculum. The atmosphere at that 1895 meeting was so tense and the sense of drama so great that, 38 years later, DeGarmo, at the age of 85, was moved to write his friend Nicholas Murray Butler, "No scene recurs to me more vividly than on that immortal day in Cleveland, which marked the death of the old order and the birth of the new" (Drost 1967, 178).

Joseph Mayer Rice and Scientific Management

Another witness to that "immortal day" and critic of Harris's report was a young pediatrician who, by 1892, had essentially given up medicine to undertake a career as an education reformer. Joseph Mayer Rice, like Hall, Parker, and Dewey, was loosely affiliated with the American Herbartians, having left the country in 1888 to study at the great university centers of pedagogy in Germany. Having observed several school systems in Europe, Rice returned to the United States with a similar purpose in mind. In a tour sponsored by an influential journal, *The Forum*, Rice undertook a survey of American elementary education that lasted from January 7 to June 26, 1892. A tireless worker, he traveled through 36 cities in that period, making careful observations of the schools and classrooms he visited. The result was a series of nine articles, published in *The Forum* from October 1892 to June 1893. Those articles created an immediate sensation, and in 1893, they were collected in book form and published under the title *The Public School System of the United States*, thereby reaching an even wider audience.

Rice's sense of outrage is present on almost every page. One passage from his observation of the lowest primary grade in a New York City school conveys his tone as well as his general findings:

> Before the lesson began there was passed to each child a little flag, on which had been pasted various forms and colors, such as a square piece of green paper, a triangular piece of red paper, etc. When each child had been supplied, a signal was given by the teacher. Upon receiving the signal, the first child sprang up, gave the name of the geometrical form upon his flag, loudly and rapidly defined the form, mentioned the name of the color, and fell back into his seat to make way for the second child, thus: "A square; a square has four equal sides and four corners; green" (down). Second child (up): "A triangle; a triangle has three sides and three corners; red" (down). Third child (up): "A trapezium; a trapezium has four sides, none of which are parallel, and four corners; yellow" (down). Fourth child (up): "A rhomb; a rhomb has four sides, two sharp corners and two blunt corners; blue." This process was continued until each child in the class had recited. The rate of speed maintained during the recitation was so great that 70 children passed through the process of defining in a very few minutes. (Rice 1893a, 34).

If nothing else, Rice's survey conveys the sense of urgency that many reformers felt about what had become a largely lifeless system of schooling. But beyond that, Rice found some school systems, such as the one in Indianapolis, to be better than some others, and Rice was determined to find the secrets of their success. Rice initially shared with the developmentalists the idea that in scientific data on the child lay the key to the relatively successful classroom techniques as well as to a rational

curriculum. But he also attacked superintendents of schools for their lack of knowledge of pedagogy and for the superficial attention they gave to what was really going on in classrooms. School boards, he thought, were also composed of unqualified people, usually political appointees. The public also was the subject of Rice's wrath. But, at least in terms of emphasis, it was the quality of teaching that seemed to Rice to be most responsible for the catastrophic state of American education. Many teachers, he contended, whose incompetence had been generally recognized, continued to teach year after year in the public schools.

Rice's first series of *Forum* articles met with almost violent public reaction. These articles began to appear, after all, a year before the generally acknowledged beginning of muckraking journalism (Curti 1951). Teachers and school administrators rushed to their defense, attacking Rice with almost hysterical intensity. Some criticism focused on his own lack of classroom experience (Schneider 1983), some on his alleged misuse of English (Author 1895, 295), and there was even a hint of anti-Semitism here and there in their replies (Author 1894, 149). Professional educators appeared to be simply unused to such open and unrelenting attack. Theirs had been a life of relative invulnerability within the walls of their schools and classrooms.

Unrepentant, Rice undertook a second survey of American schools in the spring of 1893. Although he expressed interest in those school systems that were in the process of experimenting with new curricula, in fact, he focused almost entirely on gathering data on the achievement of third-graders in reading and arithmetic. Rice was seeking comparative data that would indicate why some schools and teachers were more successful than others in these subjects. In this respect, Rice is the acknowledged father of comparative methodology in education research, a fact recognized by Leonard Ayres as early as 1918 (Engelhart and Thomas 1966, 141). In particular, Rice's work in the teaching of spelling, which he began in 1895, was a monumental effort, involving initially some 16,000 pupils, designed to discover superior techniques of teaching spelling. When that test failed to accomplish that intention, apparently because some teachers, in administering the test, gave away answers through their careful enunciation, Rice, indefatigably, undertook another comparative study involving 13,000 more pupils, this time supervising the administration of each test himself. After all that work, Rice could only conclude that the amount of time spent in drill on spelling appeared unrelated to achievement on the part of the students, but the secret of how spelling should be taught remained a mystery.

When Rice's new series of *Forum* articles was collected into one volume in 1912, that book was entitled, significantly, *Scientific Management*

in Education. Although there were still vestiges of Rice's concern for the child in the school environs, the major thrust of Rice's work had shifted from the monotony and mindlessness of school life to the themes of standardization and efficiency in the curriculum. Rice's genuine dismay and disgust at what was going on in American schools in the 1890s had evolved into a grim determination that teachers and administrators must be *made* to do the right thing. Supervision, for example, would take the form of seeing to it that the achievement of students reached a clearly defined standard (xvi), and school administration, generally, ought to be governed, Rice claimed, by "a scientific system of pedagogical management [that] would demand fundamentally the measurement of results in the light of fixed standards" (xiv). Such an interpretation of science applied to education and curriculum represented a fundamental departure from science in the interest of discovering the developmental stages through which a child passes. "The child's capital," Rice declared, "is represented by time; and whether certain results are to be lauded or condemned depends upon the amount of time expended in obtaining them" (9). It is the job of the teacher to see to it that "this capital . . . be expended on sound economical principles, *i.e.*, without waste" (9). Educational reform, Rice argued, revolved around a clear articulation of definite goals (24–25) and on finding the techniques of measurement that would reveal whether those results have been realized.

In slow but perceptible stages, Rice's position had evolved from outraged humanitarian to a zealot for the elimination of waste in the curriculum through the application of the kind of scientific management techniques that, presumably, had been so successful in industry. Almost against his will, Rice became the principal forerunner of the third of the major curriculum interest groups that was to appear just before the turn of the century: the *social efficiency educators*. Although the social ideas that were to characterize that group in the twentieth century are difficult to detect in Rice, Rice unquestionably reflected the version of science and the techniques of curriculum-making that were to become the trademark of that movement. Although it was a reform movement in most senses of that term, it proceeded from fundamentally different assumptions and pointed in different directions from the developmentalist interest group. With Hall and the developmentalists, Rice and his ideological heirs found common cause against the humanistic position that Eliot and Harris, for example, tried to articulate, but the social efficiency educators and the developmentalists ultimately were as far apart from one another as they were from their common enemy. Their bitter battles would be reflected in their professional writings, in their open debates at professional meetings, and in colleges and universities as curriculum issues and problems gained

academic respectability and were formalized into courses and degree programs.

Education as an Instrument of Social Progress

Far from the center of National Education Association proceedings and the hallowed halls of academe where the battle lines for the American curriculum were being drawn, there labored a relatively obscure, largely self-taught, government botanist and geologist whose ideas were to emerge as the major challenge to what was rapidly becoming the established dogma in social theory. By 1883, Lester Frank Ward had somehow found the time in the midst of his paleobotanical work for the United States Geological Survey to produce a two-volume tome, *Dynamic Sociology*. Although himself strongly influenced by Darwinian theory, Ward took almost the opposite position on its application to society from the doyen of the new sociology, Herbert Spencer. Spencer's enormously successful lecture tour in the United States in 1882 and his widely read works in such journals as *Popular Science Monthly* had spread the message of Social Darwinism, and his disciples, such as William Graham Sumner at Yale, were promoting his ideas in American universities. Basically, they argued that the laws that Darwin had enunciated in terms of natural selection had their parallel in the social realm. Survival of the fittest, in other words, was a law, not only of the jungle, but of civilization, and the unequal distribution of wealth and power was simply the evidence of that law's validity.

By contrast, Ward's position was that, in the social realm, "there is no alternative but to renounce all effort and trust to the slow laws of cosmical evolution" (Ward 1883, 153). The laissez-faire position that the Social Darwinists had advocated was, in Ward's view, a corruption of Darwinian theory because human beings had developed the power to intervene intelligently in whatever were the blind forces of nature, and in that power lay the course of social progress. Civilization, he argued, was not achieved by letting cosmic natural forces take their course, but by the power of intelligent action to change things for the better. For Ward, "if any moral progress is ever too [sic] be made other than that which would naturally be brought about by the secular influence of cosmical laws, it must be the result of an *intellectual* direction of the forces of human nature into channels of human advantage" (216). In many respects, Ward foreshadowed in his 1883 work significant elements of John Dewey's educational philosophy.

Critical to social progress, in Ward's mind, was a properly constructed and fairly distributed system of education. Ward liked to use the metaphor

of legacy in connection with education, and he argued in *Dynamic Sociology* that social inequality was fundamentally a product of a maldistribution of the social inheritance. Like Eliot, Ward expressed great optimism about the power of human intelligence, asserting without equivocation that native endowment was equally distributed across social class lines as well as gender, and whatever the differences that could be observed in the human condition, they were directly attributable to that maldistribution. Unlike Eliot and the other humanists generally, however, Ward saw education as a direct and potent instrument of social progress.

Dynamic Sociology did not go unnoticed. Albion Small, for example, Dewey's respected colleague at the University of Chicago, declared several years after its publication that, "All things considered, I would rather have written *Dynamic Sociology* than any other book ever published in America" (Commager 1967, xxvi). Nevertheless, on the first of January 1892, Ward resolved to embark on another ambitious project, and within about three months, *The Psychic Factors of Civilization* was nearly complete. Published in 1893, *Psychic Factors* became recognized as the most significant among Ward's voluminous writings. In it, Ward reiterated his attacks on "survival of the fittest" as a doctrine that had any application to the social world and welcomed intervention, particularly by government, in human affairs. The trouble with governmental intervention as it now exists, declared Ward, was that it was controlled by the wrong groups. The right sort of intervention would be accomplished once the influence of partisan pressure groups was eliminated and practical and humanitarian approaches to social problems were substituted.

Ward's commitment to egalitarianism was unequivocal. "The denizens of the slums," he said in *Psychic Factors*, "are not inferior in talent to the graduates of Harvard College" (290). "Criminals," he argued, "are the geniuses of the slums. Society has forced them into this field, and they are making the best use they can of their native abilities" (290). The key to progress and the great undertaking that lay before us was the proper distribution of cultural capital through a vitalized system of education.

In his *Psychic Factors*, as well as in his other works, Ward reveals himself, not only as the prophet of the welfare state in the twentieth century, but as the principal forerunner of the fourth and last of the major interest groups that were to battle for control of the curriculum in the decades ahead, the *social meliorists*. By the 1890s, Ward had already laid down the main outlines of the arguments that were to put education at the center of any movement toward a just society. To be sure, Ward's position on education was often taken to be a particularly American obsession. Spencer, for example, when asked to comment on America's future, declared, "It is a frequent delusion that education is a universal remedy for

political evils" (Commager 1967, xxxvi). Whether a practical faith or a popular delusion, it was a belief that Dewey and many American educators came to share in the twentieth century. Ward himself noted that the most perceptive review of *Psychic Factors* was Dewey's, and Dewey certainly believed that in education lay the key to social progress. While the possibility exists, of course, that Americans share an inordinate faith in the power of education to correct social evils and promote social justice, inordinate or not, it became a powerful force in the shaping of curriculum policy in the years ahead.

The Four Interest Groups in Place

When the twentieth century finally arrived, the four major forces that were to determine the course of the new American curriculum had already emerged. First, there were the humanists, the guardians of an ancient tradition tied to the power of reason and the finest elements of the Western cultural heritage. Although, in later years, the leaders of this interest group remained, for the most part, outside the professional education community, they exerted a powerful influence through their standing in the academic world and among intellectuals generally. To them fell the task of reinterpreting and thereby preserving as best as they could their revered traditions and values in the face of rapid social change.

Arrayed against this group were three different kinds of reformers, each representing a different conception of what knowledge should be embodied in the curriculum and to what ends the curriculum should be directed. Hall and the others in the child-study movement led the drive for a curriculum reformed along the lines of a natural order of development in the child. Although frequently infused with romantic ideas about childhood, the developmentalists pursued with great dedication their sense that the curriculum riddle could be solved with ever more accurate scientific data, not only with respect to the different stages of child and adolescent development, but on the nature of learning. From such knowledge, a curriculum in harmony with the child's real interests, needs, and learning patterns could be derived. The curriculum could then become the means by which the natural power within the child could be unharnessed.

The second group of reformers, the social efficiency educators, were also imbued with the power of science, but their priorities lay with creating a coolly efficient, smoothly running society. The Rice exposé's, begun in 1892, and impelled by genuine humanitarian motives, turned out to be a portent of a veritable orgy of efficiency that was to dominate American thinking generally in the decades ahead. In fact, efficiency, in later years, became the overwhelming criterion of success in curriculum matters. By applying the standardized techniques of industry to the business of schooling, waste could be eliminated and the curriculum, as seen by such later exponents of social efficiency as David Snedden and Ross Finney, could be made more directly functional to the adult life-roles that America's future citizens would occupy. People had to be controlled for their own good, but especially for the good of society as a whole. Theirs was an apocalyptic vision. Society as we know it was flying apart, and the school with a scientifically constructed curriculum at its core could forestall and even prevent that calamity. That vision included a sense that the new technological society needed a far greater specialization of skills and, therefore, a far greater differentiation in the curriculum than had heretofore prevailed.

Finally, there were the social meliorists as represented by one of their great early figures, Lester Frank Ward. Ward was the forerunner of the interest group that saw the schools as a major, perhaps the principal, force for social change and social justice. The corruption and vice in the cities, the inequalities of race and gender, and the abuse of privilege and power could all be addressed by a curriculum that focused directly on those very issues, thereby raising a new generation equipped to deal effectively with those abuses. Change was not, as the Social Darwinists proclaimed, the inevitable consequence of forces beyond our control; the power to change things for the better lay in our hands and in the social institutions that we create. Times indeed had changed, but, according to the social meliorists, the new social conditions did not demand an obsessional fixation on the child and on child psychology; nor did the solution lie in simply ironing out the inefficiencies in the existing social order. The answer lay in the power of the schools to create a new social vision.

The twentieth century became the arena where these four versions of what knowledge is of most worth and of the central functions of schooling were presented and argued. No single interest group ever gained absolute supremacy, although general social and economic trends, periodic and fragile alliances between groups, the national mood, and local conditions and personalities affected the ability of these groups to influence school practice as the twentieth century progressed. In the end, what became the American curriculum was not the result of any decisive victory by any of the contending parties, but a loose, largely unarticulated, and not very tidy compromise.

References

Author of "Preston Papers." 1894. "The Critic at Sea, V." *Education* 15: 149–57.
Author of "Preston Papers." 1895. "The Critic at Sea, VII." *Education* 15: 288–97.

Commanger, H. S. ed. 1967. *Lester Ward and the Welfare State.* Indianapolis, Ind.: Bobbs-Merrill.

Curti, M. E. 1951. *The Growth of American Thought* (2d. ed.). New York: Harper.

"Discussion of [the] Report of Dr. Harris." 1895. *Journal of Education* 41: 165–67.

Drost, W. H. 1967. "That Immortal Day in Cleveland—the Report of the Committee of Fifteen." *Educational Theory* 17: 178–91.

Eliot, C. W. 1892a. "Shortening and Enriching the Grammar School Course." *Journal of Proceedings and Addresses of the National Education Association. Session of the Year 1892,* 617–25.

Eliot, C. W. 1892b. "Wherein Popular Education Has Failed." *The Forum* 14: 411–28.

Eliot, C. W. 1905. "The Fundamental Assumptions in the Report of the Committee of Ten (1893)." *Educational Review* 30: 325–43.

Engelhart, M. D., and M. Thomas. 1966. "Rice as the Inventor of the Comparative Test." *Journal of Educational Measurement* 3: 141–45.

Hall, G. S. 1883. "The Contents of Children's Minds." *Princeton Review* 11: 249–72.

Hall, G. S. 1904b. *Adolescence: Its Psychology and its Relations to Physiology, Anthropology, Sociology, Sex, Crime, Religion, and Education,* Vol. 2. New York: D. Appleton.

James, W. 1890. *The Principles of Psychology,* Vol. 1, New York: H. Holt.

Kaestle, C. F. ed. 1973. *Joseph Lancaster and the Monitorial School Movement: A Documentary History.* New York: Teachers College Press.

Krug, E. A. 1962. "Graduates of Secondary Schools In and Around 1900: Did Most of Them Go to College?" *School Review* 70: 266–72.

Mott, F. L. 1941. *American Journalism: A History of Newspapers in the United States Through 250 Years, 1690–1940.* New York: Macmillan.

National Education Association. 1893. *Report of the Committee on Secondary School Studies.* Washington, D.C.: U.S. Government Printing Office.

National Education Association. 1895. *Report of the Committee of Fifteen on Elementary Education, with the Reports of the Sub-Committees: On the Training of Teachers; On the Correlation of Studies in Elementary Education; On the Organization of City School Systems.* New York: American Book.

"Original Papers in Relation to a Course of Liberal Education." 1829. *American Journal of Science and Arts* 15: 297–351.

Rice, J. M. 1893a. *The Public School System of the United States.* New York: Century.

Rice, J. M. 1912. *Scientific Management in Education.* New York: Hinds, Noble & Elredge.

Schneider, H. G. 1893. "Dr. Rice and American Public Schools." *Education* 13: 354–57.

Thorndike, E. L. 1924. "Mental Discipline in High School Studies." *Journal of Educational Psychology* 15: 1–22, 83–98.

Thorndike, E. L., and R. S. Woodworth. 1901. "The Influence of Improvement in One Mental Function Upon the Efficiency of Other Functions." *Psychological Review* 8: 247–61, 384–95, 553–64.

Troen, S. K. 1976. "The Discovery of the Adolescent by American Educational Reformers, 1900–1920: An Economic Perspective." In L. Stone, ed., *Schooling and Society: Studies in the History of Education,* 239–51. Baltimore, Md.: Johns Hopkins University Press.

Turbayne, C. M. 1962. *The Myth of Metaphor.* New Haven, Conn.: Yale University Press.

Tyack, D. B. 1974. *The One Best System: A History of American Urban Education.* Cambridge, Mass.: Harvard University Press.

Ward, L. F. 1883. *Dynamic Sociology, or Applied Social Science as Based Upon Statistical Sociology and the Less Complex Sciences,* Vol. 2. New York: D. Appleton.

Ward, L. F. 1893. *The Psychic Factors of Civilization.* Boston: Ginn.

Wiebe, R. H. 1967. *The Search for Order, 1877–1920.* New York: Hill & Wang.

Wolff, C. F. 1740. *Psychologia Rationalis: Methodo Scientifica pertractata . . . cognitionem profutura propunbuntur.* Francofurti: Lipsiae.

PART III

PERSPECTIVES ON NATIONAL STANDARDS

3

Implications of Subject-Matter Standards

CHRISTOPHER T. CROSS

Christopher T. Cross is executive director, the Business Roundtable, Washington, D.C.

Introduction

The idea of establishing national standards in education is not new. However, the momentum for the current thrust springs directly from a national "summit" meeting held in 1989 in Charlottesville, Virginia. For the first time in history, the nation's governors and the President of the United States came together to address a noneconomic topic. Then-President Bush, 49 governors, every cabinet member, and the heads of several subcabinet agencies attended. The topic was the crisis in K through 12 education.

The president called the Charlottesville summit, but the National Governors' Association (NGA) was centrally involved. The meeting culminated in an agreement to establish national goals in education. For the next four months, a small group fashioned the specific language of those goals. Former President Bush presented the goals in his State of the Union Address in January 1990, and they were formally adopted by the NGA in February 1990.

The governor most involved in both the Charlottesville meeting and the formulation of the goals was a governor from the South named Bill Clinton. I mention this to highlight the fact that the creation of the national education goals was not an act of one political party. Not surprisingly, the goals have been as enthusiastically embraced by the new administration as by its predecessor. President Clinton's Secretary of Education, Richard Riley, is also a former governor, although he was not in office at the time of the Charlottesville meeting.

Once the goals were adopted by both the NGA and the Bush administration, an effort to develop national standards in different subject-mat-

43

ter areas was almost inevitable. As a participant in the endless sessions devoted to writing the goals, I recall many references to the pioneering work of the National Council of Teachers of Mathematics (NCTM) in establishing standards for that field. That model was very much on the minds of the people who crafted and finally adopted the national goals.

However, it is only fair to point out that we did not focus then on the issue of different kinds of standards for different aspects of the education enterprise. At that time, NCTM had issued only its content standards. Thus, the subtle differences between performance, content, teaching, and assessment standards were not discussed. Nonetheless, everyone involved was convinced that a major failing of our K through 12 system was the lack of clear expectations of what students should know and be able to do. We were keenly aware that our trading and economic rivals had much clearer criteria for student outcomes at key points along the education continuum.

Funding the Standards Movement

Everyone involved then, and most of the people who later became involved, held the conviction that the federal government should not control the development of standards. I, among others, had serious reservations about the federal government taking a leading role in funding these efforts. The National Science Foundation and the Department of Education provided some funds for the NCTM and National Academy of Science (NAS) projects, but the impetus and early funding of these efforts had come from foundations and the professional community. No one among us saw the federal government as the primary force behind the NCTM or NAS efforts.

The situation changed in late 1991 when Secretary of Education Lamar Alexander directed the Office of Educational Research and Improvement (OERI) to fund standards-setting efforts in several other disciplines. Today, the Department of Education is funding the arts, civics, English, science, geography, history, and foreign-language standards projects, with additional contributions from the National Science Foundation, the National Endowments for the Arts and the Humanities, and several private foundations. Altogether there are now 14 different standards-setting efforts in progress, only half of which are funded by the federal government.[1]

[1]Each of the seven OERI projects has received at least $1,000,000. Some, like science, have received far more.

The projects are at different stages of development. The NCTM has already drafted its professional standards for teachers, and the arts standards were adopted in April 1994. It is expected that the English language arts and foreign language standards efforts will take far longer. In addition, the federal government is also funding the development of curriculum frameworks in 21 states.[2] Seven of these states have grants to develop multidisciplinary frameworks. Forty-five states in total are reported to be planning, developing, or implementing new curriculum standards. While some of these efforts build on the work of earlier projects like that of the NCTM, many do not. Concurrent with these efforts, the New Standards Project, an entirely private-sector effort led by Lauren Resnick and Marc Tucker, is going forward with funding from several major foundations.[3] There is also a major effort under way to upgrade the teaching profession sponsored by the National Board on Professional Teaching Standards.[4] This project was funded by private foundations and now has federal support as well. Finally, there is the College Board's own Pacesetter program, aimed at raising achievement for all high school students.

What Kinds of Standards?

The current standards-setting situation is a tangled and indecipherable web to the public and probably to most professional educators. Most projects focus on performance standards, but some are concerned with teaching standards, and others with assessment. It has been difficult to establish a common vocabulary. Developing performance, content, teaching, and assessment standards are separate and distinct activities. Performance standards define what a student should know and be able to do, whereas content standards describe the material to be taught to ensure that students can meet the performance standards. Teaching standards outline the skills and competencies that teachers need to provide learning

[2]The states that have received OERI funding for the development of curriculum frameworks are Alaska, Arkansas, Arizona, Colorado, Connecticut, Delaware, Florida, Louisiana, Massachusetts, Maine, Michigan, Minnesota, Montana, Nebraska, New Jersey, New York, Ohio, Oregon, Rhode Island, Vermont, Wisconsin, and the District of Columbia. The states that have OERI funding for multidisciplinary frameworks are Alaska, Arkansas, Connecticut, Delaware, Montana, Vermont, and Wisconsin.

[3]The New Standards Project is a private-sector organization initiated by the University of Pittsburgh and the National Center on Education and the Economy. It has been funded by the John D. and Catherine T. MacArthur Foundation and the Pew Charitable Trusts.

[4]The National Board for Professional Teacher Development is a voluntary association funded by private foundations and the federal government to develop assessments through which teachers can demonstrate advanced competencies in a variety of instructional fields.

opportunities and experiences for students to be able to master performance standards. Assessment standards identify the essential criteria for determining whether students have met specified performance standards. One of my modest proposals would be to ban the word "standards" unless it is preceded by the proper modifier so that everyone can understand what kinds of standards are being discussed.

Unresolved Issues

I fully support the idea of national education standards, but several issues still need to be addressed for this major reform to be successful. Some may be resolved, others are more philosophical and ongoing. In my article "Education Standards: A Question of Time," I argued that the single greatest problem is that of the never-ending school day.[5] Each subject-matter group has viewed the standards-setting process as an opportunity to fulfill its wish list. We know that there are not enough hours in the school day or days in the year, even if we were to expand both, to cram in everything that each group believes it is in the national interest for all students to know. We have at most 1,000 hours in each school year for teaching, including physical education and noncore academic subjects. Some schools and districts may have as few as 920 hours. Although many of the standards-setting groups are under pressure from their advisory councils and others to keep their standards lean, they are still focusing solely on their individual subject areas. The job of coordinating the school day to accommodate all these disparate efforts is inevitably left to some indeterminate person or organization.

We haven't thought enough about the number of hours it would take to teach the content standards currently being developed. To those who say that we should leave it to each state or district to resolve the dilemma by picking and choosing among elements of the standards, I would argue that we are thereby inevitably creating a situation that will not produce national standards. For example, one district may decide to emphasize literature of the Western world while a nearby district just over the state line focuses on Asian literature with special emphasis on haiku (a form of Japanese verse) for the same grade. The first district could decide that the visual arts will receive priority while its neighbor emphasizes the performing arts, especially those of ancient Asia.

In both instances, the districts may be drawing their content from the national standards, but in recognizing that there simply wasn't time to

[5]*Education Week*, April 21, 1993.

"do it all," they made very different choices. From the perspective of an employer, a college admission dean, or a book publisher, there would be no national standards. Ironically, a reform motivated by the belief that graduates throughout the nation should have the same core of knowledge could be reconfigured by the politics of local control into the pedagogical equivalent of mush.

Teachers have long complained that textbooks contain too much material, making it impossible to cover it all in a course. As a result, most youngsters never learn about the Korean War, let alone the latest discoveries in genetic engineering or the latest theories about the formation of the solar system. The current standards projects run the risk of reproducing the same results, magnified to the nth degree. The consensus-building process required to develop standards for each discipline, several of which are more contentious than math, is likely to be a logrolling exercise that results in every subdiscipline being given equal emphasis. The result will be a fragmented, chaotic curriculum that is far from world class because of the attempt to be comprehensive.

The troubling tendency to treat each subject in isolation will be exacerbated by the standards efforts under way. Some states, such as Maine, have recognized this pitfall and are designing their common cores to be multidisciplinary. Other states have not. Recently, the vice-president of a California firm wrote to tell me that an article of mine echoed her hopes and fears. "The standards projects are potentially making interdisciplinary instruction seem undoable and certainly less valued. Life *is* interdisciplinary. Good teaching usually is."

Those who advocate incorporating as much of "their stuff" as they can into the required curriculum are joined, often inadvertently, by critics of reform who are uncomfortable with anything that does not contain the familiar Carnegie units or similar standards. On the other side, we find those who, like my California correspondent, see life as interdisciplinary and realize that time will not permit each subject to be taught in isolation. Right now there are no mechanisms in place at the national level to facilitate building bridges among the disciplines. Some states are making the attempt, but leaving it to the states virtually assures the continuation of the chaotic conditions that exist today.

Many fear that a national curriculum will follow once we establish a uniform set of standards. Others believe that a "top-down" strategy will never work. However, if we permit each state or each district to choose content standards for itself, we will destroy the dream of a society in which all students master a common body of knowledge in key areas and thereby have greatly enhanced opportunities to compete for and hold jobs in what is a global marketplace for both products and labor. We have a major public relations job to do with the public and within our own ranks.

We are faced with difficult choices. We cannot leave the resolution of this problem to chance. We should not expect that as states define content standards, and as occupational groups define skill standards, that their efforts will converge on a single core on which we will all agree. Some group has to take the lead. Mechanisms that will permit us to interweave history, literature, geography, and the arts when we teach about ancient Rome, for example, are essential. Such an effort inevitably raises a more fundamental question: Are all disciplines created equal? Is it necessary that every subject area have the same status? Why not combine geography, history, and art as components of world civilizations in the eleventh grade or consider science, mathematics, and art jointly in an architecture course?

I am also troubled by the fact that the standards projects are ignoring the results of the SCANS (Secretary's Commission on Achieving Necessary Skills) report issued two years ago by the U.S. Department of Labor. While our current standards documents do explicitly cover such skills as the mastery of technical material, other skills such as the ability to work in teams and to solve complex problems are addressed only indirectly if at all.[6] The Goals 2000 legislation also calls for the creation of skills standards in a wide number of occupations. According to the legislation, these standards will be established by groups composed of representatives from labor and business. More attention must be given to articulation between the SCANS report and the national education standards-setting efforts. I fear that the public will become so confused about what is going on that it will lose interest in and withdraw support for the entire effort to establish standards and improve the educational performance of students.

We also need to recognize that we are dealing with highly controversial issues. Our society is built on the right to express dissent and on the responsibility of the power structure to listen and respond to that dissent. We may prefer to believe that critics are always wrong, politically motivated, foolish, or even stupid. We all want to think that we know what is best, and this is the heart of the problem. We should be prepared to address controversy openly and be willing to compromise.

[6]In addition to discussing such skill areas, the SCANS report also dealt with a three-part education foundation consisting of basic skills, thinking skills, and personal qualities. The basic skills include reading, writing, mathematics, listening, and speaking. Thinking skills involve creative thinking, decision making, problem solving, seeing things in the mind's eye, knowing how to learn, and reasoning. Personal qualities include responsibility, self-esteem, sociability, self-management, integrity, and honesty. The five competencies identified in the report as bridging learning and the workplace are resources, interpersonal skills, information, systems, and technology.

Furthermore, we can avoid false controversy by using clear, concise, nontechnical language. We can also avoid the controversy that results when we confuse affective and academic outcomes. Most people will support setting performance standards in key academic disciplines, but they will not endorse such standards if affective outcomes are linked to academic outcomes. Affective goals require community consensus. John and Joan Q. Public may be willing to let professionals decide mathematics content for their eight-year-old, but they will not cede decisions concerning values to others.

We should also recognize that we are engaged in an organic process. Over time, each discipline will need to revise its standards. Disciplinary groups will need a mechanism for doing this and must make it a regular part of their ongoing organizational lives.

The final element of standards reform that must be addressed is teacher training. This is a thorny issue that cannot be elaborated here; suffice it to say that we are fooling ourselves if we think this reform can succeed without a tremendous investment in teacher training and development. Schools, colleges of education, and in-service programs will have to carefully consider how to present the standards movement to teachers so that they understand, accept, and are motivated to respond to these new standards. We must also ask, and answer, what kind of financial investment will be required for teacher training and development? Where will the money come from?

Conclusion

Goals 2000 calls for the creation of the National Education Standards and Improvement Council (NESIC). This council will review the new standards and determine certification—something perhaps akin to the *Good Housekeeping* seal of approval. The 1991 report calling for the creation of NESIC recommended that states be required to ensure a "feasible, coherent" curriculum when submitting their standards for certification. Unfortunately, the current legislative language does not include such a recommendation.

Some critics believe that NESIC is already obsolete because its substantive work will have been completed before it is established late in the summer or early fall of 1994. I disagree. Much remains for NESIC to do, key among which will be to establish working relationships with participants in the standards projects. I hope each standards group will rise above its own parochial interests in helping to formulate the overall strategy and tactics of the standards and assessment movement. We need to work together to build professional and public support for our efforts. We have to identify interdisciplinary ties while thinking of the realities of the academic day for students and teachers. Subject-matter groups need not give up their autonomy, but they should embrace a collaborative process in which each organization would acknowledge the problems facing practitioners who are not specialists and students, who must, after all, cope with what we have wrought.

We need some organization, perhaps the College Board, to serve as the "honest broker" to bring all the discipline groups together with a cross-section of teachers from all education levels to dissect, try out, cross-fertilize, rationalize, and otherwise make sense of the standards-setting efforts so that practitioners can understand and fully benefit from the enormous investment of both manpower and money going into this education reform movement.

When NESIC begins operation sometime in fall of 1994, it will face a highly confusing situation. The council is likely to feel some urgency to move the standards efforts forward and will welcome the active intervention of an organization that stands aside from any particular subject-matter group, yet has the cooperation of all of them in working out commonsense solutions. I hope this will lead the disciplinary groups to put aside their "wish lists" in the interest of finding solutions that will work for all students and teachers.

The enactment of Goals 2000: Educate America Act into law legitimizes the standards efforts in the eyes of the public and of practitioners. It should also serve as a wake-up call to the education community. We need to abandon untenable curricular wish lists to make sure that this much needed reform will achieve its goals. To do this, educators will have to forge interdisciplinary ties. This will not be a simple task: training, practice, and turf battles work against it. For that reason I have proposed a mediating structure to bring representatives from the academic disciplines together in a collaborative way.

4

The Politics of National Standards

TOM LOVELESS

Tom Loveless is an assistant professor of public policy and a faculty affiliate of the A. Alfred Taubman Center for State and Local Government at the John F. Kennedy School of Government, Harvard University.

As the American schools' latest reform movement gathered momentum in the 1980s, the idea of national standards raised a noble hope, the belief that if we spotlighted the grandest peaks of knowledge in school subjects, teachers and students would strive to scale them. Congress has passed legislation establishing national standards (the "Goals 2000: Educate America Act"), but as befalls many great ideas, the codified reality is distinguished more by pragmatic compromises than by soaring aspirations. Though essential to the art of governing, in this case political compromise has dealt a potentially mortal blow to original purpose.

National education goals will succeed or fail on their ability to raise American students' and parents' and teachers' appreciation for the work that they do, to motivate the key actors in schooling by placing their day-to-day labors within a larger, national mission. It is not the conservative complaint that national standards usurp local authority over education that tarnishes the latest effort. Nor is it the liberal complaint that standards supply new justifications for condemning the historically disadvantaged members of our society. Both are legitimate concerns. But, unfortunately, in accommodating these and other concerns, Goals 2000 lost its focus. What we have now looks more like 2,000 educational goals—and a missed opportunity to debate and to resolve what our schools are about, a lost opportunity to sharpen the purpose of schooling in America. Moreover, the failure of the standards to speak directly to teachers and stu-

dents renders the recent debate largely irrelevant to the nation's classrooms. School personnel are not the audience for this legislation; more
than anything else, Goals 2000 consists of a conversation among governments—federal, state, and local. How did this happen?

The three sets of educational standards—content, performance, and
delivery—have their own interesting political histories. Content standards
define the curriculum schools are to offer; performance standards establish content-mastery levels and include assessments to measure whether
students meet acceptable thresholds; and delivery standards spell out the
quality of services schools must provide so that students have a reasonable opportunity to achieve the expected levels of learning. Under the
legislation, a National Education Standards and Improvement Council would
set voluntary national standards in the three areas, with states submitting
their own standards to the council for certification that they meet or ex-
ceed the national benchmarks. The emphasis on state autonomy is designed to allay fears of an intrusive federal government.

Content standards in core academic subjects (English, mathematics,
science, history, and geography) were originally suggested by the education summit convened by President Bush and the nation's governors in
1989. After complaints from professional educators' groups representing
other subject disciplines, foreign languages and the arts were added to
the core group, and standards development is proceeding in civics and
physical education as well. Faced with choosing between a spare or ex-
pansive core curriculum, educational leaders have opted for the latter.

Performance standards require tests of some kind to measure student
achievement. After the public outcry following *A Nation at Risk* in 1983,
most states instituted assessment systems to monitor student learning.
For the most part, these tests are used to determine if minimum competency in basic subjects has been attained, with high school graduation
or grade promotion dependent upon the results. Responding to concerns
for equity, Goals 2000 would bar states for the first five years from using
assessments under the new program for such high-stakes outcomes. The
lesson from the states' experience with testing poses a conundrum. If tests
are to be taken seriously, they must have important consequences; however, they tend to be designed so that most current students can pass
them, set at the level of minimum competency, not at the level of world-
class standards. The five-year moratorium only delays confronting this
dilemma.

Delivery standards mark a departure from reform legislation pushed by
Republican administrations in the past and from the original legislation
offered by the Clinton administration. When the reform bill was introduced on Capitol Hill in early 1994, several Democratic members of Con-

gress, led by Representative William D. Ford of Michigan, the chairman of the House committee considering the legislation, rejected the bill's sole emphasis on educational outcomes, insisting that it also address systemic inputs (for example, class size, expenditures per pupil, school facilities). One amendment adopted by the House committee mandates that states establish time lines to remedy school districts not meeting these service and facility requirements. Another forbids states from implementing the other standards—content and performance—until delivery standards are in place. These provisions are designed to promote a level playing field for all students before judgments are made about who has succeeded and who has failed. Unfortunately, however, they provide no new revenues to assist states or local districts in bringing impoverished schools up to standard. Notwithstanding their voluntary nature, the delivery standards smack of federal mandate without crucial federal funding. In addition, as Albert Shanker of the American Federation of Teachers has correctly warned, delivery standards are an invitation to excuse resource-poor schools from meeting national expectations for achievement. If this happens, it is our nation's most disadvantaged students who stand to lose.

The legislation relies upon the elaborate machinery of governmental bureaucracies to operate as a catalyst for school reform. The federal government will tell state governments that they need to do better, state governments will tell local districts that they need to do better, local districts will tell school principals that they need to do better, and principals will tell teachers that they need to do better—trickle-down school reform. This fundamental flaw in the legislation is exacerbated by the political pressures mentioned above—pressures from liberal and conservative politicians, state interests, and professional groups. It originates, however, from the federal government's trying to alter, without incentives or sanctions, the inherently local nature of school governance and finance. For the legislation to succeed, either creative implementation or future amendments need to connect the federal government with local school personnel in a useful, purposeful manner. Three improvements would begin to forge this connection:

Redefine the Audience and Narrow the Standards.   Diminish the intergovernmental thrust of the act. Talk to teachers and students and parents, not just governments. National standards should clearly lay out what the nation expects students to learn and teachers to teach in a way that teachers, students, and parents can understand. If this can only be done in a few school subjects, so much the better. Trying to describe everything a fully enlightened individual needs to know in a complex society entering the twenty-first century should be left to others.

Develop and Distribute a Useful Test.   Another test that identifies the students who have not learned material is not very valuable to teachers; they already know. Another test that identifies struggling schools is not very valuable to district and state administrators; they already know. What would be valuable is a test that tells teachers, students, and parents the knowledge an individual student has learned and the knowledge remaining to be learned in core subjects. If this information is made available early enough in the school year, teachers could build it into their curricular planning. Diagnostic testing is extremely expensive, but the potential payoffs are enormous. Schools that can afford such information already purchase it from private testing companies. This approach would require that we change the posture of national performance standards from monitoring and compliance to gathering information and sharing it with the most important people in learning.

Collect and Publicize Information on School Services. This information is already in the hands of savvy real estate agents, but the real audience for such information is parents. Let them know schools' average class sizes, whether teachers are teaching in the subject areas for which they were credentialed, and if rigorous Advanced Placement courses are offered. Forget setting national delivery standards that dictate specific features. There is too much variation in the local contingencies affecting critical school characteristics, too much within states to set enforceable state standards, let alone national standards. In addition, the provision of adequate school services is ultimately a political decision made by states and localities, involving taxation and revenue distribution, or a local judicial decision, involving state constitutional requirements. The federal government cannot force local governments to provide schools with challenging curriculum and productive environments, but parents might be able to do so if they were armed with data documenting glaring deficiencies.

The educational reform movement began with great hope, and national standards represent one effort to satisfy our yearning for better schools. Unfortunately, political compromises have diminished the promise of Goals 2000, the national standards legislation. By responding to powerful interests, the act proclaims to layers of government that education needs fundamental reform, ignoring the teachers, students, and parents who sit at the center of educational efforts. Like a puff of smoke on a distant horizon, the political battle over Goals 2000 was a remote event to those who should have been involved, but were not.

5

The Threat to Freedom in Goals 2000

STEPHEN ARONS

Stephen Arons is a professor of legal studies at the University of Massachusetts, Amherst. He is the author of *Compelling Belief: The Culture of American Schooling* (University of Massachusetts Press).

The Goals 2000: Educate America Act, which President Clinton signed into law, has eight lofty goals for systematically improving the quality of American schooling. But the law also has one deep and probably fatal flaw: It will lead to the creation of a national curriculum as a means of reaching its student-achievement and citizenship goal. In setting model national content and performance standards in English, mathematics, science, foreign language, civics and government, arts, history, and geography for K through 12 students, as well as certifying standards and assessments submitted by states seeking federal school-reform grants, the government will be provoking a storm of conflict, which it can neither resolve nor control.

The self-destructive conflicts which now plague California reading tests and Texas health textbooks are signposts for what we may expect on the federal level as this national curriculum takes shape. Californians are confronting a dispute over the state's removal of two stories by the Pulitzer Prize-winning author Alice Walker from a reading comprehension and analysis test. One story, involving the marriage of a Christian and a Muslim, was alleged to be antireligious; the other was apparently considered propaganda for a fifth column of militant vegetarians. (See *Education Week*, March 9, 1994.)

Meanwhile, Texas has been continuing its tradition of looking for a secular humanist under every textbook cover by ordering changes demanded by conservatives in state-authorized health texts. (See *Education Week*,

February 23, 1994.) The battle over whether students in Texas ought to be permitted an informed discussion of AIDS, divorce, drug abuse, human sexuality, and physician-assisted suicide appears headed for the state legislature. There a majority vote will presumably distinguish between official truth and dissenting propaganda, and inform the teachers and children of Texas of which ideas and opinions they should adopt as their own.

By creating a mechanism for the establishment of a national curriculum, Washington is tooling up for its own zero-sum conflicts over conscience and belief in schooling. Senator Jesse Helms, Republican, North Carolina, got it started even before the new law was enacted. His amendment to Goals 2000, adopted by the Senate but modified in the final version of the act, would have barred federal aid to any school district that prohibited voluntary, "constitutionally protected" student prayer in schools. It is clear that the ideological and epistemological battles over schooling are likely to be even more detached from reality on the national level than they have been on the state and local levels.

Under the Goals 2000 law, political-interest groups, politicians with local followings and national aspirations, and associations of education experts are given new forums—including the politically appointed National Education Standards and Improvement Council—in which to engage in a democratic struggle over what Michael Apple has called "official knowledge." In the federal government, as in California and Texas, the more we submit these matters of intellect and conscience to political determinations, the less respect for intellectual freedom, cultural diversity, and critical thinking we should expect our children to learn.

Many in the Clinton administration and in Congress will deny that such a substantial shift of power over curriculum content to the national government is intended or possible under Goals 2000. They will point to the clearly stated voluntary nature of national content standards in the act and to the prohibition the law contains against conditioning federal school aid on state acceptance of the national curriculum. But these assurances ought to be given no more credence now than Americans of 1789 gave to the argument that the new U.S. Constitution contained sufficient checks and balances to make a Bill of Rights unnecessary for protecting individual freedom. There is no education "bill of rights" in the Goals 2000 attempt to reconstitute schooling in the United States.

Once the political and bureaucratic specification of official knowledge is in full federal swing, the conflict over whose beliefs will be reflected in a national curriculum may become so intense that it cripples the entire federal school-reform effort and weakens intellectual freedom and cultural diversity around the country. Here is how the U.S. Supreme Court saw the problem in 1943 when, in *West Virginia v. Barnette*, it declared the compulsory flag salute in public schools to be an unconstitutional "confession of belief":

> Probably no deeper division of our people could proceed from any provocation than from finding it necessary to choose what doctrine and whose program public educational officials shall compel youth to unite in embracing. . . . If it [public education] is to impose any ideological discipline, however, each party or denomination must seek to control, or failing that, to weaken the influence of the educational system.

The Goals 2000 act adopts a top-down, authoritarian, and systematized model of schooling, and it ought probably to be rejected by teachers, students, families, and subcultures on educational grounds alone. But by moving control of the goals of education and the content of schooling ever further from individuals, and by linking performance testing of all students to national content requirements, the act also raises serious constitutional issues.

Establishment of a national curriculum—or of 50 state curricula—would be broadly inconsistent with the principles of constitutional democracy. Those principles hold that if political majorities are empowered to manipulate the content of communication or to regulate the individual freedom to form and express opinions, majority rule itself, and the "just consent of the governed" it is supposed to express, would be rendered meaningless.

An analogy to religious freedoms is incomplete but helpful. The creation of a national curriculum would be as contrary to the fundamental freedoms of intellect and belief protected by the First Amendment as would the establishment of a national religion or the approval of an official catechism. Suggesting that a national curriculum would be inoffensive to the First Amendment, as long as the knowledge and skills students must demonstrate are value-neutral, ignores a fundamental reality of learning and teaching. Government technocrats would be as convincing if they claimed that an established religion would be constitutionally acceptable as long as it were based on monotheism. In a pluralistic society, value-neutral schooling is a contradiction in terms.

These are serious problems with a long-overdue federal commitment to improving the quality of teacher–student interactions around the country. But perhaps an urgent concern for freedom of conscience in schooling is unwarranted here. After all, the law was crafted by two presidential administrations and two political parties, has mobilized much of the education establishment, and probably would be approved by most educators if put to a vote. What's more, right-wing fundamentalists have had increasing success in gaining a foothold in local school board elections, so a nationalization of education policy might slow the trend of intolerance that threatens individual freedoms.

But the fact that there has been virtually no public debate about the fate of intellectual freedom and cultural diversity under Goals 2000 does not inspire confidence in the wisdom of this reform program. Nor should those who appreciate the complex connection between democracy and education be reassured by the tacit approval a national curriculum has received from educators.

If there are significant reasons for putting the principles of constitutional democracy at risk by creating a national curriculum, they ought to become part of the public discourse before this juggernaut gets under way.

Only one argument for taking this risk appears important enough to be taken seriously—the need to reverse the widely acknowledged inequalities in schooling that have brutalized large segments of the rising generation. Among the most harmful of these inequalities are the disparate expectations which mark some students for success, consign others to frustration and broken dreams, and are all too often the silent justification for gross inequalities in the resources available for schools. The imposition of a national curriculum might be advocated as a means to ensure that the same high expectations are held and pursued for all students, regardless of poverty, race, ethnic or linguistic heritage, gender, or other status.

But the essential goal of eliminating these individually and culturally destructive inequalities can be effectively achieved without resorting to a national curriculum. It isn't necessary to impose the conflict-inducing, freedom-restricting, diversity-inhibiting uniformity of official knowledge on every teacher, student, school, and subculture in the country. The alternative, a thorough program for updating and improving the professional skills of teachers, would neither cause the kind of conflict which would undermine all of Goals 2000, nor restrict the freedoms essential to professional teaching, active learning, and a healthy, pluralistic democracy.

The curriculum provisions of Goals 2000 ought to be repealed. In their place should be created a 10-year program during which every teacher in the United States receives two summer scholarships for continuing education in the substance and pedagogy of his or her field, whether elementary reading or advanced physics. Every teacher would be required to participate, but each would be free to choose from among many continuing-education offerings created by decentralized, nongovernmental consortia, each of which would include a college or university. Goals 2000 already calls for some grants for professional-development programs, so the idea is hardly revolutionary.

In addition to scholarships, which would empower teachers and induce colleges and universities to offer continuing education for them, what is needed is to make the choice of which continuing-education program to attend entirely voluntary, and to leave the content of the offerings to the professional judgment of their sponsors. There would be no national curriculum standards to systematize these offerings, and other government content controls at the state or federal level would be prohibited. The program could be set up so that every teacher could use it within its 10-year life. The program of required continuing education would begin with teachers working in schools in which inequalities have taken their heaviest toll. States would be required to provide the in-school resources necessary for a reeducated teaching profession to function at a higher level.

Adoption of a teacher-scholarship program as a substitute for national curriculum standards would provide what the principles of constitutional law would call a "less restrictive alternative." That is, it would attain the legitimate and compelling goals of the legislation, but by a means that would impose fewer restrictions on constitutional rights than a national curriculum would. By this mechanism we might not only avoid prolonged conflict and litigation, but also improve schooling, preserve diversity, secure the freedom of belief, and protect the sphere of intellect and spirit which is at the core of education and which the First Amendment excludes from majority control.

6

Developing World-Class Education Standards: Some Conceptual and Political Dilemmas

J. Myron Atkin

Professor of Education, School of Education, Stanford University

Introduction

There may not be many issues on which politicians from both parties profess as much agreement as on the need to develop world-class standards for U.S. education. Governors, the president, and a large number of legislators all have concluded that improvement of schools requires establishing explicit standards for the major subject-matter fields: science, mathematics, English and literature, history, and geography. The agreed-upon objectives, they believe, will set a needed and overdue direction for a national education agenda and provide a framework within which subsequent concrete steps can be taken to improve the nation's schools.

In 1989, then-President Bush and the 50 governors issued a declaration from Charlottesville, Virginia, that articulated six broad goals for U.S. education. Among them were the following:

> By the year 2000, American students will leave grades four, eight, and twelve having demonstrated competency in challenging subject matter including English, mathematics, science, history, and geography. . . . U.S. students will be first in the world in science and mathematics achievement.

This manifesto was followed in 1991 by an administration document prepared by the secretary of education and submitted to the president; it declared:

> New World Standards: Standards will be developed ... for each of the five core subjects [that] represent what young Americans need to know and be able to do if they are to live and work successfully in today's world. These standards will incorporate both knowledge and skills, to ensure that, when they leave school, young Americans are prepared for further study and the work force. (U.S. Department of Education 1991, 11)

Bill Clinton was one of the key governors who participated in drafting the Charlottesville statement, so it is no surprise that there was hardly a pause in the drive toward standards when he succeeded George Bush.

In a few other countries, too, a decision has been reached to define education standards (though other labels are usually used), and, as in the United States, the sentiment supporting such a policy encompasses the full political spectrum. On the right, talk of subject-specific expectations seems to stimulate nostalgia about the way schools once may have been: serious students, unambiguous and broadly accepted objectives, demanding teachers, high levels of performance. On the left, the press for standards usually stems from the fact that schools vary widely in their apparent success. In particular, schools in poor neighborhoods—and especially those that serve children from minority groups—are not considered to be as successful as schools in more affluent neighborhoods. In the name of fairness, *all* children should be expected to reach the same levels of achievement; a primary task is to identify those levels.

Whatever the accuracy of the perceptions that have led to near-unanimous political agreement in the United States about the need to establish education standards, there is no mistaking the seriousness with which they are being discussed and designed. Specific groups have been designated to develop standards and several have been working diligently for more than a year. The federal government (primarily through the Department of Education but typically with other agencies joining in the effort) has begun investing millions of dollars in the standards movement at a time when money is unusually tight and there is no shortage of children's causes with plausible claims for public dollars. Draft materials regarding possible new standards are being circulated, and legislation has been passed to create a 20-member National Education Standards and Improvement Council (NESIC) to monitor and coordinate the effort.

There are two major conceptual obstacles, however, to this earnest resolve to set a direction for U.S. education by identifying standards. First, there is uncertainty about what the range of standards might actually look like and the functions they would serve. Second, no one knows what is meant by "world class." Compounding these dilemmas, political issues and conflicts have arisen, some associated in the United States with traditional debates about federal as against state-level prerogatives and some associated with determining who has the credibility and the authority to determine the standards in the various subject-matter fields. Adding to these problems is the serious possibility that professional perspectives—those of subject-matter experts, teachers, and school administrators—may, in the end, conflict with political expectations and enthusiasm. Such an outcome was indeed the result in one nation, England,[1] where a massive attempt was made to institute a national curriculum where none had existed before.

Thus there is a sharp escalation of effort but no guarantee that it necessarily will lead to education improvement or calm a nervous public. In fact, in some circles, there is growing skepticism about what might be accomplished and increasing concern that the standards enterprise might, in the end, fall short of its declared goals or even prove counterproductive.

This section attempts to outline and illustrate some of the key issues and challenges besetting the standards movement. The point of view proffered here is that the unprecedented national standards exercise now under way in the United States has the potential for making significant contributions to the improvement of U.S. education, but not in the fashion that many advocates of more precise education standards seem to think, and not without certain risks. And the term world class has little operational meaning because virtually every country in the world, especially those to which the United States likes to compare itself, is trying to change its education system in significant ways. The perception in the United States of the superior educations offered elsewhere is illusory, at least in the eyes of the public and politicians in the countries we tend to admire. In some countries envied by the United States, significant education reforms are moving in directions diametrically opposite to those reflected in the U.S. standards movement.

The proposed standards themselves are beginning to precipitate useful debate. Broad discussion of them, during both the development and implementation processes, can lead to significant improvement in many classrooms. For standards to achieve their potential, however, the groups

---

[1]Scotland, Northern Ireland, and (to a lesser degree) Wales have independence in education matters. The British developments highlighted in this paper pertain only to England and Wales, which constitute one jurisdiction.

with a stake in the matter—especially teachers—must have plenty of time to deliberate on the education vision that precise subject-specific standards reflect and project and the most sensible ways to achieve it. Also, ways must be found to avoid dampening education initiatives that do not fit easily within the subject-by-subject approach that now has the full force of federal government approval.

Not least, an assessment system must be devised that comports with the high-quality education the new standards will demand. The challenges to the development of an educationally defensible examination system however, are formidable, if experience in the United States, as well as other countries, is any indication.

Who Defines Standards?

The first group to develop curriculum standards in the sense in which the term is currently used was the National Council of Teachers of Mathematics (NCTM). Indeed, the NCTM effort was a prime factor in inspiring and shaping today's standards movement. The mathematics standards were the product of a multiyear effort to articulate a vision of improved mathematics education in U.S. elementary and secondary schools. It was a carefully engineered exercise that involved hundreds of participants and resulted in a 258-page document that was generally acclaimed within the mathematics and mathematics education communities, as well as by the informed public. The timing of the report (Working Groups of the Commission on Standards for School Mathematics 1989) of this voluntary, professional association could not have been more propitious for those interested in building a national consensus around curriculum changes. The report provided a model at a time when persistent and growing concern about the quality of U.S. education was crystallizing and political leaders were being urged to take action.

Unlike some previous bursts of attention to education, public interest in education did not abate during the 1980s.[2] The public, galvanized in part by the Reagan administration report decrying a "rising tide of mediocrity" in the schools (National Commission on Excellence in Education 1983), perceived a direct link between the quality of U.S. education and the state of the economy. Since the condition of the economy was seen

---

[2]Post-Sputnik efforts to ameliorate problems in science and math education, the mid-1960s focus on children in poor neighborhoods, and the back-to-the-basics movement in the 1970s all represented attempts to deal with education improvement. After the initial flurry of attention, however, public interest tended to wane.

as parlous (and still is), education reform moved toward the top of the national agenda. Spurred by public anxiety about the state of the schools, and after a long period of apparent inability to influence curriculum matters, government officials at the federal level were searching actively for answers.

The Federal Role

By statute, since the creation of the republic the federal government has had a minimal role in education in general, and certainly in matters of curriculum. During the First World War, however, the government began supporting vocational education programs. After the Second World War, special programs were established by the federal government to stimulate improvement of science, mathematics, and foreign language education because of their presumed relationship to national defense. During the height of the civil rights movement, Congress (and the courts) became forcefully involved in the schools to ensure equal access, but only peripherally with respect to curriculum content. Even with all these efforts, however, the federal government's contribution to support of elementary and secondary schools stands today at only about 6 percent of the total cost of education. And, with constitutional prohibitions against deep and continuing involvement, especially with respect to curriculum matters, it will be difficult to carve out a prominent role for the president or the Congress.

State Involvement

In the states, education debates traditionally revolved around finance and, in recent decades, access. True, there has always been some attention focused on the curriculum—in response, for example, to pressures to teach about the dangers of alcohol consumption in the early part of the century and a broader range of substance abuse in the latter part, or to downplay the teaching of human evolution, or to instruct adolescents about careful driving, or to attend to other concerns for which there was an identifiable and vocal constituency. Legislatures also acted from time to time on changes in state-level examinations. But, in general, issues of subject-matter content were left to those who staffed the state education departments and to local districts. The districts, in turn, tended to turn matters of subject-matter content over to the teachers and school administrators.

Almost surely, these factors underlie the enthusiasm with which the governors and the president embraced the NCTM standards report. Here was a voluntary, national effort intended to raise the quality of mathematics education in all U.S. schools. Its spirit reflected the traditional role of government in education: there were no compulsory requirements with respect to what was to be taught; content was a matter for local school districts. Yet the report had the potential to articulate a vision for U.S. education and to stimulate necessary local action that would comport with that vision. The standards issue seemed an ideal vehicle to display political leadership. Elected officials, governors, and the president quickly adopted the term employed in the title of the mathematics report—standards—and issued the call for establishment of analogous statements for all core school subjects.

Subject Areas

Currently, about a dozen groups are trying to articulate subject-matter standards. Among those furthest along in the process are the National Research Council (NRC) of the National Academy of Sciences (science), the American Association for the Advancement of Science (AAAS, also science), the Center for Civic Education (civics), the National Council for the Social Studies (social studies), the National Council for Geography Education (geography), and the Consortium of National Arts Education Associations (the arts). Most, but not all, are supported by the federal government as well as private agencies. In the case of the National Research Council, most of the money is coming from the Department of Education and the National Science Foundation. The National Council for Geography Education receives funds from the Department of Education and the National Endowment for the Humanities. The civics effort is supported by the Department of Education and the Pew Charitable Trusts. The work in the arts receives funding from the Department of Education, the National Endowment for the Arts, and the National Endowment for the Humanities.

Some of the most active players, however, such as the AAAS, are not receiving government funds in support of their efforts to define standards. The American Association for the Advancement of Science standards effort is a by-product of its Project 2061, a major initiative to articulate a vision of excellence in science education for the nation's schools. Project 2061 predates the current flurry of activity about standards. But when establishment of standards began to claim the center of the education stage, the project gave priority to the issue and, in record time, translated and extended its previous work into a statement of desirable "benchmarks" (virtually synonymous with standards) for science education (Project 2061, American Association for the Advancement of Science 1993). The benchmarks were designed to influence the schools and, most particularly, the government-supported effort at the National Research Council.

When they were released, with considerable skill and fanfare, in the fall of 1993, the press, often on page 1, reported the benchmarks as representing the new science standards (probably to the consternation of the NRC, which is the designated agency for developing science standards and is still actively at work on the task).

The standards project of the National Council for the Social Studies is another self-initiated activity with no support from federal authorities at present. In this case, the lack of financial backing may stem from antipathy in the Bush administration to the concept of social studies as a school subject (in contrast to history and geography). Indeed, the interest in standards by the National Council, and its attempt to claim a position for the field by articulating standards, reasonably can be seen as a defensive reaction by those associated with a jeopardized subject. It remains to be seen whether the council can capture the same sort of public interest as the AAAS benchmarks have.

What Kinds of Standards?

Once the drive toward establishment of standards began in earnest and various groups started to allocate resources to the task, it soon became apparent that the very concept of standards was somewhat problematic to those given the responsibility of defining them. Is a standard a guideline? A minimum expectation? An aspiration? A measuring stick? A vision of a desirable state? And are there not standards associated with the quality of all the different elements of the education system, rather than just the formal curriculum?

Politicians meant initially to launch an activity that identified what children were expected to know as a result of their formal schooling. The wording of the Charlottesville statement makes clear that their concern was with subject matter. School programs were seen as unchallenging, student achievement as unimpressive, teachers as possessing marginal competence. Demand higher levels of performance, and educational quality will rise. Or so most politicians who addressed the issue assumed.

Standards-makers, however, quickly expanded their charge as they began to wrestle with details of the task. They saw the job as considerably more complex than just specifying curriculum content, although that assignment became the primary concern and was extraordinarily challenging in its own right. We soon began to hear not only about curriculum (or content) standards, but also about performance standards, assessment standards, teaching standards, program standards, and—a partic-

ularly controversial matter—support (sometimes called delivery or opportunity-to-learn) standards. Many of these seem to overlap.

In hindsight, this outcome should not have been a surprise. Professionals in a field, and they are the ones given the task of articulating
education standards, almost always view matters in more complicated
terms than those without daily involvement.

Content and Performance Standards

In most cases (but not all), the starting point for standards development
has been a consideration of the subject matter of the various disciplines
usually taught in school—the curriculum. What should children study?
According to a draft statement of civics and government standards:[3]

> A standard is a rule or principle used as a basis for judgment and com-
> parison. . . . Content standards are statements of what students should *know*
> and *be able to do* in relation to a specific discipline such as civics, history,
> or geography. Thus, they include content or knowledge and understandings
> and skills. Skills include intellectual skills as well as those essential to read-
> ing, writing, speaking, and participating in the governance of their class-
> room, school, and the larger communities of which they are a part. (Center
> for Civic Education 1993)

The National Research Council group working on science standards put
it this way:

> Science content standards describe what all students should know and be
> able to do in science as a result of their school science studies. Although
> we honor the fact that the intellectual character of the science curriculum
> is derived in large part from the knowledge base of the natural sciences,
> we also believe that "science content" in schools should not be limited just
> to the concepts, principles, facts, laws, and theories that represent the body
> of scientific knowledge.
>
> Instead, four general categories of *school science content* serve to define
> the breadth of science content and to provide organizers for these stan-
> dards:
>> Science as Inquiry
>> Science Subject Matter
>> Scientific Connections
>> Science and Human Affairs (National Research Council 1993, 3)

[3]Almost all the examples of standards in this section are drawn from draft material distributed for comment and criticism. All of it is subject to revision before final publication,
and many of the examples, almost certainly, will not appear in the final versions.

"To know and be able to do"—which boil down to subject matter content and student performance—are the common elements in the definition of an education standard. The draft material from the different standards-setting groups indicates, however, that there is not always consistency among the groups about definitions, usage, or even priority. One group, geography, appears to have moved more rapidly than the others toward the development of performance standards. That is, a draft of performance standards appeared before the content standards. The two types of standards are closely linked, of course. *Performance* emphasizes action by the student and so is linked more closely to assessment. The distinction is drawn by the geography group as follows:

> Content standards for K through 4, 5 through 8, and 9 through 12 will identify essential subject matter, skills, and perspectives that students should know and be able to use to be competent individuals and citizens. Performance standards will describe ways in which students should be able to demonstrate cumulative mastery of geography's content, skills, and perspectives upon exiting grades 4, 8, and 12. If students master the content of geography and can demonstrate that mastery, they will have acquired knowledge and skills equal to or better than those required of top students in other nations. (Geography Education Standards Project 1993, 1)

Standards have also been developed for the arts. After a justificatory statement about the centrality of arts in the education of all students, content and achievement standards were proposed for consideration. The arts (dance, music, theater, and the visual arts) are categorized under the main headings Creating and Performing, Perceiving and Analyzing, and Understanding Cultural and Historical Contexts. Standards are offered for grades K through 4, 5 through 8, and 9 through 12. (Consortium of National Arts Education Associations 1993.)

The performance standards promulgated by the geography group are indistinguishable in style and intention from the *achievement* standards proposed by the arts group. Note, however, that some of the standards groups do not formally distinguish between content and performance. In one prominent case, the content standard is elaborated in the form of discursive narrative, making the standard difficult to describe adequately in a list of bulleted items. Then performance elements, which do lend themselves to a succinct list, are used to illustrate what students might be expected to do.

In a fall 1993 draft, the NRC offered sample content standards. For example, for grades 9 through 12 studying earth and space science: "As a result of their activities in grades 9 through 12, all students should develop an understanding of:

- matter and energy in earth systems;
- processes and cycles in earth systems;
- the evolution of earth systems; and
- the earth in the universe."

This statement is followed by several pages of text that suggest the spirit and intent of the standard by expanding on key earth science concepts. Then some "indicators of student understanding" are listed:

> As an indication of their understanding of earth and space science, students should be able to:
> - Design and carry out an activity showing that energy can be transmitted by radiation from a candle, light bulb, or other source, and use the results to explain how the same process brings radiation, mainly in the form of light, across space from the sun to earth;
> - Investigate the absorption and reflection of solar energy by various materials;
> - Describe the causes and general characteristics of convection as observed in a fluid. Explain how convection moves energy received from the sun through the oceans and atmosphere of the earth system, giving rise to clouds, global winds, and ocean currents;
> - Discuss the evidence for convection currents in earth's mantle, driven by heat rising from earth's core, causing the motion of the crustal plates; and
> - Identify situations where energy is transmitted by conduction and explain how this process spreads energy through portions of the earth system.

Teaching Standards

Recognizing that no new set of curriculum standards is likely to lead to higher-quality education unless teachers receive a high-quality education, at least one group, again the NRC committee working on science standards, has begun to draft standards for professional development. The focus is on what science content teachers should learn and how they should learn it, on how teachers learn to teach science, on lifelong learning for teachers, on teachers' development programs, and on teachers' development policies.

With respect to learning science, the draft standards propose (among many suggestions) that teachers become actively involved in scientific investigations themselves, collaboratively, as part of their introduction to science content. Regarding teachers' development policies, the accent is on the need for consistency (in certification, curriculum, and examinations) in terms of federal, state, and local actions, and on the need to ensure correspondence between governmental initiatives and those of voluntary professional groups of scientists and teachers.

Opportunity-to-Learn Standards

Many educators who became involved in articulating national standards took the position early in the process that fairness demands that schools not be held to account unless teachers and school administrators are provided with the resources necessary to achieve the new goals. They asked, for example, can a school with 35 students in a class can be held to the same standards as a school with 25? Can a school without a licensed science teacher be expected to demonstrate the same achievement levels as a school with qualified teachers? Can a school with a language laboratory or state-of-the-art computer equipment be compared fairly to a school without these resources?

At the first meeting of the National Committee on Science Education Standards and Assessment (NCSESA) in 1992,[4] several members of the new committee indicated that they had professional and moral reasons for insisting that standards for *support* of children and teachers be a part of the National Research Council effort. This suggestion was not unanticipated. As a direct result of previously initiated education activities at NRC, the organization had established a committee on a Nationwide Education Support System for Teachers and Schools (NESSTS) "to examine the merit and feasibility of a national delivery system for science and mathematics education." NESSTS' report identified the requirements associated with "a standards-based support system," including:

> The support system must include assistance to schools in adapting their programs to the diverse needs of students and teachers. . . . [It] must address the needs of teachers for substantial noninstructional time devoted to planning, assessing progress, and consulting other teachers within the school and beyond. (National Research Council 1993)

The NRC science group (which next to mathematics probably promulgated the most comprehensive of the standards initiatives) then went on to draft "program standards" to reflect the levels of support for teachers and students expected of standards-driven science programs. Supplementing the statement about professional development cited very briefly in the preceding discussion, program standards reflect concern about the *context* in which high-quality science education is to take place. In an informal, working document by this group, issues were raised that em-

[4]The author of this paper is a member of NCSESA.

phasized the importance of providing the full range of science experiences for students K through 12. What about the nature of the curriculum as a whole? Is it consistent across grade levels? Does it match what is known about children? Does the science relate appropriately to other subjects, especially mathematics? Does the learning environment reflect "scientific attitudes and habits of mind as well as the social values conducive to scientific learning"?

One standard states: "The K through 12 science program should give students access to appropriate and sufficient resources including time, space, materials, equipment, and personnel." This standard is elaborated in five paragraphs of text; one of which reads:

> Science learning that is based in collaborative inquiry requires space as well as time. There must be space for students to work together in groups, to engage safely in investigation with materials, and to display work in progress as well as finished work. At the younger levels, science need not have a laboratory setting. Integration with the rest of the curriculum may well be enhanced if science is an integral part of the students' environment. At the older levels, laboratories become important and provide a safe location and appropriate space for inquiry.

This strong emphasis on the support and resources that are necessary to meet newly articulated curriculum standards has engendered two kinds of reservations. One centers on the matter of who pays. Several governors and legislators—looking toward the not-too-distant future—see the probable acceptance of some sort of national content standards and, possibly, a national (voluntary) examination system. Content and achievement standards are one thing. But if the standards directly address the matter of required resources, where does the money come from? Is the standards movement one more example of federally initiated expectations without accompanying federal funds? States and localities are strapped financially. Formal agreement about the conditions that are necessary to achieve the new education standards legitimates and fortifies one more demand on strained local treasuries.

Another reservation about opportunity-to-learn standards, one with the potential to alter the concept dramatically, is that they are too vague and unrelated to outcomes. Andrew Porter, a University of Wisconsin education professor, argues that such standards should focus more on factors that are "known" to have a strong connection to student achievement:

> What is a good indicator of OTL (opportunity to learn)? Amount of instructional time on specific topics? Availability of equipment (computers, lab materials)? Access to good teachers? The main criterion for selecting in-

dicators should be utility for predicting student achievement. The best predictors of student achievement that are within a school's control are the content actually taught, the instructional strategies used, and the standards for achievement evident in testing and grading. . . . Recently developed curriculum standards are a good start, but they are too general and incomplete to describe the enacted curriculum in ways that predict student achievement. (Porter 1993)

Porter, in stressing factors that are within a school's control, shifts the ground back to teachers. He suggests they should be required to keep logs that indicate how much time they devote to subjects like cellular biology, chemistry, magnetism, and light. They might also keep track of the modes of instruction they employ, such as exposition, pictorial models, conceptual models, graphing, and lab work. With respect to learning outcomes (in mathematics), they would keep records of the percentage of time spent on matters such as memorization of facts, collecting data, ordering and estimating, and novel problem solving. These elements, Porter says, relate directly to the opportunity to learn.

This interpretation of opportunity-to-learn standards differs sharply from that enunciated by groups like the NRC—in fact, it turns the notion of support standards on its head—because it places the matter of resources for teachers and schools in the background and teacher performance in the foreground. If one or both of the two standards concepts survives, they will have to be disentangled, with subsequent delineation of both program standards and opportunity-to-learn standards.

World Class?

The present standards movement in the United States is powered partly by a sense of competitiveness with other countries. The nation is concerned about becoming second-rate economically, and a strong relationship is seen between industrial productivity, a favorable balance of international trade, and the quality of education. It is true that there is almost universal anguish about the quality of education; education reform is a global phenomenon. But the initiatives that are developed for making things better in any country depend primarily on local perception, circumstance, tradition, and opportunity. Each country tries to reach its own evolving ideals by modifying its education system, using the policy tools at hand. But each one also tries to exorcise its own demons. In the United States, many of those demons are seen to lie in the questionable quality of the work force: education must be improved to increase national productivity.

In only a very few countries, however, has acute public concern about the schools taken the form of a drive toward identifying national standards and the establishment or strengthening of a national examination system. That particular direction for education reform seems to arise in countries with the greatest distrust of those who now staff the education system. It stems from the conviction that many teachers and school administrators are of questionable competence, and that progress lies in holding them to greater account.

The British Example

England and Wales have moved more aggressively and rapidly toward a national curriculum and assessment system than has any other nation where no such system had existed before. They have also suffered the most pain in the process. Deep traditions of local control in Britain date back for more than a century. The national government historically has remained aloof from curriculum matters. But state-supported schools gradually began to be seen by large segments of the population as soft at the primary level and chaotic at the secondary. Labor prime ministers were almost as assertive as Conservative politicians about the need to raise curriculum quality by more direct government action. Over a period of about 15 years, beginning in the mid-1970s, the stage was gradually set for drastic reforms, culminating in 1988, when the Thatcher-led Conservative government instituted a national curriculum in 10 subjects.

There was broad involvement in designing the new curriculum (as there has been in the United States). Education experts from many spheres— subject-matter specialists, teachers, teacher educators, school inspectors—devoted countless hours to the task of devising new courses. And they acted with a pronounced sense of urgency spurred by short government deadlines in completing and distributing new curricula.

In a surprisingly short time, however, the initiative foundered. There were two primary reasons. One was disagreement about content. (The other, a sharp and even more destructive controversy about assessment, will be highlighted in the following discussion.) The history curriculum took the brunt of criticism, though not alone. It had been developed primarily by inspectors and teachers and stressed the importance of major concepts in the subject, like cross-national interdependence and interactions among individuals, groups, and institutions. By implication more than by direct assertion, it also deemphasized memorization of dates by placing greater value on identification of patterns and other contextual factors.

To make the story quite short, the prime minister herself was affronted and infuriated when she examined the new proposed curriculum. Not one to shy from details, she entered the debate personally and forcefully by ridiculing the suggested history program in a major speech that made the front page of most national newspapers. The current problem with history education, she said, is that children are not taught enough facts. The British education system needs more rigor, thus facts are to be emphasized. The proposed curriculum was another indication of education gone soft.

She, and the press, highlighted the issue as "concepts versus facts," with no doubt about which were superior. The perception reflected in much of the British press was that creation of the new national curriculum gave too much influence to the very people who were responsible in the first place for the problems of British education: the professional educationists—teachers and those who prepare them.

Implications for the United States

Analogous sentiments may underlie the U.S. decision, at least at the federal level, not to support standards development in social studies, but instead to emphasize geography and history. And it takes no particular prescience to foresee heated debates (with similar caricatures of the issues) in the United States when standards are released that reflect a vision of education at variance with the personal educational experience of most of today's adults. The National Council of Teachers of Mathematics standards apparently are supported by a surprisingly broad array of professionals, politicians, and parents. But it is by no means clear that such consensus will be sustained when many of the details are worked out and the populace learns that the professionals' views of appropriate standards are a major shift from remembered practice; there are already rumbles in several communities about the NCTM's approval of the use of hand-held calculators. It is unlikely that the British experience will prove unique.

Any debate about curriculum has the potential for deep political controversy. That is not to say that debate about education goals is undesirable. School subjects represent a society's definition of how it wants its young people introduced to the adult world. Discussion of what to teach touches on deeply held feelings about what a country values. But the risks are great if the conflicts swirl around slogans and become grist for even deeper ideological divisions—as, for example, opposing views about the role of schools in sex education or the teaching of evolution.

Almost certainly, some of the education standards proposed in this country will be lightning rods for such conflict. Primarily for this reason, many of the standards-development efforts encourage extended discussion of draft material. At the NRC, the critique and consensus process involves scores of organizations whose opinions are sought at regular intervals along the way to a final report. It remains to be seen, however, how successful this effort will be at warding off simplistic public debates after the standards are made final.

The Japanese Example

Almost always, decisions about curriculum content are reached as much in reaction to perceived problems as in pursuit of a fresh vision. Existing problems, however, are defined differently in different countries. Many in the United States seem to look enviously at Japanese education. Japan, however, has recently revamped its curriculum because of internal dissatisfaction. ("Courses of Study" are revised regularly in Japan, about once every 10 years.) Two concerns among the Japanese when the current round of curriculum revision was initiated in the late 1980s were, first, the country's perception of a lack of creativity and originality in its students and, second, increasing alarm about problems of environmental degradation.

Consequently, Japan's latest science curriculum is undergirded by several principles that may appear surprising and anachronistic to some critics of U.S. education. Among them are "that importance be attached to the fostering of capability of coping positively with social changes and to the cultivation of foundations of creativity, and that the willingness to learn by oneself be encouraged" and the "need to lay greater stress on closeness to nature, observation, and experiment . . . and to develop a more positive attitude toward nature as a whole."[5] A new, required subject has been introduced, life environmental studies. It stands now as the sole science subject in grades 1 and 2. In grades 3 through 6, the science curriculum consists of living organisms and their environment, matter and energy, and the earth and space. One hundred and fifty 45-minute hours are devoted to science in each elementary school grade. Problem solving is emphasized throughout.

The Japanese example (and others could be cited) reflects the fact that science education is in extraordinary flux there, as it is in most countries. Priorities shift. They always will. Standards setting in such a situation is difficult. Even if agreements are negotiated, it is not clear how long they will last. Because each country identifies somewhat different problems in

[5]The information presented here about changes in Japanese science education is drawn from a paper prepared by Takashi Yamagiwa, chief school inspector, Primary and Secondary Education Bureau, Ministry of Education, Science, and Culture of Japan (MONBUSHO), for a November 1991 conference of the Organization for Economic Cooperation and Development (OECD) in Paris.

its education system and in its society, each copes in a different manner. There is no international standard guiding the selection of curriculum content, and it is unlikely there ever will be.

One further point in understanding U.S. developments in an international context: it may be important to note that many of the countries trying to forge greater consensus about the goals of education use softer imagery than is suggested by the term standards. Even Britain has used "attainment targets." Spain also uses "targets," but ministers state they are intended to be suggestive only. Officials assert, further, that the targets are flexible. The claim is credible inasmuch as Spain has no national examination and is taking systematic and significant steps to give more authority for education (and almost everything else) to its autonomous regions.[6] In British Columbia and some other Canadian provinces, "reference sets" is the term employed, also connoting guidelines rather than compulsory requirements.

In partial summary, no one knows what world class means. It is true that many countries are trying to change their education systems in significant ways. However, in every case, policymakers are responding primarily to internal pressures. In England and Wales, there is a major effort to nationalize the curriculum, but none in Scotland, nor in Spain, Norway, Austria, Germany, Italy, or most other countries. Most policymakers are interested in what goes on elsewhere in the world; parallel developments sometimes profit from the exchange of ideas. But few countries pattern their reforms in any specific sense on what goes on elsewhere. It seems that "world class standards" is a slogan, probably intended to be inspirational. It carries little operational meaning and it is unlikely that it ever was intended to be taken literally.

The Heart of the Matter: Assessment

Standards and examinations are not identical, of course, but they are closely related. As noted, "achievement standards," "performance standards," or "indicators of student understanding" are an integral part of each of the U.S. efforts to develop educational standards. They are intended not only to add instructional specificity to what may otherwise be general statements of content-related goals, but also to provide guidance for student assessment. With "voluntary" national examinations on the horizon, these statements are likely precursors of the kinds of specifications we might

[6]Personal conversation with Alejandro Tiana Ferrer, director, Center for Investigation, Documentation and Evaluation, Ministry of Education, Madrid, December 12, 1993.

expect for standardized tests of the future. This impression is fortified by the fact that all the standards work focuses on grades 4, 8, and 12, which happen to be the grades selected by the National Assessment of Educational Progress and which represent the most likely levels for proposed new national examinations.

As the United States moves toward nationalization of the curriculum and a possible new examination system, and in view of U.S. interest in being world class, it may be instructive briefly to examine the nature of testing practices and related developments in other countries. A recent report by the congressional Office of Technology Assessment (OTA) highlights several points that are noteworthy in this regard (Office of Technology Assessment 1992, see especially Ch. 5). First, national, standardized examinations are an increasing rarity in Europe and Asia—and they are seldom administered before students reach age 16. Second, these examinations are almost always used for purposes of selection for university admission and hardly ever for feedback to teachers or for monitoring education systems. (Instead, some variation of an inspection system is the primary method of ensuring overall accountability in most countries.) Third, teachers in other countries play a major role in developing, administering, and scoring national examinations.

Furthermore, the OTA report states, "the trend in several countries has been to allow schools a greater say in the definition of curricula during the compulsory period of schooling" (Office of Technology Assessment 1992, 138). Germany leaves matters entirely to the individual states, but, in practice, to the schools. So does Austria. So do Switzerland and Denmark. Trends may change, of course. But at a time when the United States is seriously considering identification of standards, and probably more standardized testing, to define and gauge the quality of the education system, it should be remembered that the practice elsewhere is quite different, and, in fact, has moved in the opposite direction during the last 15 years.

The British Experience

Again, the major exception to greater devolution of curriculum and assessment responsibility to localities, schools, and teachers has occurred in England and Wales, where the new National Curriculum was instituted with the Education Reform Act of 1988. Conflicts about facts versus concepts in history have already been cited. They were mild, however, in comparison to the furor about testing.

In connection with the new National Curriculum that, for the first time, gave central government direct control over what was to be taught in the school subjects, it was proposed that every student be tested at ages 7, 11, 14, and 16. The initial job of making recommendations about how the plan was to be put into effect was given to a special committee: the Task Group on Assessment and Testing (TGAT), chaired by Paul Black, a physicist and professor of science education at King's College London.[7]

Among other recommendations, TGAT suggested that national assessment be based on a combination of teacher assessment and externally set tasks, to be called Standard Assessment Tasks (SATs); SATs would often resemble carefully designed classroom work. Deliberation among teachers (group moderation) was suggested to enhance the comparability of standards among teachers in their own assessments and to reconcile results of the SATs with teacher assessments. The main aim of assessment should be formative, not summative, said TGAT. The assessments at the four ages should be interrelated, with later stages building on those that come before. There should be 10 levels for each subject in order to address performance criteria in a sequence that corresponds to a desirable learning progression. Assessment results should be reported in terms of aggregated achievement consisting of no more than four profile components; the profile in each subject, rather than a single result, would be the educationally significant outcome.

A few months after accepting the main recommendations in the TGAT report, the Department of Education and Science established new councils to consider the recommendations and further develop curriculum and assessment policy and practice. Several changes were made to the TGAT recommendations. It was decided that the results of the externally developed SATs would be provided for each student and not used only in conjunction with teachers' assessments. The weight of teachers' judgments in student assessment was thereby significantly reduced.

Against this background, government officials were becoming increasingly hostile to the proposed examinations, particularly the SATs, which did not look familiar. They were based on teachers' judgments about student performance, not on how children made clear choices based on written questions devised by independent assessors. In a speech, Kenneth Clarke, minister of education in 1991, said the following:

> The British pedagogue's hostility to written examinations of any kind can be taken to ludicrous extremes. The British Left believe that pencil-and-

[7]Much of this material about assessment in England and Wales has been obtained through conversations with Black and, especially, from his invited address at the April 1993 meeting of the American Educational Research Association, "Performance Assessment and Accountability: The Experience in England and Wales," *Educational Evaluation and Policy Analysis*, June 1994.

> paper examinations impose stress on pupils and demotivate them. We have tolerated for 20 years an arrangement whereby there is no national testing or examination of any kind for most pupils until the General Certificate of Secondary Education (GCSE) at the age of 16. . . . This remarkable national obsession lies behind the more vehement opposition to the recent intro-duction of [testing of seven-year-olds]. . . . [The tests] were made a little too complicated and we have said we will simplify them. . . . The complications themselves were largely designed in the first place in an attempt to pacify opponents who feared above all else "paper-and-pencil" tests.

Largely on Clarke's insistence, the character of the SATs was altered so they more closely resembled traditional tests. This modification made them less burdensome to administer, but also more objectionable edu-cationally to many teachers.

In the turmoil, and for some of the reasons outlined above (and many others, including the excessive assessment load on teachers), the as-sessment plan in England and Wales collapsed completely. Teachers had become demoralized. Some of the teacher unions refused to participate in the examination program and they were upheld in the courts. The pub-lic was angry and confused.

In a personal communication, Paul Black, from his admittedly self-in-terested position, summarized the problems of a national assessment sys-tem as follows:

1. The limitations of external written tests are not understood.
2. Better summative tests take longer and cost more, and they don't look like "proper tests."
3. There is confusion about the distinction between formative and summative assessment.
4. Nostalgic models of learning underlie public perception and policy.
5. Assessment schemes can drown in a sea of reference criteria.
6. There is confusion about assessment for the purpose of school ac-countability as against certification of individuals.
7. Radical reform cannot happen quickly.
8. Designing a coordinated assessment system that works and com-mands confidence is a formidable task.

In late 1993, the timetable for the entire assessment effort was extended, and a decision was reached to revise the specifications for every National Curriculum subject—just four years after the monumental effort, includ-ing the expenditure of millions of pounds, to create the first one! As-sessment was the fault line along which the National Curriculum structure finally fractured; it clearly exposed a lack of sufficient correspondence between professional vision and political desires.

Some Challenges Ahead

Right now, most U.S. standards are in the development stage. Professional groups are busily engaged in generating defensible goals. The entire country has the benefit of a respected exemplar in the seminal NCTM report. Well-regarded and diligent figures have been enlisted in the effort. Good intentions abound.

Perhaps the U.S. standards effort will move ahead for several years with the same steady purposefulness. The three-year time line for most of the separate subject-matter efforts is certainly more reasonable than the hurried schedule followed in England and Wales. Deliberate attempts are being made to ensure consensus about the results, and there is no rush toward the examination system, voluntary or otherwise, at least not yet.

Potential Pitfalls

But there is also the possibility that conflicts will erupt publicly, as well as internally, along any of several significant dimensions. Some have been foreshadowed earlier in this section. For example, will all subjects get their due? What about economics? Anthropology? Psychology? Will the standards produced by education experts match the expectations of the politicians who are providing the funds? How rapidly will the country move toward national examinations, and what will be their purpose? Will the operational consequences of a national exam, when it comes, alienate teachers if they see their professional latitude reduced? Will some states object to further federal involvement in education, especially if they do not receive more money? All of these questions carry the seeds of deep and loud disagreement.

There are additional potential disputes. Underlying several of them is the confusion about the meaning of the term *standard* itself. On the current education scene, the word can be taken in at least two senses. In one, a standard is a sort of measuring stick, a point of reference for comparison purposes. In another, a standard is a flag or banner under which people march. The prime mover in the NCTM standards effort, Tom Romberg of the University of Wisconsin, asserts that the mathematics curriculum standards that spurred the entire U.S. movement were intended in the latter sense.[8] The aim was to proffer a vision of high-quality mathematics education. While that kind of goal undergirds all of today's standards-development efforts, every one of them has moved significantly toward articulating standards as measuring sticks—hence the talk about performance and achievement. There is considerable potential for controversy in the transition from one definition to the other because of the greater precision that is required for assessment. People often find it easier to agree on general goals than on the specific operational consequences.

At a completely different level, the issue of what subjects are worth teaching has not been resolved and is sure to become more contentious. Within a subject, there is the matter of how much of each subspecialty is to be included. As noted, the science work encompasses all science disciplines, but there is extended discussion and little consensus about how much physics, earth science, technology, and meteorology (to name just a few disciplines) to include. Then there is the special case of social studies. Seemingly, it is a well-established subject. However, social studies is now under threat because it is seen as less rigorous (and perhaps potentially more controversial) than history, civics, and geography.

And what about the crucial matter of cross-disciplinary activity? Much research and intellectual excitement, as well as public concern, is focused on areas where the disciplines intersect. Those fields often offer the greatest potential for meeting human need: in health and environmental improvement, for example, or in enhancing economic productivity. One clear curriculum trend everywhere is a move toward the study of such matters in school, partly to demonstrate to students that there are important connections between intellectual effort and practical results. At the moment, however, there is no national standards-setting committee in fields like environmental or technological education. The U.S. efforts may constrain the curriculum in undesirable ways if a subject-by-subject approach to education standards is overemphasized.

The Teachers' Role

Most crucially, identification of even the most educationally justifiable standards will be a force for improving the quality of U.S. education only if teachers understand and support them, as the British experience demonstrates. That means, in part, that the standards must reflect what teachers see as desirable for their students. It means also that teachers must

[8]It is questionable whether the NCTM report would have received the attention it got if the authors had used a term like "guidelines" or "framework." "Standards" has the kind of bite politicians like.

consider the standards as sanctions to teach in a fashion that they consider attractive and professionally satisfying. Such perceptions are unlikely to come solely from reading the written documents produced by the standards committees. Teachers will need to have extended opportunities to discuss the standards among themselves so that the standards can meaningfully be incorporated into their own visions of high-quality education and how it might be provided.

As just one example, but a significant one educationally, many teachers are attracted to small-group activity and project work to better engage students in their academic and practical studies. (There is also a pronounced trend toward project work and research in Europe and Asia.) If the published standards and the examination system that is likely to follow do not seem to emphasize such activity, teachers are less likely to embrace them.

Project work is also a style of instruction that is more heavily grounded in teacher prerogative and independence than textbook-based education. Yet some of the impetus for world-class standards is the belief that such standards are necessary precisely because the United States has a teaching force that is unreliable and perhaps inept. A dilemma arises. Will a distrusting public accept standards that accord teachers greater latitude if the whole standards exercise was intended, at least in part, to hold teachers to greater account? If the standards do not accord teachers the professional scope they believe they need, will teachers accept them?

All this further underscores the need for teachers and other important stakeholders to have the opportunity to examine the proposed standards in considerable detail and over a relatively long period of time. They must be discussed, debated, made operational, and understood. The consensus to be gained through such an approach is worth as much as the standards themselves. Without such deliberation and at least a minimum level of agreement, the standards will fall far short of whatever potential they might have to improve the quality of U.S. education.

References

Black, Paul. 1993. "Performance Assessment and Accountability: The Experience in England and Wales." Address at meeting of American Educational Research Association, April. *Educational Evaluation and Policy Analysis*, June 1994.

Center for Civic Education. 1993. *National Standards for Civics and Government*, draft, April 28.

Clarke, Kenneth. 1991. Speech available from Department of Public Education in France.

Consortium of National Arts Education Associations. 1993. *National Standards for Education in the Arts: What Every Young American Should Know and be Able to Do in the Arts*. Draft. Boston: August.

Geography Education Standards Project. 1993. *National Geography Standards*, draft. June 30.

National Commission on Excellence in Education. 1983. *A Nation at Risk*. Washington, D.C.: U.S. Government Printing Office.

National Research Council. 1993. *National Science Education Standards*: July 1993 Progress Report.

National Research Council. 1993. *Report of the Committee on a Nationwide Education Support System for Teachers and Schools*. Washington, D.C.: March.

Office of Technology Assessment. 1992. *Testing in American Schools: Asking the Right Questions*. Washington, D.C.: U.S. Government Printing Office (OTA-SET-519).

Porter, Andrew. 1993. "Opportunity to Learn." *Brief* (Number 87), Center on Organization and Restructuring of Schools, University of Wisconsin, Fall.

Project 2061, American Association for the Advancement of Science. 1993. *Benchmarks for Science Literacy*. Oxford, England, and New York: Oxford University Press.

U.S. Department of Education. 1991. *America 2000: An Education Strategy*. Washington, D.C.: U.S. Department of Education.

Working Groups of the Commission on Standards for School Mathematics. 1989. *Curriculum and Evaluation Standards for School Mathematics*. Reston, Va.: National Council of Teachers of Mathematics.

7

Curriculum and Assessment Standards: Common Measures or Conversations?

DENNIE PALMER WOLF

Dennie Palmer Wolf is executive director of Performance Assessment Collaboratives for Education (PACE) and senior research associate at Harvard Graduate School of Education.

Introduction

In an article on the fiftieth anniversary of D-day, there is this paragraph:

> In Italy, the anniversary of Mussolini's death in April 1945 was marked at his grave by neofascist salutes and protest. Hundreds of thousands of other Italians are deeply upset by the current political resurgence of the neofascists, who last month entered the new government, and these people marked the end of the war in Italy (April 25) differently, as the forty-ninth anniversary of the liberation from Fascism. (New York Times 1994, 1)

Reading, I think of being there—in Modena—a year ago. It was the eve of "XXV Aprile"—that day of liberation. It was the hour between the end of the day and dinner, and I was going over the stones of the ancient central city, stone by stone, with an architect and his son. Talking, we circled the cathedral. The south and pagan, sun-facing wall had panels out of Aesop, not the saints, carved by a nameless Romanesque sculptor who left his signature on every medieval cathedral along the Via Romagna—each one built a day's march apart on the pagan ground of legion campsites. At the north-facing portal—the one that pilgrims would have entered on their way to Jerusalem—Tulio, the father, points to the walls rising toward the bell tower. The stones are not pristine, but nomadic, pilfered. Now and again, acanthus leaves belonging to Jupiter, maybe to Venus, break out in the masonry like history lessons. Tulio runs his hands along a set of graduated channels in the stone. Below them, on a shelf, are a series of hemispheres dished into the stone—bowls running over with shadow at this hour. "This was the market square, before there was a church. These were the measures . . . Convivere." The common measures that make it possible to live together translated to stone.

But it is the western wall that startles. It is paved with a mosaic of tiny black-and-white photographs under glass. The letters running in the bronze say, "For those who died." "No," Tulio says, "not for *all*, the *partizans*. Some of the images have the hats and shirts of farmers, as if somewhere at their feet you can imagine lambs and apricots with the leaves still on. Stars float over the pale, rabbinical faces of others. They, too, must have had bodies—ones that half a century ago stood up from books, or pianos, or ledgers to race across streets or unforgiving flat fields, from poplar to poplar.

Tulio walks away, broad and Romanesque in his jacket. In his studio, the model hanging on the wall—from his first *concorso*—was the *partizan* cemetery at Urbino, built as catacombs under a slope, cracking the grass like some eruption of memory that will not be quietly buried. The underground.

I turn and ask Michele, Tulio's son, if the *partizans* are still live history for his generation. There is silence. And he, who only moments ago, formed perfect English nouns like "apse" and "buttress" and "rib"—stumbles. "They are . . ." He throws his arm back toward the grooves and the half-spheres on the far side of the cathedral. "How do you say? . . . The real standards?"

The dictionary shows half a dozen meanings for standards. The first entry is "a pole or spear bearing some conspicuous object (as a sculptured figure or a banner) at the top, formerly used in an army or fleet to mark a rallying point, to signal, or to serve as an emblem." It is only the fourth entry that reads: "something that is set up and established by authority as a rule for the measure of quantity, weight, extent, value, or quality; *esp.*: an original specimen measure or weight (as the international prototype meter and kilogram of the International Bureau of Weights and Measures)." (Webster's Third New International Dictionary of the English Language, 1968).

The grooves and the *partizans* are two distinct faces of what we mean when we speak of standards. The grooves are stable, civic inventions of the first order: reliable tools that work across different goods, buyers, days, and times. Like the kilogram, the teaspoon, or the footcandle, they are international, declarative, and firm. In that way, they ensure even-handed dealing, certain kinds of everyday justice just as Tulio says. They yield common measures. But the photographs under glass are an equally necessary kind of standard: that first mentioned conspicuous object or *emblem* that raises the question, "But what is worth measuring?" Because they are nominations about what is best, or brave, or worth following, such standards work by provoking allegiance, resistance, conversation, even debate. Tulio's and Michele's awe could be questioned. Someone might ask, "Weren't the *partizans* equal partners in a bitter cycle of strikes and reprisals? Didn't they steal bread, abduct wives and brothers, commandeer attics?" In the wake of the recent election news, someone else might ask, "If they understood the dangers of Fascism so fiercely, why didn't they establish an Italian democracy that would not splinter and falter?" The debate would last long into the night.

Why *partizans* and channels in the stone? Because we are about to play out a great educational wager based on standards. The bet is that national standards for what students should know by when and how well are an electric surge to the heart, capable of stimulating a dying U.S. public school system back to life. Only three-quarters of a year separated the announcement of former President Bush's "America 2000" proposal in April 1991, and the January 1992, National Council on Education Standards and Testing report to Congress which concluded that a national testing system, based on national standards for what students know and can do, is both desirable and feasible. Two years and a change of administration later, the impulse is constant. Congress has passed the legislative package associated with Goals 2000, wherein funding is dependent on a state improvement plan centered on standards. But as rapid-fire and surefooted as these initiatives seem to be, they constitute a tense triple gamble. First, there is the bet that if minimum competency standards and standardized testing could drive the curriculum down to rote learning, then the inverse is possible. If we can formulate demanding national standards and equally demanding performance assessments, we can drive achievement up. The second bet is that, armed with national standards, we can achieve what years of desegregation have not yielded, equitable access to worthwhile educational activities like writing, problem-solving, and scientific experimentation. And finally, there is the bet that crisply formulated content and performance standards will operate exactly like kilograms or footcandles, stimulating widespread agreement and equally clear implications.

But, to date, such wagers have been formulated largely, if not wholly, with reference to the common measures definition of standards. Perhaps the most marked evidence of this is the stunning activity around the development of new performance assessments (and corresponding psychometrics) to measure the acquisition of the capacities called for in the standards, whether that be in Vermont, Kentucky, Delaware, New York, or California.

Such common measures in the form of public content and performance standards for student learning are important, possibly even necessary. We have largely lost the high expectations Thomas Jefferson and Horace Mann had for common schools, falling into routines of minimum competency and neglect. In the four decades since "separate but equal" schooling was struck down, we have proven chronically unable to guarantee anything but equal access to the same school buildings. Standards for student performance could become one among the many tools we need to move beyond what desegregation could yield. And demanding assessments based on those standards might drive home the seriousness of the standards.

Still, the much more vulnerable side of the equation is that of the *partizans*—the question of thinking about what is *worth* all that measuring. To understand that, we need standards that remain alive to the ongoing conversation about what knowledge is—that preserve a spectrum of opinions, even doubts. Without that, the standards will freeze in place accounts of knowledge and standards for performance when, in fact, both are problematically alive and changing. In addition, as our shelves fill with separate, almost selfish subject-matter standards, each listing its own strands and major ideas, we have to pause. We are speaking of performances, not grocery lists of atomically separate items. Finally, and ironically, worthwhile standards require humility—the sense that they are not a miracle cure, but one turn in what ought to be a much wider conversation about what will permit substantial educational reform. We are not after the small white truck that travels through the county recalibrating meat scales. Instead, we want for education something like the workings of a Supreme Court that could hand down the separate but equal ruling of *Plessy v. Ferguson* in 1896, but then, barely half a century later, could write *Brown v. the Board of Education*. A way of asking what is worth measuring.

Insisting on the Dynamic Nature of Standards

The literary critic, Kenneth Burke, reflecting on the nature of knowledge in his field, once wrote:

Imagine that you enter a parlor. You come late. When you arrive, others have long preceded you, and they are engaged in a heated discussion, a discussion too heated for them to pause and tell you exactly what it is about. In fact, the discussion had already begun long before any of them got there, so that no one present is qualified to retrace for you all the steps that had gone before. You listen for a while, until you decide that you have caught the tenor of the argument; then you put in your oar. Someone answers; you answer him; another comes to your defense; another aligns himself against you. The discussion is interminable. The hour grows late, you must depart. And you do depart with the discussion still vigorously in progress. (Burke 1974, 110–11).

Burke was writing about the back and forth of a literary world, but he could easily have been talking about scientific debate over the utility of unified theory or the biochemical bases of schizophrenia. Our accounts of Islam, Vichy France, and atomic theory have all been unstable in the best sense. It is important to look at this dynamism closely in order to think wisely about the proposed national standards.

The subject we know as "English" makes an excellent case in point. As a school subject, English was born at a very particular moment in the late nineteenth century. In Great Britain, the political and industrial revolutions of the eighteenth and early nineteenth centuries reaped harsh realities more than promised new orders. The England of Wordsworth became the London of Dickens: increasingly industrial, urban, competitive, and gritty. Visiting Haymarket, Dostoyevsky had to tear his coat loose from the hands of mothers hawking their daughters. And events in the larger world without promised even greater danger: Marx, writing in the British Museum, threatened the apocalyptic revolt of the world's workers, and events like the Paris Commune seemed to ratify his prophecies. London newspapers were glutted with eyewitness accounts of the Crimean wars; the city overflowed with homeless and crippled refugees.

But the British reaction, both to internal dislocation and to events overseas, was a determined recoil from, rather than entrance into, the modern world. Tennyson wrote of the Paris Commune as "the red, bloody fury of the Seine." Ruskin argued that industrialization had forced workers descended from the sculptors of Gothic cathedrals to become the automatons of Leeds and Sheffield, who knew no better than to build and then crouch within brutish row houses. But, utterly unlike Marx, Ruskin counseled a return to what he imagined as the medieval values of craft and art. He was not alone. After labor demonstrations in West End London parks left workers, bystanders, and police bloodied, Matthew Arnold, the socialist and author, wrote not about labor legislation, but a manifesto for literature:

It is of itself a serious calamity for a nation that its tone of feeling and grandeur of spirit should be lowered or dulled. But the calamity appears far more serious still when we consider that the middle classes, remaining as they are now, with their narrow, harsh, unintelligent, and unattractive spirit and culture, will almost certainly fail to mold or assimilate the masses below them, whose sympathies are at the present moment actually wider and more liberal than theirs. They arrive, these masses, eager to enter into possession of the world, to gain a more vivid sense of their own life and activity. In this their irrepressible development, their natural educators and initiators are those immediately above them, the middle classes. If these classes cannot win their sympathy or give them direction, society is in danger of falling into anarchy. (quoted in Super 1962, 22)

Arnold had a tool for salvation: the sword against the "barbarism" of industrialized life and the "Philistine" nature of the middle class was to teach literature ("the best that has been thought and said in the world") to every child in each year of school. As he developed the argument, he suggested that the common experience of becoming literate was an initiation into exemplary models of human conduct and could convey to all citizens the elegant, measured forms of expression, even the exact words and images, that would ensure civility. Great books, like the Bible and Shakespeare, if closely studied, would provide a vital antidote to the cheap literacy of dime novels, advertising supplements, want ads, and "For Sale" signs. By 1920, virtually every almanac of knowledge and English textbook argued that literature opened a transcendent realm in which it was *human nature*, not the dangerous, divisive topics of class, gender, and nationality, that was at stake:

Literature presents us *not merely* what individual men found to interest them in a *particular* epoch, but also the *general laws* which have been gradually formulated by long-continued observation of *the processes of nature*. . . [what] Homer has given us in an Aegean of sunlit islands and purple seas; Dante, in a dark and mysterious Inferno; Milton, in a Garden of Eden; Shakespeare in an Elizabethan England. (Ruoff 1916, 20)

The result was that in Victorian times, the English language, abetted by literature, became a kind of *lingua franca* in which the scripts, morals, and diction of England were exported to the colonies. To this end, Victorian civil service exams carried questions about literature; children in Burma knew all the verses to "Rule Britannia," and generations of Jamaican students remember writing poems about "the snow on the cane fields" mimicking what their teachers imagined were the practices of faraway places like Devon and Suffolk. The reward for being a British colonial was lifelong membership in an "English-speaking union." As one 1916 reference book put it:

> English is the most remarkable as well as the most prolific of modern literatures. . . . The institutions and language of the conquerors were largely imposed upon the natives, but so great has been the vitality of the Saxon speech that about two-thirds of the words now composing the English language are, radically, or derivatively, of Saxon origin. . . . There have been many influences brought to bear upon its speech; yet in this composite texture, the Anglo-Saxon element is dominant. That is the first outstanding fact of importance. (Ruoff 1916,)

The habits that developed were these: Nothing other than literature entered the classroom for examination. No literature outside of English was read. Nothing appeared written in the English of Australia, India, or Nigeria. African literature is Conrad; Asian literature is Pearl S. Buck. Indian characters are Kim and the narrator of *The Jungle Book*. Little that was modern, nothing that was contemporary broke the surface. And the duty of the reader was awe.

But certain as Arnold and his colleagues were, only 100 years later, our sense of what literature is, and who creates it, and the interaction between works and readers has changed utterly. Increasingly, English is one among many languages—even in London and Cleveland. In an increasingly international context, teaching literature/literacy is no longer as simple as unfolding *the* narrative of an Anglo-American tradition. The closed circle of British and American literature has been pried open to admit a world literature including writers in English from quite other traditions (Achebe, Soywinke, Gordimer), writers across languages (Solzhenitsyn and Cisneros), and writers in translation. At the same time, the once unquestioned definition of a text as print on the page has broken wide open to include the digital literacies of film, video, and computer imagery. And the clean, assured sense of *the* meaning *in* the text has evolved to a commitment to meaning-making on the part of a variety of readers' readings. Consequently, writing and speaking have increasingly displaced the hegemony of reading and listening in English classrooms. In this way, the transfer of awe has, in many contemporary classrooms, been largely replaced by a concern that students become active constructors of meaning. As a result, contemporary English teaching is described in terms that Arnold would barely recognize:

> Accomplished teachers command specialized knowledge of how to convey and reveal subject matter to students. They are aware of the preconceptions and background knowledge that students typically bring to each subject and

of strategies and instructional materials that can be of assistance. They understand where difficulties are likely to arise and modify their practice
accordingly. Their instructional repertoire allows them to create multiple
paths to the subjects they teach, and they are adept at teaching students
how to pose and solve their own problems. (National Board of Professional
Teaching Standards 1994, 4–5)

This dynamism surrounding standards is not some awkward result of
long-term cultural change, but an intrinsic—and indispensable—part of
thinking about what is worth knowing and consequently, what is worth
teaching and learning. A college teacher, Gerald Graff, provides an example in his book of essays, *Beyond the Culture Wars*, where he describes
the transformations in his reading and teaching of *Heart of Darkness*, particularly after his reading of Nigerian author, Chinua Achebe's essay, "An
Image of Africa: Racism in Conrad's *Heart of Darkness*." In his own essay,
Graff writes:

> When I teach *Heart of Darkness* now . . . I assign Achebe's essay, I do not
> simply teach Achebe's interpretation as the correct one, however, but ask
> my students to weigh it against other interpretations. Nor do I discard my
> earlier reading of the novel as a contemplation of universal truths about
> the human soul. I also assign another critical essay that argues for that
> interpretation. I also assign several essays . . . by critics who take issue with
> Achebe. These critics—and I agree with them—grant Achebe's thesis up to
> a point about Conrad's racism and colonialism but argue that Achebe ig-
> nores or minimizes the powerful critique of racism and colonialism that
> coexists in the novel with these more sinister attitudes.
>
> After Conrad, my class reads Achebe's novel *Things Fall Apart*, which
> presents a counterview of Africa to Conrad's, as if Achebe were trying to
> wrest the power to represent Africa away from the great European. I sup-
> plement these materials with short essays representing opposing sides in
> the past and present debate over the place, or nonplace, of politics in the
> arts, illustrating the fact that the debate has a long history dating back to
> Plato's founding of the history of criticism in an act of political correctness,
> his expulsion of the poets from his republic for corrupting the morals of
> the state. Also included in the reading list are several recent neoconserva-
> tive polemics . . . I also invite conservative colleagues into my class to debate
> the issues with me and my students. To make sure my students enter the
> debate rather than watch passively from the sidelines, I assign a paper on
> it or ask them to prepare class presentations in which they give their views.
>
> In short, I now teach *Heart of Darkness* as part of a critical debate about
> how to read it, which in turn is part of a larger theoretical debate about
> how politics and power affect the way we read literature. Without claiming
> to be neutral or disguising my own leanings, I try to help students adju-
> dicate between competing arguments and make informed choices on the

key points of contention: Is literature a realm of universal experience that transcends politics, or is it inevitably political, and in what sense of "political," a word too often brandished today without being defined. (Graff 1992, 30–31)

It is no accident that Graff describes a kind of encounter with Achebe. Nor is it a whim that he asks his students to weigh Achebe against other interpretations. Much of what a community or culture decides is worthwhile—its implicit content standards—evolves from a matrix of shifting technology and training or emerges from the literal back and forth exchanges of conversation or argument, or in some analog to that process: letters to the editor, appeals in courts of law, or conflicting book reviews. And this is not some peculiarity of the humanities. The Manhattan Project, the human genome project, accounts of the birth and evolution of the universe were and are the sites of similar back and forth motion. The interchange is, in fact, a source of change.

Similar points could be made about the dynamism of our evolving sense for what counts as poor, acceptable, or fine work—the continuous setting of record times for running the mile or the escalating record heights in pole vaulting created by diet, training, and Fiberglas. But literacy is effectively no different. At one time, to be acceptably literate was to be able to make an X or other sign on a document. In the nineteenth century, many readers only spoke aloud familiar texts, using the print to jog a failing memory. The reading passages featured in Army intelligence tests ushered in the notion that a reader ought to be able to decode even unfamiliar and out-of-context materials (Wolf 1988). Now, with the advent of on-line libraries, hypertexts, and the Internet, our standards for literacy are likely to shift again. It will be possible to expect that students will consult, not just the text and the stalwart encyclopedia, but numerous sources or distant readers. We will expect of them a command of search and sources unprecedented in an era when Britannica and Compton's set the standard.

If we are going to implement national education standards, but skip this concern for conversation, there are costs. At the national level, two are already clear. The first cost is evident in the declarative, rather than interrogative, approach taken to the content and performance standards recently set in mathematics, the arts, and other subject matter. While standards committees certainly fight tooth and nail about what counts, what has emerged from that contentiousness is a smoothed surface of agreed-upon strands or large ideas. No standards have been published carrying a minority report. Nor—to date, anyway—do the standards include a discussion of open questions that communities have to take up if they are to implement the standards. This all takes its toll on how we portray learning. For example, none of the subject-matter standards—at least to date—includes a set of questions that ought to be on any given young artist's or scientist's mind.

The second cost is timidity. Standards can be academically bold while on neutral ground demanding an emphasis on problem solving or collaboration. But where standards verge toward values, mentioning critical thinking or points of view, they cannot offend major—or loud—constituencies. These are the long-standing lessons of textbook adoptions in Texas, the battles over outcomes in Pennsylvania, and the recent rescinding of state assessments based on controversial texts in California. But suppose we think that questions such as what ideas students have access to, what they read, and whether we insist that students consider matters from multiple points of view are an important part of the education conversation, not just sidebars? Then we have to rethink the current model of trickle-down standards, where the national standards provide the basis for state frameworks that localities then mimic. Instead, we have to find structures that not only permit, but encourage, schools to take up these vital issues. Suppose, for instance, that national or state standards included the insistence that questions concerning "habits of mind" or "cultural values" be set at the community (district or school) level using the kind of town-meeting process Vermont pioneered in setting up its system of portfolio assessments.

The issues are not contained in the usual policy realm. They affect what occurs in classrooms. Here the danger is that the recurrent phrase "meeting the standards" will become a literal-minded reality with teachers and students being trained/ educated to take the standards as given as immutable rather than as highly negotiable descriptions of what is "good." Classrooms have to be sites for the active discussion of standards. Consider the following essay on the Harlem Renaissance written by a high school senior.

Harlem Renaissance

It was a phrase by Woodrow Wilson, former president of the United States that surprisingly gave the "Negro race" hope in 1917. It was the beginning of World War I. The reason given by this president for the American involvement in the was "to make the world safe for democracy." This phrase had special meaning for the "Old Negro" because for so many long, incredibly long, years they were deprived of the promised, documented, and signed freedom right for "man." So when the white president of that time came right out and said "safe for democracy," most Black Americans of that time thought the president meant them also. In fact, he did not. I say, "surprisingly gave hope" because Black Americans are people too and when the constitutions and amendments and bills said "... for all," they found out that these free will notes excluded them. So, in went Black makes to fight in World War I for their reasons. In they went—straight to segregated boot camps. They were used for clean-up jobs. Again, Black Americans were used for America's dirty work.

This now sets the Black mood of the early 1920's.

World War I was over. Middle and upper class white people were clapping and flapping and trying to forget that past war. On the other side of town in Harlem, New York, the greatly gifted Black people were writing, drawing or singing their blues away. Sure they clapped and flapped, and danced carelessly until daybreak, but after, their creative abilities transported to a paperback or onto a wall of an art exhibition. (The student author continues to describe the range of work undertaken in the Harlem Renaissance, particularly that of Langston Hughes.) [*sic*]

The distinct profile of strengths and weaknesses evident in this essay is, the writing (particularly as it continues), which resists the sorts of summary characterizations that appear in many holistic rubrics that figure in numerous scoring systems. The essay also eludes the usual dimensions for appraising essays: information, organization, argument, and control of the conventions of written English. It makes all kinds of trouble for the assumption that a student is either writing an expository or an imaginative/ creative piece. Its deliberate and effective use of dialect and oral language wreaks havoc with what is usually meant by phrases like "the student exhibits strong/some/little control of the conventions of written English." The point is that the piece is not an anomaly. Versions of it are being written in San Diego, Detroit, and Miami. In order to think about this kind of writing productively, students and teachers need to address standards as occasions for discussion, even debate. The danger under the current system is that the demand to "meet the standard" will drive out substantial conversation about the viability and inclusiveness of the standard itself.

Here the notion of the *partizans* resurfaces. It is difficult to measure the emblem-like quality of their lives: it was provoked by their circumstances; it was an invention. The whole point is that they surprise. Writers like Eisner (1994) and Stake (1976) have long insisted that in such circumstances models of judgment from the arts, not from commerce, are the right calipers. After all, they argue, wholly new and rare rules and dimensions are being invented. In a culture where change and diversity are regularities, we are going to need discussion. It is the only way that standards can be protean enough.

The Mutuality of Standards: Performances of Thought

In his book *The Mismeasure of Man*, Stephen Jay Gould discusses the history of the concept of IQ, stressing how, once Terman and others posited, made measurable, and tested it, the original concept acquired a durable sort of reality like the humors did in Elizabethan England. So it was that Terman could write about the consequences of IQ scores as if they were as real as height and weight:

> Preliminary investigations indicate that an IQ below 70 rarely permits any-thing better than unskilled labor; that the range of 70–80 is pre-eminently that of semi-skilled labor; from 80–100 that of skilled or ordinary clerical labor; from 100–110 or 115 that of the semi-professional pursuits; and that above all these are the grades of intelligence which permit one to enter the professions or the large fields of business. Intelligence tests can tell us whether a child's native brightness corresponds more nearly to the median (or one or another of these classes). This information will be of great value in plan-ning the education of a particular child and also in planning the differen-tiated curriculum. (Terman 1922, 62)

In the wake of this reification, an entire technology grew up: IQ testing, tracking based on scores, and educational materials allegedly tuned to the mental abilities of the student. In turn, these technologies served to guarantee evidence for IQ by creating or at least amplifying just the va-rieties of performance the concept predicted. The currently proposed na-tional standards are just as virtual as the concept of IQ ever was.

One of the outstanding features of the current discussion of standards as common measures is that it is built on a similar reification: a concep-tion of parallel and separate subject matters. The separate committees, publication dates, and formats of the standards guarantee that we will continue to think of learning as occurring in the school subjects of mathematics, English, social studies, etc. This same conception of learn-ing will be verified by the technologies of testing and the reporting of results in the same domains. But before we buy this parallel architecture lock, stock, and barrel, it is important to pause to examine its usefulness.

In a lecture to the literary translators of the United States, Robert Ly-ons Danly gave this account of his current struggles to translate the cul-tural, not just the linguistic, content of the short stories of Ihara Saikaku, a seventeenth-century businessman, poet, and fiction writer. He rum-inated especially on his dread of the apparently transparent lists of details that Saikaku uses, Faulkner-like, to produce the "feel of the score and the manners and morals of his people." Danly writes:

Now a list might not sound like a very hard thing to translate, and, linguistically, it is not. But lists—which are nothing but pure, concentrated
detail—have a way of going very flat in translation. I used to dread it every
time I came to one of these lists. Then I began to realize what Saikaku was
doing. His lists are a kind of shorthand, a streamlined form of wit. They are
not so different, in fact, from the urbane and tightly packed lyrics of a Cole
Porter song. . . . But most important, being a distillation of concrete detail,
Saikaku's lists capture the period and the place as acutely as Cole Porter's
lyrics capture the 1930s. Listen to a record of Ethel Merman singing "You're
the Top," and you know what was in and what was out in 1934, what made
news; you know the cultural level of New York cafe society, not to mention
the level of American technology and commerce. . . . Just imagine translating Cole Porter's lyrics into Japanese:

> You're the top!
> You're a Waldorf salad.
> You're the top!
> You're a Berlin ballad.
> You're the baby grand of a lady and a gent,
> You're an old Dutch Master,
> You're Mrs. Astor,
> You're Pepsodent.
> (Danly 1981, 20–26).

Very little in schools would prepare students to navigate through these
historical and cultural waters. They would have taken their Japanese in
a curriculum where language learning is set off sharply from history, and
where their U.S. history would have been taught as if the rest of the world
were only a dim and static backdrop. Yet much of what students will do
as adults demands just this kind of work across borders. Medical treat-
ments must consider the diet and culture of patients; engineers have to
design within the demands and limits of human factors; journalists have
to know—or find out—enough about science to investigate a rumored
asbestos crisis.

So what would it look like if we parted company with this reification?
What if education standards exhibited some of the mutuality that Danly's
translation problem calls for? In this spirit, it is worth noting that in the
name of such connections, states like Vermont and New York are blurring
the separate sanctity of subject matters. New York has created joint
standards for mathematics, science, and technology. Vermont is thinking
about reporting student progress as a set of "vital results" cut as broadly
as "communication" or "problem solving." To take root, such a notion
would have to be supported in accompanying assessments. This is not
impossible, if we are willing to undo the narrow ecology to which we have

assigned crucial learning tasks. For instance, currently, reading and writing instruction occurs overwhelmingly in the context of English or language arts classes, even though what it takes to write a science report or an essay based on primary historical sources has its own genre and knowledge constraints. What if the tasks used in state assessments increasingly demanded integrated performances like Danly's? Or what if states reported on students' literacy, using data generated in multiple contexts: a short story, a critical reading of a set of experimental results, and the selection of a newspaper article demonstrating the continuity of certain basic issues in U.S. history? If the current move toward portfolio-based assessment doesn't crash under the weight of its own demands, it could offer another compatible place to begin. To urge schools and students to think about literacy, not just the essays written in English 10 between 10:05 and 10:55, we might ask them to produce evidence that they have a critical and imaginative literacy that operates powerfully in a range of contexts.

Again, these conversations across subject-matter borders are not just niceties. There are crucial educational issues that we cannot think our way through armed only with the canalized standards we presently have. The most pressing is that independent subject-matter learning is unlikely to prepare students for work or further study. If we value people who make connections, we cannot wait until they enter college or the workplace to start nurturing that capacity. There are also pressing issues of education policy that separate standards will never fit us out to resolve. First, unless we think broadly about language acquisition across English and "foreign" languages, it is inconceivable that we will ever have a coherent and productive approach to second-language learning. The second instance is no less urgent. Currently, many state standards cordon off vocational or technical education, giving it a separate framework and its own standards. But in the last 10 years, the distinction between the workplace and academic study, the scholastic and the real, the theoretical and the applied, has blurred. Everyone wants students who can work with noisy and applied problems and employees who can collect data, draw inferences, and take a position. We need, therefore, a genuine conversation, not just rhetorical ties, across the schooling that is a preface to work and that which is a preface to college.

Humility in Standards Setting

Nineteen ninety-four marks the fortieth anniversary of the Supreme Court's landmark decision on school segregation, *Brown v. the Board of Educa-*

tion. In that decision, the justices sought to undo "separate but equal" as the impoverished realization of the Civil War, the Emancipation Proclamation, and the Fourteenth Amendment. In framing their decision, the justices of the Supreme Court sought a basis for enforcement—a foundation for immediate change in who attended what public school. Racial balance via desegregation was that tool. To this day, school districts are still before the courts arguing that they have—at last—met those standards for equal access formulated in *Brown v. the Board of Education*.

But even as we continue to use what Marshall handed us, we have come to understand some of the limits of racial balance rulings as *the* tool for equalizing educational opportunity. Any but the most cursory look at schools reveals that just below the surface of integration lies a network of programs (special education, vocational tracks in high schools, gifted and talented seminars) in which racial imbalances thrive. In addition, recent commentary and research make the point that it is status, or income segregation, as much as, if not more than, racial imbalance, that is pernicious. Poor and isolated schools, in abandoned neighborhoods, away from social services and resources, foster a next generation of inequality—no matter what their racial composition. Change in these schools demands addressing what author Jonathan Kozol referred to as savage inequalities, not just busing. But the message from desegregation efforts is not an isolated case: consider the difficult and unproductive use of Chapter I initiatives to improve the school performance of poor children.

The implications seem clear: major education change is not produced by single-shot, silver-bullet solutions. Yet most recently national education goals, standards, and testing have been offered as the next set of tools to cure educational inequalities. And, in fact, the discussion of standards initially sparked a vigorous insistence that content and performance standards be accompanied by the parallel development of opportunity-to-learn standards. Simply put, this is the issue of who, among U.S. students, has access to acquiring the skills and strategies so touted in the *2061* national science reform benchmarks, the NCTM standards, or the vision laid out for twelfth-grade citizens by the National Council for the Social Studies. But, with increasing frequency, discussions of learning opportunity have been cast as obstructionist: a stick in the spokes of national standards. The argument is that we cannot afford to slow the momentum toward the realization of the proposed standards.

But what if we resisted this arrogant logic by insisting that the standards not be written as a forced choice between excellence and equity? In its work, the English Language Arts Standards Project provided an example of how we might go about this—although that effort played a role in the discontinuation of the project's funding. The effort was to build standards from the ground up as tools for equity, rather than expecting a neutrally written set of standards to *become* a tool for equity by way of enforcement. The guiding principles of the project stated quite frankly, "Our intent is to move forward with challenging educational standards and to redress the imbalance of learning opportunities for those students who have been least well served by education." (English Language Arts 1994, 8). The innards of the document were written to bear witness to that preamble. Thus the list of language standards included items such as:

- Students will build upon the language skills that have been developed in the home and the community.
- Students will develop abilities in and appreciation for more than one language.

However, it was not just the content of the standards, but their literal anatomy that aimed at coupling content and opportunity-to-learn standards. To make this clear, it is important to look closely at a specific standard. Each standard began with a short statement of its focus. For instance:

> *Standard.* Students will understand and make thoughtful use of the forms and features of language that vary within and across different speakers, cultural communities, and contexts.

Each standard was followed by an elaboration. The purpose of the elaboration is to point out that we seek these qualities across ages, levels, and contexts. Thus, the elaboration of the above-quoted standard reads as follows:

> *Elaboration.* All effective communication depends on speakers and listeners understanding how language use varies widely across audiences and contexts. This understanding allows all language users to tune talk, gesture, and expressions to home, work, or school communities and to choose the right language and dialect for the moment. But in school, students often use and study only the narrower range of language characteristic of formal schooling. By turning to the rich language performances occurring in families and neighborhoods, we can often provide stronger illustrations of the full range of choices any communication demands.

This elaboration was then deliberately followed by a section designed to focus readers' attention on *the conditions under which* it was likely that large numbers of students would be able to attain this standard. This represents a sharp departure from most standards-related activity.

Meeting the Standard. Teachers and schools must provide:

- occasions for students to look at language use in a wide range of communities and contexts;
- the materials and tools to understand and study how language use varies;
- interactions (conversations, models, etc.) that urge students to think about and apply what they observe about language variations.

Evidence That Students Meet the Standard. Students who meet this standard can:

- observe variations in language use thoughtfully;
- discuss what they observe;
- draw inferences from and raise questions about what they observe; and
- think, talk, and/or write about the implications for their own language use.

Each standard was illustrated to show what high, common levels of performance would look like in elementary, middle, and high school. What follows is an illustration of the same standard at the middle school level.

In the Middle School Years. In a middle school classroom that contains students from 18 different countries, the students develop oral histories centered on experiences many of them have in common, such as surviving a civil war or immigrating to a new country. To prepare for their independent work, students practice interviewing a guest speaker on this topic. In the process they learn about conducting interviews, about taking notes, and about using tape recorders. Later, students interview a person they know about the topic. They then turn their transcript, notes, and observations into a narrative. Finally, they revise with the help of a peer group and publish a group collection, *Lives beyond the Border.*

In the context of this work, a student interviewed her uncle in Spanish, then transformed the transcript and her notes into a first-person narrative written in English, thinking all the while about how to translate her uncle's spoken meaning into writing, his Spanish conversation into English.

Interpretation. Here a teacher has made thoughtful use of the fact that students come to the classroom speaking a number of languages. She has constructed an assignment that insists that students think across these languages. For instance, in class students use English to formulate a shared set of interview questions, but often in their interviews, students must adapt these questions to the situation and speaker. All of them must think about the versions of questions that would work with a neighbor, a grandparent, or an older sister. Students coming from other nations and cultures must translate the questions into linguistically and culturally effective forms. As students turn their transcripts into narratives, they must make decisions—

both as writers and editors—about how to move from spoken to written language.

On the grounds that literacy is a demanding capacity that is constructed in diverse contexts, the English Language Arts project standards also argued that the work of helping students to meet these standards had to be the joint task of an entire school and community, not just personal language arts in classrooms. Therefore the three language arts vignettes were followed by a fourth vignette in which the same standard was being worked on in a class or setting other than language arts.

Changing the language and format of the standards is only an emblem—one of those "conspicuous objects used to mark a rallying point, to signal, or to serve as an emblem" that Webster mentions. Two further things must occur if the standards are to be anything but pious declaration. First, the standards are, in fact, virtually useless unless they become one of many initiatives increasingly building a level playing field. Uncoupled from the provision of fair funding, youth services, work apprenticeships, and other opportunities, the push for academic excellence is hollow. Second, the standards need embodiment—educators and the public have to see how it is that teachers and schools make it possible for students to meet such standards. Part of the responsibility in writing standards lies in demonstrating that it is possible both for schools and for students to meet the standards in a range of ways, using the materials they have, or resources their particular community offers. This is the critical difference between parochial belief or prescription and a productive set of standards that a diverse nation with differing communities of professionals could use to inform practice. In this vein, we have to think more concertedly about initiatives that have done just this: the British model of regional examining boards, the International Baccalaureate schools, the writing projects, and the networks of Advanced Placement and Pacesetter teachers sponsored by the College Board.

These standards, written thus, proved unacceptable to the federal government in the spring of 1994. At the time of this decision, there were any number of contentious debates stirred by the early drafts and the writing still needed to mature. But among the chief reasons cited for ceasing to fund these standards was that the authors had stepped outside the bounds of the contract by addressing questions of opportunity to learn. But standards divorced from questions of who has access to understanding seem barren, without conscience. Arrogant about their singular power.

Conclusion

In many matters of quality—the granting of Ph.D. degrees, the reviewing of grants in science, the use of second opinions in medical diagnosis, the research process over time—are based on the interplay of multiple opinions. In fact, that interplay is seen as the driving force in refining understanding or performance. Think about the review processes at many journals or of many plays, even while still trying out in Connecticut. There are key features to such processes: review rather than certification, a place for majority and minority opinions, and mechanisms for sustaining, rather than suppressing, questions.

But currently we are entering an era when the content and level of standards are no longer a matter of discussion between Graff and his colleagues, but a matter of legislative and fiscal import. Certainly, this will rivet attention on questions of what students should know and how deeply they possess it. At the same time, as standards become part of a system of public funding and policy initiatives, they will have to behave as consensus documents able to get out of committee, receive legislative endorsement, or withstand public hearings. A recent conversation regarding literature standards is revealing. The particular discussion was sparked by a phrase in a proposed document that called for students "to have a broad and deep knowledge of different genres of literature and the best authors and illustrators in those categories."

> *Speaker 1:* "Best" gives me trouble here. Who determines what's best, the state? the school, the teacher?
> *Speaker 2:* Maybe it is better to say outstanding.
> *Speaker 1:* But I keep wondering who says what's outstanding.
> *Speaker 2:* What if we say important, that covers a lot of categories.
> *Speaker 1:* I don't get it, it's still a list. I know the kids in my class, and the kinds of books that are going to engage them in reading. If I want them to leave me reading, then that's what's best.
> *Speaker 2:* So how about popular?
> *Speaker 3:* I don't know what's wrong with best. Aren't there just some works that every kid ought to read? Isn't that what we want for our kids?
> *Speaker 2:* We have criteria later on [hunts for the language in the document]. Here they are; "important" and "engaging." Why doesn't that cover what you are talking about?
> *Speaker 1:* It's still going to turn into somebody's list.
> *Speaker 2:* So how about "talented"? Or "specific"? Does that do it?
> *Speaker 3:* No, look, if you have limited resources, like almost any school district I know, are you going to go into the bookstore and just choose every fifth volume? You think there is some literature that is better, don't you?
> *Speaker 2:* So can we solve this by saying "a variety of literature and illustration"? [Both other speakers nod assent, and this is the wording that is entered in the draft copy.] (Wolf, unpublished field notes, 1994)

There is a very clear diversity of opinions here, but the political press for developing widely acceptable standards, against a background of a frayed cultural fabric, did not permit frank discussion to be preserved, or dangerous topics to be admitted.

In Education 2000, all proposed standards will be certified by a federally appointed central council, the National Education Standards Improvement Council (NESIC). With education and a strong support staff, the members of this government-appointed body are likely to be able to make decisions based on common measures: validity, comprehensiveness, equity, and the like. But framed and peopled in this way, it seems unlikely that the proposed federal system will be either informed or perturbed by serious debates in the fields that it has been designed to oversee. For example, how will this federal body think its way through to the realization of the national goal that all students come to speak more than a single language? How will it sort through what scholars, linguists, and researchers view themselves as still finding out about language acquisition? Finally, how will they arrive at decisions? Surely majority vote is not a complex enough response to the question of whether language and literature standards must cite core works.

If we want the equity of common standards, are we bound to give up a vision of standards as conversations? Not necessarily. Imagine CEICAS— a Council on the Excellence and Integration of Curriculum, Assessment, and Standards. It is nongovernmental, but rather is funded independently by participating educational organizations such as the National Council of Teachers of Mathematics or the National Council of Teachers of English, possibly in conjunction with foundations. It has a national board of overseers drawn from focused groups working on mathematics, science, literacy, etc. The working groups would not be synonymous with familiar subject matters. Instead of an English/Language Arts group, we might want a working group on literacy, language, and literature. Their membership could draw on the full range of professional organizations (the National Council of Teachers of English, International Reading Association, National Reading Council, American Council of Learned Societies, and Modern Language Association). But to that it might add representatives from government-funded institutions such as the National Endowment for the Humanities, members from the United Nations Council on Literacy, independent researchers, or authors.

The function of such an organization would be to provide the conversation that is fundamentally missing in present proposals. At the level of a conjoined board of overseers, the work would be to ask questions that are unlikely to be asked in the common measures environment proposed in NESIC: How can the standards be sensitive to the changing and debated nature of knowing? For instance, how effectively do the standards reflect a world where many literacies—textual, visual and digital—now exist? If we look across the standards, what kinds of articulation are there—what kinds of schools are we creating? If we look to the world of postsecondary education, what kind of preparation do these standards provide? The working groups could be deliberately designed to provide a broad-based critique and reflection on the nature and consequences of the national standards. They could act as an independent review board helping states or regions think hard about what they want for standards—rather than merely copying the national standards. This might happen in several types of reviews: for example, a mentoring review in early phases of development, a juried review for more nearly finished materials, a review for materials that have proven problematic at NESIC or in implementation. Throughout such reviews, those reviewed would have access to the full range of reviews of their materials—both majority and minority opinions. Critics will say, "But we need progress, not academic dithering." To that perhaps the sharpest reply is the earlier example of the workings of the Supreme Court, where decisions of tremendous moment are made, but go public with the possibility of dissenting opinions and the prospect that later cases will continue to develop our understanding of where justice lies. Commonality need not drive out conversation.

There are two very different kinds of standards—common measures and highly debatable emblems. We could also call them regulation and perturbation—precedent and debate. Both are integral sides of any robust *system* for assaying questions large enough to matter. It is no mistake that Tulio's cathedral carried both—some day, if we are insistent enough, we might claim the same.

References

Burke, K. 1974. *Philosophy of Literacy Form*. Berkeley and Los Angeles: University of California Press.

Danly, R. L. 1981. "Translating Local Color." *Translation Review* 10: 20–26.

Eisner, E. 1993. Presidential address. The annual meeting of the American Educational Research Association, San Francisco, Calif.

"Fiftieth Anniversary of D-Day." New York Times, May 8, 1994, Section 4, 1.

Graff, G. 1992. *Beyond the Culture Wars: How Teaching the Conflicts Can Revitalize American Education*. New York: W. W. Norton.

National Board of Professional Teaching Standards. 1994. Statement of guiding principles. Detroit, Mich.

Ruoff, H. W., ed. *The Circle of Knowledge*. Washington, D.C.: The Standard Publishing Company.

Stake, R. 1976. *Responsive Evaluation*. Champaign-Urbana: University of Illinois Press.

Standards Project in the English Language Arts. 1994. *Public Sampler*. Champaign-Urbana: University of Illinois.

Super, E. H., ed. 1962. *Democratic Education*. Ann Arbor: University of Michigan Press.

Terman, L. M. 1922. *Intelligence Tests and School Reorganization*. Yonkers-on-Hudson, N. Y.: World Book Co.

Webster's Third New International Dictionary of the English Language, 1968.

Wolf, D. P. 1988. *Reading Reconsidered*. New York: The College Entrance Examination Board.

Wolf, D. P. 1994. Unpublished field notes. The PACE project. Harvard Graduate School of Education.

PART IV

STANDARDS AND EDUCATIONAL POLICY

8

Policy and Practice: The Relations Between Governance and Instruction

DAVID K. COHEN

David Cohen is professor of Public Policy and John Dewey Professor of Education at the University of Michigan.

JAMES P. SPILLANE

Jim Spillane is a research associate at the College of Education at Michigan State University.

Ours is a time of remarkable ferment in U.S. education. The recent school reform movement initially focused on the "basics," but then took off in a dramatically new direction in the late 1980s. Reformers started to demand more thoughtful and intellectually ambitious instruction. Leaders in politics and business argued that students must become independent thinkers and enterprising problem solvers. Educators began to say that schools must offer intellectually challenging instruction that is deeply rooted in the academic disciplines.

These ideas are a dramatic change. For most of this century, politicians and businessmen ignored public education or supported only minimum programs for most students. And most leaders in education long have

We are grateful to Carol Barnes, Linda Darling-Hammond, Robert Dreeben, Robert Floden, Susan Fuhrman, Harry Judge, James Kelly, Magdalene Lampert, George Madaus, Barbara Neufeld, Andrew Porter, Daniel Resnick, Brian Rowan, Lauren Sosniak, Marshall Smith, Gary Sykes, Teresa Tatto, Suzanne Wilson, and Rona Wilensky for comments on earlier drafts of this essay. Gerald Grant and Linda Darling-Hammond offered especially helpful suggestions on the next to last draft.

been inclined to the view that most students need basic and practical education rather than more high-flown and demanding stuff. These tendencies were entirely representative. Though the American people have been enthusiasts for schooling, few have been keen on intellectually ambitious education.

More unusual still, recent reformers have proposed fundamental changes in politics and policy to achieve the new goals. They argue for the creation of state or national curricula, to push instruction to new heights. Or they advocate state or national tests or examination systems, to pull instruction in the same direction. Or they propose to link examinations and curricula so as to gain even more leverage on teaching and learning. Prominent politicians, businesspeople, and professors have endorsed one or another of these proposals. Several state and national agencies have begun to implement them. Major efforts are under way to mobilize much more consistent and powerful direction for instruction from state or national agencies.

These developments seem hopeful to some and unwise to others. But everyone agrees that they mark an astonishing reversal, and many therefore wonder whether the new proposals are attainable. One set of problems concerns politics. Power and authority have been extraordinarily dispersed in U.S. education, especially in matters of instruction. Could state or national agencies actually mobilize the influence required to steer teaching and learning in thousands, or hundreds of thousands, of faraway classrooms? That would require extensive new state or national infrastructure in education, as well as a radically new politics of education. Are such things possible?

A second set of problems concerns instructional practice. The new proposals envision much more thoughtful, adventurous, and demanding instruction. But most instructional practice in the United States is quite traditional: Teachers and students spend most of their time with lectures, formal recitations, and worksheets. Intellectual demands generally are modest, and a great deal of the work is dull. Only a small fraction of public school teachers have deep knowledge of any academic subject. Hence, even if state or national agencies accumulated the infrastructure and influence required to steer teaching and learning, could teachers be steered so sharply away from long-established practice?

To answer these questions about how things might change, one must ask others about how they now work. How do instructional policies made in state and national agencies play out in local classrooms? What are the relations between policy and practice? What might it take to change them? Have central agencies ever tried to promote innovative and adventurous teaching? If so, with what results? These seem crucial issues for America today and tomorrow, but our knowledge about them is limited by what we did yesterday. The dispersed organization of American education rendered the connections between policy and instruction inconsequential for most of our history. The topic barely entered educational inquiry because it seemed so distant from educational reality. There is little American evidence about the structure or consequences of much greater state or national control. Similarly, American disdain for intellectually challenging education has left us with only modest evidence on how such education might turn out in this nation's schools. In order to learn much about such matters we must look beyond the U.S. education mainstream, and to studies of other national school systems.

We tackle the issues in four chunks. First, we probe the relations between state and national government on the one hand and instruction on the other. We explore how the structure and activities of central government affect classroom practice. But in some systems, key decisions about instruction, like what texts to read or what tests to use, are made by no central agency. Hence, in the second chunk of the essay we identify the specific sources of guidance for instruction, including tests, texts, and other things. We explore how such things interact with governance structures, and we probe their effects on classroom practice.

In the third chunk of the essay we scrutinize change in classroom practice. The recent U.S. reforms propose very ambitious shifts in instructional purposes, processes, and content: We inquire about the prospects for such change in teaching.

Finally, we consider nongovernmental influences on instruction. Recent reformers have proposed radical changes in policy, politics, and instructional guidance, seeing these as potent influences on classroom work. Yet studies of schooling here and abroad often suggest that social and cultural influences may be no less significant. For instance, some researchers report that Japanese families tend to support children's hard work and academic achievement, while Americans tend not to. Such differences may account for many of the effects often ascribed to policy and institutions.

Government Structure and Policymaking

The formal institutions of government are widely supposed to shape the relations between education policy and instructional practice. In France and many other nations, central agencies have enormous authority and power (Holmes 1979; Lewis 1985). Ministries of education make most policy for local education, and they often do so in great detail. But the U.S. political system was specifically designed to frustrate central power. Authority in education was divided among state, local, and federal governments by an elaborate federal system, and it was divided within governments by the separation of powers. These divisions were carefully calculated to inhibit the coordinated action of government, and they gained force from the country's great size and diversity (Kaufman 1969).

The U.S. federal government thus has had relatively weak influence on education, as a matter of both law and tradition. But since World War II the central government has accumulated increasing influence on state and local decisions about funding, education for disadvantaged groups, civil rights and civil liberties in schools, research, and curriculum improvement. Despite these changes, direct federal governance of education is marginal. Federal agencies directly operate few schools and contribute only a little more than 6 percent of school operating budgets, on average (U.S. Bureau of the Census 1989).

State governments are the constitutional center of U.S. education. But most states delegated most authority to localities, for most of their history. States supported the establishment of public schools with enabling statutes and, sometimes, a bit of money in the nineteenth century, but most of the pressures to establish public schools lay outside of state government. There has been some variability in states' influence in education. Hawaii has no local districts, and southern states have tended to be stronger than those elsewhere (Wirt and Kirst 1982). But until 15 years ago the general pattern was extensive delegated state power. Most state agencies were small and weakly staffed (McDonnell and McLaughlin 1982; Murphy 1974). State governments have begun to exercise more power during the last decade (Cantor 1980), but most are still far from what, in world perspective, could be called central control.

Such weakness in higher-level agencies is quite unusual. In many nations the national ministry is the senior and often sole partner, managing all education programs and paying most or all operating costs. In modern France, the schools have until recently been a creature of the national government in Paris, not of local or departmental governments (Cameron, Cowan, Holmes, Hurst, and McLean 1984b; Holmes 1979; Lewis 1985). Even state or provincial governments in other federal systems have much greater power and authority. Australian state governments hold most constitutional authority in education, as they do in the United States. But the six Australian states also are the basic operating units in education (Boyd and Smart 1987; Cameron, Cowan, Holmes, Hurst, and McLean 1984a). Each state operates all the public schools within its boundaries, performing all the functions that Americans associate with both state and local school government.

The United States thus has a remarkably fragmented governance system. Many important education decisions are made in the nation's roughly 110,000 individual schools (U.S. Bureau of the Census 1989). These include decisions about educational programs, student assignment, teacher assignment, and resource allocation among students (Wirt and Kirst 1982). One result is remarkable variation across schools (Cusick 1983; Powell, Farrar, and Cohen 1985). Recent efforts at local "restructuring" and "school-based management" will almost certainly enhance the influence of many schools.

Local districts are the fundamental governance agencies, by tradition and practice. There are some 15,000 local districts (U.S. Bureau of the Census 1989), and their influence is extraordinary in world perspective. Despite the recent growth of state and national power, these districts make a great range of decisions, including those that bear on levels of funding, the nature of educational programs, and the teachers to be hired (Travers and Westbury 1989). Financial support for most U.S. schools is still tied to local tax bases and taxation decisions, which produces enormous variation in education resources and, thus, instructional programs. The key role of local districts builds many differences into U.S. education (Firestone 1989).

Individual schools and districts have had much less influence in many other nations (Travers and Westbury 1989). The French and Singaporean ministries of education have until recently monopolized decisions about education programs, teacher assignment, and resource allocation (Cameron, Cowan, Holmes, Hurst, and McLean 1984b, 1984d). Local schools have had little leeway within central guidelines, a condition that some nations have begun trying to change (Cohen 1990a; Resnick and Resnick 1985, 1989). And many nations simply have no local districts. Australian state education departments deal directly with each school (Cameron et al. 1984a), although some use regional offices for some administrative purposes. Funding decisions typically are made by national or state agencies, greatly reducing or eliminating fiscal and programmatic variation among schools. Some nations with strong central governments do have local jurisdictions that are supposed to play a large role in education. The postwar Japanese constitution guarantees local authority in such education decisions as teacher hiring and curriculum (Cameron, Cowan, Holmes, Hurst, and McLean 1984c). But the influence of local prefectures is constrained both by the broad authority of national agencies and by centuries-old habits of deference to the center. The result limits educational variation of many sorts (Cameron et al. 1984c).

In most nations, the relations between policy and practice are framed by systems of central power or by a small number of powerful state or provincial governments. The authority of the state is immense and, in many cases, theoretically unlimited. Schools are creatures of the nation-state or the province, and usually were created in the process of consolidating those entities (Meyer 1983; Ramirez and Rubison 1979; Ramirez and Boli 1987).

The connection between central power and public education is a world pattern to which the local mobilization of schooling in the United States is one of the few great exceptions. Despite growing state and federal power, local government still is the key element in U.S. schooling. And the relations between policy and practice are framed by sprawling government structures in which fragmented power and authority express a considered mistrust of government.

If government structure frames the formal relations between central policy and classroom practice, policymaking fills that frame with specific content. The two are often at odds. While the design of American government incarnates a deep mistrust of state power, the design of most education policy expresses an abiding hope for the power of government and a wish to harness it to social problem solving. Collisions between the two were precipitated by the proliferation of state and federal education policies and programs in the last three decades. These included federal efforts to improve curriculum and instruction in the 1950s and early 1960s and to eliminate the racially dual school system throughout the South in the 1960s and 1970s. They also included federal and state efforts to improve education for disadvantaged students, to reform the education of handicapped students, to provide bilingual education for non-English-speaking students, and to ensure sex equity in schools across the nation. Nearly all of these policies and programs sought to solve problems that crossed jealously guarded jurisdictional boundaries among and within governments.

To speak of the relations between policy and practice in the United States is thus to speak both of collisions between policy and governance and of the consequences in education institutions. Those collisions have affected the relations between policy and practice in several ways. New education policies expanded central authority and drew the agencies of policy and practice closer together. But these policies did not commensurately reduce the autonomy of "lower-level" agencies. The flood of state and federal policies and programs coursed through a large and loosely jointed governance system, and agencies throughout the system retained much of their operating independence. For instance, the states depend on localities for political support and policy execution, as any higher-level agent depends on subordinates. State governments, therefore, should be constrained by what localities will accept. Yet the states often act with remarkable independence. The state education reforms of the last 10 years have in some respects been quite offensive to local educators, but many still have been enacted with little difficulty (Fuhrman, Clune, and Elmore 1988). Similarly, the national government has only a modest constitutional role in education, and it has long deferred to state and local authorities. Nonetheless, federal agencies have taken various dramatic initiatives designed to greatly change state and local education. Many were taken over local and state opposition, some over fierce and even violent opposition (Orfield 1969). Despite the constraints that lower-level agencies can impose on their superiors, agencies above have regularly pushed far beyond the presumed limits.

The same phenomenon obtained in reverse: state and local autonomy has been only modestly constrained by higher-level policy. Researchers have documented the states' great flexibility in responding to the dramatic federal policies and programs of the 1950s and 1960s (Murphy 1974). Researchers also have shown that local schools and districts retain considerable latitude in coping with state and federal policies (Berman and McLaughlin 1977; McLaughlin 1987). Despite the increasing flow of high-level requirements, advice, and inducements, lower-level agencies have much room to interpret and respond. Relations among state, federal, and local agencies therefore remain quite attenuated despite decades of effort to bring them closer together. Centers of organization and governance are widely dispersed and weakly linked, despite the growth of policy. Central agencies can make serious demands on others with relative ease; they need only mobilize the political resources to enunciate a policy or begin a new program. But the costs of enforcing demands are much greater. A great distance remains between state or federal policymaking and local practice (Firestone 1989).

Yet policymaking has complicated educational organization. In order to make contact with local education organizations, state and federal agencies have had to bridge vast political chasms artfully designed to frustrate central power. To increase general governance authority in education was politically unthinkable for the federal government. What is more, federal agencies were weak. They had no general capacity in curriculum, instruction, school personnel, or assessment, since both the Constitution and political practice were thought to forbid it. State agencies had much more authority, but with a few exceptions they had little more capacity. A majority of states had delegated most operations to local governments and private test and text publishers. Traditions of decentralization, suspicions about central power, and deference to local authority meant that higher-level authority could grow only by way of individual, freestanding programs, each of which promised to solve a specific education problem (Bankston 1982; Meyer 1983). But these individual programs were located in agencies that had little general operating capacity in the "technical core" of education.

Hence, when weak federal and state agencies tried to implement such ambitious programs as Head Start and Title I of the Elementary and Secondary Education Act (1965), each program had to be outfitted with its own minimum core of administrative operations (budget, personnel, evaluation, and the like). Furthermore, each program had to coordinate operations across many levels of government, owing to the lack of general administrative capacity above the local level. And each policy or program had to do so in ways that did not require much capacity in such key areas of education as curriculum or instruction, since such things were regarded as off limits to central government. Lacking general central authority and capacity, leaders of each program had to establish their own systems. How else could they hope to mobilize tens or hundreds of thousands of educators, in hundreds or thousands of jurisdictions, across several levels of government?

Work in such policies and programs therefore was confined within specialized administrative subunits organized around oversight tasks within each program (Wise 1979). Administrative capacity grew, within programs rather than across entire governments. Administrative burdens therefore multiplied as the same or similar administrative work was repeated across programs (Bankston 1982; Cohen 1990a; Meyer 1983; Rowan 1982, 1983). Central agencies grew, but in a fragmented fashion (Clark 1965; Scott and Meyer 1983; Stackhouse 1982). And the adminstrative expansion added little to central capacity in the core areas of education such as curriculum and instruction. The collisions between optimistic policies and cautiously designed government have produced fractured and duplicative administration.

These fractures were reflected in the organization of agencies outside of government. As policies and programs took shape, networks of interested agencies—advocacy organizations, professional groups, and special-purpose research and development agencies, among others—grew up around them. Examples include the loose network that helped to build support for the legislative proposals that became PL 94–142 and Title I of the 1965 ESEA (now Chapter I). Each network has helped to coordinate and stabilize program operations and mobilize support for programs across governments and among many sorts of agencies (Cohen 1982; Peterson 1981; Peterson, Rabe, and Wong 1986). Like the programs and policies that they grew up around, these policy networks are ingenious, for they support state and national efforts to solve local problems in a political system that was designed to frustrate such efforts (Kaufman 1969). But these clever inventions also encourage political fragmentation and multiply administrative work (Bankston 1982; Cohen 1982; Meyer 1983; Rogers and Whetten 1982). For they support fractured authority within education agencies, as managers in each program attempt to build their own bridges across great political chasms. The ingenious devices that cope with fragmentation among governments tend to exacerbate fragmentation within them.

Collisions between cautious designs of government and hopeful designs for policy also complicated local education practice, because administrative work grew as localities coped with increasing state and federal policies and programs. Since higher-level authorities are so distant from local practice, they are rarely held accountable for their actions there. Hence state and federal initiatives were generated with little regard for the relations among them, or for their cumulative local effects (Kimbrough and Hill 1981; Kirst 1988; Wise 1979). Indeed, some of the most potent local effects of state and federal programs or policies had no intended programmatic content. The best case in point is underfunded mandates. Federal legislation for handicapped students placed unaccustomed procedural and substantive burdens on local education agencies, but the legislation carried less than half the estimated costs of compliance. Initially, it was thought that full funding would soon follow, but it never did. Federal requirements were never relaxed, though. Local and state school agencies had to allocate their own funds to this area of program support, often with grave results for other education activities.

Yet requirements have limits. State and federal officials rarely can effectively oversee local program implementation. No state or federal education agencies have the inspectorates found in Britain, France, and their former colonies. At best, U.S. state and federal agencies use oversight-at-a-distance, such as written program evaluations, grant recipients' reports on operations, and the like. Such things multiply work without producing fruitful contacts among public servants at different levels of government (Bardach and Kagan 1982). And local schools retain considerable autonomy. Administrators and teachers usually can tailor higher-level programs to local purposes and conditions if they have the will and take the time (Berman and McLaughlin 1977). Often they can cope with higher-level directives simply by ignoring them. Inattention is a ubiquitous management tool (Kiesler and Sproull 1982), and it can be especially efficient in a fragmented governance system.

These patterns contrast sharply with many foreign education systems. The ministries of education in France and Singapore deal with schools on a broad range of education matters, as do the state departments of education in Australia and provincial governments in Germany. There are administrative subunits in these agencies, but they are broadly defined by the key areas of schools' operation (i.e., curriculum, instruction, personnel, and the like). The subunits have extensive general authority, and new initiatives typically subsist within them rather than being set aside in independent units, because the operating units make the key decisions about education and have the resources. That is what might be expected in nations founded on *étatist* traditions. Policy initiatives are not organized as though they were at war with government, or on the assumption that they can have little to do with the core operations of education.

The collisions between rapidly expanded policymaking and fragmented governance are a hallmark of U.S. education. Few nations have such dispersed authority and power in education, yet few have such intense higher-level policymaking. Americans complain more than any other people about state interference with education and centralizing forces in schools, but authority and power are more dispersed here than in nearly any other nation. Perhaps that is why we complain more.

Instructional Guidance

State and federal governments have made many efforts to improve instruction. They offer financial aid to local districts, sponsor child health and nutrition programs, and support efforts to improve education for the disadvantaged. Yet such policies rarely make broad or close contact with instruction. Teaching and learning are more directly affected by the texts that students and teachers use, the examinations that assess students' academic accomplishments, the standards teachers must satisfy in order to secure a post, and the like. These instruments constitute the means so far invented to guide classroom work. We lump them under the rubric of instructional guidance and sort them into five categories: (a) instructional frameworks, (b) instructional materials, (c) assessment of student performance, (d) oversight of instruction, and (e) requirements for teacher education and licensure.

Nations use these instruments very differently. In some cases guidance is designed and deployed by governments, while in others private agencies play a large role. Additionally, the arrangement of government-sponsored guidance varies greatly across nations (Broadfoot 1983). and while all school systems adopt some stance toward guiding instruction, often that stance includes offering little advice.

Instructional guidance also mediates the effects of other policies that seek to affect practice, because the effects of all government policies that try to influence instruction—including those that do so by offering extra aid to the disadvantaged or holding schools "accountable"—are mediated by such things as instructional materials, teachers' professional capacities, and methods of student assessment. Intentionally or not, the aggregate of instructional guidance is a medium in and through which many other education policies and programs operate.

In what follows we compare instructional guidance in the United States with its counterparts in other national school systems. We focus on the instruments of guidance; while these are governed in many different ways in national school systems, we do not try to describe that variety here. Instead we use a few key categories that describe variations in instructional guidance. These variations can be produced by many different governmental and administrative arrangements (see Porter, Floden, Freeman, Schmidt, and Schwille 1988).

Consistency.   Given different domains of guidance, one important issue concerns the extent of agreement within and among domains. In some systems instructional frameworks are consistent internally, and consistent with texts or teacher education. But in other systems they are not.

Specificity or Prescriptiveness.   Teaching and learning are complex enterprises, and there are many different ways to enact them. Teachers and students are offered clear and detailed guidance about content coverage or pedagogy in some systems, while in others guidance is very general or vague.

Authority and Power.   To offer guidance is not to decide what weight it carries. Advice for instruction is presented in ways that have great authority with students and teachers in some systems, but in others such advice is presented in ways that carry little weight.

Instructional Frameworks

Instructional frameworks are general designs for instruction (i.e., broad conceptions of the purposes, structure, and content of academic work). Frameworks can set the terms of reference for the entire enterprise. In some school systems they guide course structure and content, the nature of textbooks, the purposes and content of examinations, and the like. They can be quite prescriptive: In some former French and British colonies such frameworks offer extensive and focused guidance about instructional content, and in some cases approaches to teaching as well. In France many curriculum decisions are made in the national ministry of education (Horner 1986), which often details the topics to be studied, the teaching materials and methods to be used, and even time allocations (Beauchamp and Beauchamp 1972; Lewis 1989). The Japanese central ministry issues frameworks for each subject (Kobayashi 1984), prescribing content and detailing the sequence of topics (Kida 1986; Organization for Economic Cooperation and Development 1971).

Such guidance often seems to carry great authority and power. In France, many curriculum decisions are made by the national assembly, while others are ministry decrees. But authoritative guidance need not be governmental. In Holland it is offered by autonomous agencies that are supported by government but are not part of it.

Frameworks have been unusual in the United States. The most common instructional designs have been bare listings of course requirements by states or localities. Apart from the New York State Regents, it was long uncommon for state agencies to offer advice about the material to be covered within particular subject areas, or about the structure of courses. This passivity was not unique to state governments. Until quite recently, few local systems seemed to prescribe topics within courses or curricula. And guidelines about pedagogy have been even more rare. Relatively weak state and local guidance concerning course content and pedagogy has meant that students and teachers have had great latitude in shaping the content and purposes of their courses (Cusick 1983; Porter et al. 1988; Powell, Farrar, and Cohen 1985; Schwille et al. 1983, 1986; Sedlak, Wheeler, Pullin, and Cusick 1986).

A few states recently have moved more aggressively into instructional design. Florida, South Carolina, and a few other southern states instituted statewide basic skills curricula in efforts to improve students' performance during the past decade. These included guidance for content coverage and pacing, and at least implicitly for teacher education. Several states have published evaluations that claim gains in student achievement, although no independent evaluations seem to have been done. At the same time, several other states have pressed guidance for a radically different sort of content. In 1985, California issued the first of a series of curriculum frameworks that were intended to make teaching and learning intellectually much more ambitious and demanding. Arizona and Michigan have taken some similar steps, as has Connecticut.

Some local school systems also began to move toward instructional frameworks in the 1970s and 1980s, with the news that test scores were declining and mounting demands that schools get "back to the basics." Local districts came under unfamiliar pressure to improve performance, and some began to devise minimum instructional programs in response— Washington, D.C., Chicago, and Philadelphia among them. There is little systematic research on these matters, so we cannot gauge the depth or extent of these changes. Additionally, several cities that adopted such schemes recently announced their demise. But officials in a few districts that we recently visited reported a move to greater central control. Schools can no longer determine their own instructional programs, and central offices have written rudimentary curriculum frameworks, usually blueprints for "essential skills."

Instructional Materials

Texts and other materials are found in all systems, but the extent of guidance for their content and use varies enormously. In many systems, the national ministry sets the terms of reference for text content, and/or authorizes the textbooks to be used based on curriculum frameworks (Kida 1986; OECD 1973). In such cases, there is a good deal of consistency between the guidance teachers receive from textbooks and from national curriculum frameworks. In some nations ministries actually publish texts, while in others texts are privately published. But in either event, materials are closely tied to curriculum frameworks.

Decisions about instructional materials have been much more fragmented in the United States. Since there have been few instructional frameworks until recently, publishers had little or no consistent, content-oriented guidance. Instead, they were guided by what had been done before, by official and unofficial expressions of state or local preferences, and by their own sense of the market. Texts have improved in many ways over those that were available in the 1920s, but most commentators regard most texts as intellectually shallow. Many states and localities officially adopt textbooks, and Americans often have thought this to be highly prescriptive for instruction. But lacking much official guidance for topic coverage within texts, save for such matters as evolution, these texts seem not to have been highly prescriptive for topic coverage (Floden et al. 1988). Researchers report that many texts mention many more topics than could be dealt with, which leaves open extensive topic choice by teachers (Tyson-Bernstein 1988). Additionally, there seem to be appreciable inconsistencies in content coverage among the different texts for most subjects at most grade levels (Freeman et al. 1983). Hence texts have offered many opportunities for teachers and students to vary the content they cover (Freeman and Porter 1989; Porter et al. 1988; Schwille et al. 1983).

As several states recently moved toward more explicit instructional designs, they tried to make them count for textbooks. California used its new curriculum frameworks in mathematics, and in literature and language arts, to press publishers to revise texts. Publishers were told that if they did not make satisfactory revisions their texts would not be approved for adoption. But the state's guidance still was general. The mathematics framework, for instance, offered little specific guidance about topic coverage. Casual comparisons of the new and old literature and language arts texts with the revised framework suggest that the state has won some significant changes, although systematic analysis remains to be done. Studies of the mathematics texts and framework suggest only modest change thus far (Putnam, Heaton, Prawat, and Remillard in press).

Some local districts also have begun trying to promote greater consistency between instructional frameworks and materials. Several that devised such frameworks also specified the knowledge and skills that students and teachers should cover in texts and other materials, often doing so in compilations of "essential skills." In at least one case, local officials tied their guidance to recently published texts that seemed to fit with the local instructional frameworks. The district specified the material to be covered in the common text, and when it should be covered. This constitutes an extraordinary change for U.S. schools, but we have found no studies that gauge its breadth or depth.

Assessment of Results

Assessment of instructional results is an essential element of instructional guidance in most school systems. Though assessment practices are changing in European systems (Kellaghan and Madaus 1991; Madaus 1991), many nations tie assessment closely to curriculum. In France and many former French and British colonies, examinations are referenced to national curricula, instructional frameworks, or both. The examinations thus provide both a visible target for instruction and a means of checking its results (Madaus 1991; Resnick and Resnick 1985, 1989). The nature of assessment in these cases varies greatly among nations, but it all differs from American approaches. The examinations probe students' performance in specific curricula. Many systems mix multiple-choice questions with extended essay or problem-solving performances, though some—Japan, for instance—rely entirely on multiple-choice questions (Cheney 1991). In contrast, U.S. schools employ standardized tests that are referenced to national norms and are designed to be independent of curricula. Performance has been limited to answering multiple-choice questions (Noah and Eckstein 1989).

In France, Great Britain, and Japan, examinations count in very specific ways. Students' promotion and further education depend partly or entirely on their exam performance (Eckstein and Noah 1989). Indeed, many school systems that employ examinations are highly selective, and the exams are the key agent of selection (Kellaghan and Madaus 1991). In Singapore, exams are used to make nearly irrevocable decisions about streaming in both the primary and secondary grades and thus to influence decisions about students' careers and further education. This use of examinations sharply limits students' opportunities to recoup earlier poor performances. The United States lacks such a selective examination system, which is one reason why students here have more "second chances" than they do in any other nation. But the use of examinations for student selection does enhance the examinations' authority (Madaus 1988, 1991; Madaus and Kellaghan 1991; Resnick and Resnick 1985, 1989). In New South Wales, Australia, for example, students' performance on the school leaving exam determines their opportunities for further education. Differences of a tenth of a point in exam scores can be crucial. In Japan, scores on both national secondary school leaving exams and university entrance exams determine which high school students will go on to university and determine the quality and prestige of the universities that students will attend (Ohta 1986; OECD 1973; White 1987). Secondary schools' prestige also is tied to students' success in examinations for prestigious universities (OECD 1971). The social and economic significance of exam performance offers many incentives for students and teachers to take exams seriously.

Matters are very different in the United States. There is a great deal of assessment, but it has an uncertain bearing on instruction. One reason is that most tests have been designed to minimize their sensitivity to specific curricula (Madaus 1989; Resnick and Resnick 1985; Smith and O'Day 1990). What is more, many different tests are designed, published, and marketed by many different private testing agencies. And most decisions about which test to use have been made by thousands of local and state school agencies, each of which adopts tests of its own liking independent of the others' decisions. All of this has made for inconsistent guidance from assessment.

Variation in content coverage has been another source of inconsistency in the guidance that U.S. tests offer for instruction. Standardized tests often have been seen as interchangeable, but one of the few careful studies of topical agreement among tests raised doubts about that view. Focusing on several leading fourth-grade mathematics tests, the authors observed that "our findings challenge. . .th[e] assumption. . .that standardized achievement tests may be used interchangeably" (Freeman et al. 1983). They maintain that these tests are topically inconsistent and thus differentially sensitive to content coverage.

Inconsistency has been further enhanced by the widespread local practice of using one publisher's test in one grade and others in other grades. This problem has been magnified by the increase in testing during the past several decades, as local- and state-sponsored minimum competency and essential skills tests have spread. American students are now tested much more often than they were 20 years ago, but they are tested with more different tests.

Thus, established U.S. approaches to assessment would have impelled consistency among the elements of instructional guidance, had consistency been sought. Until recently, however, it was not. The guidance for instruction that tests offered was general, and probably more a matter of the form of knowledge (i.e., it exists in multiple-choice formats and is either right or wrong) than its content. This guidance also was vague, since the test results were rarely known. Test results were kept from teachers, partly on the designers' view that they were not designed to guide instruction.

Indeed, decisions about test design, marketing, and adoption typically have been made apart from knowledge of specific school curricula, teacher education, and the like. Test theory and practice have held that such independence is crucial to test validity, but this has further weakened consistency between tests and instructional materials. Research seems to bear out the weak relations between the subject-matter content of standardized tests and of texts. Several investigators concluded: "If a fourth-grade teacher limits instruction to one of the four books analyzed, students will have an adequate opportunity to learn or to review less than half of all topics that will be tested" (Freeman et al. 1983).

To the extent that tests have guided instruction, then, they have done so inconsistently. This has weakened the instructional authority of the tests. It is thus not surprising that many teachers report they rarely take test results into account in instruction (Floden, Porter, Schmidt, and Freeman 1978; MacRury, Nagy, and Traub 1987; Ruddell 1985; Salmon-Cox 1981; Sproull and Zubrow 1981).

But two qualifications are in order. First, there have been a few exceptions to these patterns, notably the New York State Regents exams and the Advanced Placement (AP) program. The AP program is a special subsystem within public education in which high-achieving students take advanced courses. The AP exams seem to strongly influence instruction, in part because they are tied to a suggested curriculum and readings. The exams also seem to be taken seriously by most students and teachers, partly because the scores count for college entrance as well as college course taking. But these have been anomalies in American education (Powell 1991).

Second, the patterns described above have begun to change. Rising public interest in testing and other political pressures led many states and localities to begin publishing scores in the early 1970s, after decades of secrecy. By now, many do so as a matter of course and often conviction. State and local school agencies also increasingly turned to tests in efforts to improve instruction. The favored method was to institute "accountability" schemes, often based on minimum competency tests. Many of these schemes included only a high school graduation requirement, but some also included tests for promotion. Some were hastily contrived under political pressure. The tests often were adapted from standardized norm-referenced tests designed for other purposes.

State and local use of tests to guide instruction marked a dramatic turn in assessment practices. But the fragmentation characteristic of U.S. education was evident here as well. Many minimum competency tests were unrelated to other elements of instructional guidance, such as curriculum. The tests effectively became the curriculum in some cases (Darling-Hammond and Wise 1985). Recently, however, that has begun to change as well, as some publishers have brought out test series that are accompanied by criterion-referenced test systems. These link curriculum and instruction to testing. In several cities that we have studied, these text and text series are the heart of the instructional program. Students' performance is monitored by regular testing keyed to text pages, and sometimes students are retested until they achieve "mastery." We have discovered no studies that probe the frequency of such practices, though they seem to be found chiefly in cities with many disadvantaged students. In such cases, tests offer much more specific and prescriptive guidance than ordinarily has been the case in the United States.

How does such testing affect instruction? There has been surprisingly little research on the issue. Several researchers assert that the tests have had a powerful effect on teaching (Darling-Hammond 1987; Darling-Hammond and Wise 1985; Resnick and Resnick 1989; Romberg, Zarinnia, and Williams 1989). Competency tests are said to drive instruction in a mechanical and simplistic direction. Teachers orient instruction to the test items, and if students do poorly on the test, remediation consists of drill on the items they do not know (Kreitzer, Madaus, and Haney 1989; Madaus 1988). A recent U.S. Department of Education report claims that "accountability systems . . . are very powerful policy tools that have changed school-level planning and teaching activities" (OERI 1988, 31).

But it also is often said that these claims hold only for situations in which the tests carry "high stakes" (i.e., that they count for students' academic progress, or for schools' or teachers'). This condition does not hold for many minimum competency testing programs (Ellwein, Glass, and Smith 1988), or for many students in high-stakes testing programs. It also seems to be accepted that such tests are much more likely to affect poor and minority group children, since more advantaged students pass the tests with little effort. These considerations suggest that the effects of minimum competency testing have been quite uneven, and are significant for a particular segment of the school population. Additionally, we do not know how significant the tests have been, because there have been no observational studies of teachers' responses to tests. The little research on competency testing thus far is based on interviews with teachers who describe the effects of testing in rather global terms, and the evidence they present is very mixed (OERI 1988; Romberg, Zarinnia, and Williams 1989).

The effects of testing have been complicated by recent reforms. Minimum competency testing has come under sharp attack, and standardized testing itself is the object of unprecedented criticism. Several states recently have begun to use novel testing programs in efforts to strengthen and radically change guidance for instruction. The California State Education Department has begun revising its statewide testing program in an effort to "align" the state's tests with its ambitious new curriculum frameworks. State officials hope that if the tests are changed to assess thinking and understanding rather than facts and memorization, they will "drive" instruction in the new directions. Connecticut has been making similar changes, although it seems to rely on tests much more than on instructional designs. Florida has dropped its minimum competency testing program in favor of a radically different approach to reform. Proposals for authentic assessments and performance assessments have become common, and many education agencies claim to be implementing them. This ferment is quite unprecedented, but the developments are so recent that little is known about the operation of innovative assessments, let alone their effects.

Monitoring Instruction

The inspection of students' work, the observation of teaching, and other sorts of monitoring constitute a fourth type of instructional guidance. Monitoring also varies dramatically among nations. French and British central school agencies long included inspectorates, whose duties extended to checking on the topics that teachers covered, their pedagogy, and the materials they used. British inspectors visited schools to maintain standards of work and offer advice on content and pedagogy, though this role has fallen into disuse in Britain (Lawton and Gordon 1987). They still publish reports and conduct continuing professional education for teachers. Such arrangements are common in one form or another in many former French and British colonies.

Monitoring has been extremely modest and inconsistent in the United States. Few states and localities systematically monitored either teachers' coverage of curriculum or the quality of classroom work. There were no education inspectorates, nor was it common for principals to keep tabs on students' and teachers' academic work (Schwille et al. 1983). Indeed, it was uncommon to keep the detailed records that would permit such monitoring. Even if such records were kept, few principals involved themselves in instruction. Hence there have been few checks on what materials are used, how they are used, or what instruction is provided. In this respect, U.S. teachers have had quite extraordinary autonomy.

Many observers believe that U.S. teachers nonetheless teach more or less the same thing anyway. They often point to the use of textbooks, believing that the text determines instruction in most classrooms. If teachers use the same texts, it is expected that they will teach the same thing. Though there has been little research on this matter, the assumed homogeneity of content coverage is unsupported by the available evidence. Even when teachers use the same texts, their content coverage seems to vary greatly (Putnam et al. in press; Schwille et al. 1983). The authors of one study concluded that "this investigation challenge[s] the popular notion that the content of math instruction in a given elementary school is essentially equal to the textbook being used" (Freeman and Porter 1989, 418).

There are some recent signs of change. Many state and local systems attempt to monitor instruction with minimum competency tests, though the evidence suggests that these efforts are quite inconsistent and often ineffective. But at least one local school system that we visited went further: As it adopted more centralized instructional guidance, the district also devised a way to monitor teachers' coverage. Teachers fill out forms that report chapter and page coverage in required texts, and the forms are read by principals and central office officials. Some states also have begun monitoring of a sort. South Carolina has used test scores to identify both low-performing schools and districts that need special attention, and high-performing schools and districts that can be released from various state requirements. But there are few studies of these schemes, and we could find no investigations of their effects on instruction.

Teacher Education and Licensing

Guidance for instruction in this realm also varies greatly among nations. In many countries, the guidance offered by teacher education is quite consistent with other sorts of guidance. One key connection is with the schools' curriculum; for instance, in Singapore, teachers' professional education is closely tied to the curriculum of the schools. Additionally, in many nations the requirements for licensure are national rather than local, and teacher education is consistent across institutions. That seems to be true at the national level in France, partly because the ministry's inspectors play a central role in the preparation of elementary school teachers in the Ecole Normale (Lewis 1985). This tends to create consistency in the professional education of teachers and in the messages they receive from different elements of the system.

Such guidance is more of a hodgepodge in the United States. States are the agency for licensure of virtually all occupations; however, unlike medicine, teacher certification requirements are inconsistent across states and often within them. Chicago and New York City, for instance, have different certification requirements than do the states in which they are located. The interstate differences are so considerable that one recent study concluded that "a teacher certified in one state is unlikely to meet the certification requirements in another" (Haggstrom, Darling-Hammond, and Grissmer 1988, 12).

Most requirements for certification focus on teachers' education, and virtually all concern higher education. But the state agencies that set certification standards are remote from the colleges and universities that conduct most teacher education. Moreover, certification agencies usually have little connection with the state agencies that govern colleges and universities. Certification agencies, in addition, have tended to act purely in terms of course requirements rather than course content or students' performance. Hence there is room for considerable variation in how colleges and universities interpret the same requirements.

Another source of inconsistency is the loose relation between college and university requirements for teacher education and the schools' curriculum. Schools' curricula vary within states, as well as within local districts. The variety of local instructional programs cannot be accounted for by teacher education departments. And in many cases members of those departments regard the schools' curriculum as a collection of errors that prospective teachers must learn to avoid.

Against this background, the mere idea of consistent guidance for teacher education and licensing seems revolutionary. Yet, recently there have been moves in that direction. Most notable is the National Board for Professional Teaching Standards (NBPTS), which has begun efforts to develop a voluntary national examination system for teachers. If successful, this could lead to a partial national system for teacher certification, which could profoundly affect teacher education.

Instructional Guidance: An Overview

Instructional guidance in the United States has been inconsistent and diffuse. Many private and public agencies issue advice for instruction, but few take account of one another's advice. Hence much guidance for instruction has been unrelated, divergent, or contradictory. It also has been largely decoupled from government. Public agencies have extensive authority to guide instruction, but they delegate most of it to private firms or local schools. The influence of U.S. school governments pales when compared with central or provincial agencies elsewhere.

Instructional guidance also filters the effects of other initiatives that aim to influence classrooms. Prolific and inconsistent guidance in the United States has muffled and diffused such initiatives. Since government officials could not turn to an established system of guidance in efforts to shape instruction, individual programs or policies could not exert a powerful and consistent influence on instruction. Each program or policy was on its own, each competing with a buzz of other advice. Federal and state policymakers dealt with this problem by trying to mobilize special arrangements (e.g., program guidelines, evaluation, and technical assistance). But these are ancillary to the core instruments of guidance, and have been no more than modestly influential.

The result is paradoxical. Public and private agencies prolifically produce guidance, more than in societies with much more potent advice for instruction. But this does not press instruction in any consistent direction, because when guidance is inconsistent and diffuse, no single test, curriculum, or policy or program is likely to have a broad or marked effect. Many teachers and students are aware of different sorts of advice, but few are keenly aware of most of it. Many know that most guidance is either weakly supported or contradicted by other advice and that much can safely be ignored. The din of diverse, often inconsistent, and generally weak guidance opens considerable latitude to those who work within it.

Teachers' habits and decisions are important in any system of instruction. But absent plain and strong guidance, they become unusually important. The result in U.S. classrooms is curiously mixed. The forms of instruction are generally traditional, and the intellectual level usually is low, but the specific content is remarkably variable. There are many reasons for the variation, including differences in students' inclinations and teachers' judgment. But one additional reason is that students' and teachers' preferences are not informed by a plain system of common purposes and content. Classrooms around the world are of course traditional in form as well, often much more so than in the United States. But classrooms here exhibit a distinctive sort of diffuse, academically relaxed traditionalism. Yet the content is highly variable. Teachers' work is guided more by inherited practices and individual decisions than by any clear and common view of what is to be covered, how it is to be covered, and why. In this sense, American schools have the worst of both worlds.

Our point is not that instructional guidance has been irrelevant in U.S.

schools. Rather, it has been relevant only when someone chose to notice it and to do something about it. In a sense, this is true anywhere: Teachers in Singaporean or French schools must notice guidance and choose to do something about it before it can shape instruction. But the consistency, prescriptiveness, and authority of instructional guidance in such places increases the chances that teachers will notice the same advice. In contrast, teachers' and students' autonomy have been enhanced in the United States because they work in such a diffuse system of instructional guidance. The classroom doors behind which teachers labor are no thicker here than elsewhere, but teachers in the United States receive fewer strong and consistent messages about content and pedagogy. Hence, they and their students have found it relatively easy to pursue their own preferences once the doors have closed behind them.

The situation has begun to change as recent school reformers seek to cure the ills of U.S. education by mobilizing more consistent guidance for instruction. We know little about the effects of these efforts, but the cures bear an uncanny resemblance to the disease. Several states are trying to promote some form of consistent guidance, but quite naturally do so independently of each other. Many localities are trying to promote some version of consistent guidance, but do so with no reference to one another or to state policy. Federal education officials recently have begun trying to create more consistent guidance for instruction, but their efforts so far have been independent of many state and local endeavors. Several national groups—the National Governors Association, NBPTS, the National Council of Teachers of Mathematics, and others—also are trying to promote more consistent guidance. Each, of course, is carrying on independently of the rest, and none are much related to state and local efforts. Some professional associations also have taken up the idea, as have several academic disciplines; however, there is modest contact among these endeavors as well, and little relation to state and local initiatives. We live in a blizzard of different, divergent, and often inconsistent efforts to create more consistent guidance.

There also are deep divisions over the content of the recent reforms. Proposals for more lively and demanding instruction are circulating in various political, disciplinary, and education circles, but there are many versions of the new ideas. These novel schemes also compete with established ideas and practices, for "back to basics," "effective schools," and "direct instruction" all are alive, well, and firmly rooted in school and classroom practice.

All of this is par for the American course. Government structure has not been changed by recent reforms, nor has political practice. The power of our ingeniously fragmented political system is evident even in efforts to cure fragmentation. Some attack fragmentation as a barrier to more effective instruction, but others celebrate it as a source of vitality in American institutions. Similarly, today's disagreements about the aims and methods of education are only the most recent expression of old tensions between our practical and anti-intellectual bent and our occasionally more elevated aspirations. The dispute has deep roots in both popular culture and the institutions of education, and it would be astonishing if it were settled easily or soon.

Effects of Instructional Guidance

If instructional guidance is worth noticing, it must be because it makes a difference to teaching and learning. Does it?

Many educators around the world would think the answer obvious and affirmative. That guidance affects instruction is the working assumption of many European and Asian school systems. But many U.S. social scientists argue that it is difficult or impossible to steer education toward consistent practices or results, owing to weak knowledge of education processes and other uncertainties (Berlak and Berlak 1981; Floden and Clark 1988; Jackson 1968; Lampert 1985; Lortie 1975). John Meyer and his associates contend that school systems therefore create elaborate rituals, building a "logic of confidence" to replace evidence of rational relations between education resources and processes on the one hand, and results on the other (Scott and Meyer 1983). School systems "buffer" themselves by offering evidence on attendance and degrees instead of evidence on performance. Oddly, there is little evidence on these contending assumptions. For all the variation in instructional guidance, there is little research on its effects.

Teaching

Many scholars assert that guidance affects teaching. In writing of the effects of the French Baccalaure´at examinations, for instance, Patricia Broadfoot notes that "examination questions virtually become the [schools'] syllabus" (Broadfoot 1984). But guidance from one source can be offset by guidance from another. Hence we put the issue more specifically: Is teaching more consistent in school systems with more consistent instructional guidance? The only direct way to answer this question would be to connect evidence on the structure and content of guidance in education systems to evidence on teaching within them. The only study that permits such comparisons is the Second International Mathematics Study (SIMS). And while SIMS contained evidence on math teaching and curriculum for 15 nations, it offered little data on system structure. David Stevenson and David Baker compiled such data, focusing on the degree of central curriculum control. They tied this to SIMS data on the consistency of topic coverage among teachers within nations. They found that cross-national differences in the degree of central curriculum control were positively related in consistency in the topics that teachers reported they taught. Teachers in nations with more centralized curriculum control reported greater agreement on topics taught than did teachers in systems with less central control. More centrally controlled systems also had fewer teachers who reported teaching little of the prescribed curriculum. There was less within-system variation in the amount of mathematics instruction in systems with more national curriculum control than in those with local or provincial control. Finally, teachers in more locally controlled systems were more likely to report that they adjusted instruction to local conditions, including their perceptions of students' ability and mastery of mathematics (Stevenson and Baker 1991). While modest, these differences all suggest an effect of consistent guidance. But Stevenson and Baker point out that they had no direct measures of consistency in guidance.

SIMS seems to be the only data set in which system-level effects can be explored, but instructional guidance operates at many levels of education. Many recent studies of school effectiveness have focused attention on school-level consistency in guidance. While the studies are of varying quality, they show that schools differ widely with respect to consistency in instruction. Some adopt a laissez-faire style, permit diverse offerings and approaches, and thus create many choices for teachers about what to teach and how, and for students about what to study and how much. Others offer more consistent instructional guidance, thus limiting both instructional offerings and faculty and student choices (Bryk, Lee, and Smith 1990; Cusick 1983; Powell et al. 1985).

What explains the effects of instructional guidance on teaching? Researchers who study individual schools offer varied answers to the question. Some point to school heads' leadership in forging consensus about goals and methods. Others focus on school "climate" or shared norms for instruction among faculty and students (Bryk et al. 1990). Levels of faculty collegiality and cooperation sometimes are offered as another sort of guidance for teaching (Purkey and Smith 1983). But other analysts point as much to structural as cultural factors; that is, some schools are committed to less differentiation in the curriculum, and thus to fewer choices for students and teachers, creating more consistency by organizing the curriculum around a common core of courses (Powell et al. 1985). Not surprisingly, such schools tend to be smaller (Bryk et al. 1990), which suggests another influence on consistency. Researchers who study school systems offer a different sort of answer: More central control of curriculum produces more consistent topic coverage (Stevenson and Baker 1991). But it is possible that such consistency only expresses what teachers learned as students. If elementary and secondary schools are the prime agencies of teacher education, as many scholars argue, then the curriculum that teachers present may reflect their earlier school learning, rather than current official directives. The difference could be consequential for reform. If official directives are a potent influence on teachers' actions, then recent state and national reforms might quickly affect classroom work. But if consistency is more the result of inattentive curricular hand-me-downs, then changes in policy could take much longer to find their way into classroom practice.

Learning

Our interest in the effect of instructional guidance on teaching is partly instrumental: We want to know whether it affects learning. There is, unfortunately, no cross-national evidence on this issue, nor do we expect anything persuasive very soon. For researchers would have to connect evidence on the large structure of education systems with evidence on the fine structure of teaching, and connect both of those to learning. Furthermore, they would have to do so across many different nations with different school systems. It would be an immensely complex task to make those connections while also taking other salient influences into account. If the prior history of research on school effects is any precedent, knowledge will grow slowly.

But many U.S. schools have tried to improve learning by increasing guidance for instruction, and many researchers have investigated the effects. One body of evidence arises from studies associated with the movement for "effective schools." Researchers reported that students' achievement improved, or was higher than expected, in schools in which leaders focused on common goals and faculty had high expectations for students (Purkey and Smith 1983; Rowan 1990). But these studies usually involved only a few schools, and most offered very limited data on school organization and culture (Purkey and Smith).

More systematic evidence on the effects of school-level guidance arises from reanalyses of the High School and Beyond data set. Bryk and Driscoll (1988) probed the relations between various measures of schools as "communities" and students' performance. Community included shared values, common curriculum and other activities, and an ethos of "caring" for students. Schools that were high on these dimensions had significantly lower dropout rates and absenteeism and slightly higher gains in mathematics achievement. Lee and Bryk (1989) used the same data set to probe differences in schools' constraint of curricular choices. Schools that channeled most work into a common curriculum created consistency by increasing the amount of work that students did in common. Lee and Bryk argued that such schools tended to reduce performance differences among students over time, particularly for minority group students. In a later article they wrote that schools can "minimize the normal differentiation effects that accompany wide latitude in course choices. . . . Initial differences among students' [performance] can be either amplified or constrained" (Bryk et al. 1990, 178).

John Chubb and Terry Moe also reanalyzed High School and Beyond and stressed consistent instructional guidance even more. They argued that high-performing high schools are marked by "coherence," in which principals "provide a clear vision of where the schools are going . . . [and] encourage . . . cooperation and collegiality." They opine that these attributes add up to "organizational coherence" (Chubb and Moe 1990, 91). They also found that students performed better when school staffs had a coherent vision of academic goals and were collegial and cooperative, although the magnitude of the effect was quite modest.

What can we conclude about the effects of instructional guidance? For one thing, consistency means somewhat different things, or is a construct with quite different dimensions. One line of thought focuses on culture and values, another on the organization of curriculum choice, and a third on leadership. For another, most research on the effects of instructional guidance is recent, and the evidence is modest. One cross-national study seems to show that more central curriculum control is modestly associated with greater topical consistency in teaching, and various U.S. school studies claim that more consistent instructional guidance is associated with more consistent instruction. But there are no field studies that make a convincing case for the causal power of guidance, and no cross-system studies connect consistency at the system level with student performance. Both are crucial gaps. A diverse body of research seems to show that more consistent instruction and instructional guidance in schools are associated with higher student achievement. But the causal ambiguities remain, and there are significant problems in inferences from schools to systems. Additionally, most studies reveal only modest effects, yet scholars argue fiercely about them (Witte 1990).

Even if the studies were more extensive and convincing, there is another problem: The measure of student achievement in all this research has been traditional standardized tests. These tests entail a version of academic accomplishment that is said to depend heavily on recall of isolated facts and mastery of routine mental operations. This is just the sort of work that recent reformers wish schools to put aside in favor of more sophisticated endeavors. Can we assume that a positive effect of consistent guidance on such tests would hold for more challenging versions of achievement? It seems doubtful. Some would argue that the ambitious academic work recent reformers seek would be inimical to consistent guidance. With Theodore Sizer, they would say that if schools are to cultivate sophisticated and independent instruction, they must be sophisticated and independent.

Do we conclude that instructional guidance affects teaching and learning? Plainly it does, somehow. But how? Are the effects of guidance fragmentary or systemic? Specifically, are teaching and learning more consistent in systems that have more consistent guidance for instruction? Evidence on this question is thin. There is some support for the idea in one cross-national study, as well as in many smaller studies of schools. But these studies are limited in many ways, and the authors of the cross-national study caution their readers against making too much of the results (Stevenson and Baker 1991). There is, for example, no evidence that would permit us to distinguish the effects of formal guidance from teachers' earlier learning. Research on this matter does not offer much support for recent U.S. efforts to use instructional guidance to press teaching and learning toward greater consistency.

Change in Teaching

Uncertainty about the effects of instructional guidance looms even larger when we consider the content of guidance that reformers wish to offer teachers and students. For they propose to transform teaching and learning from relatively dull and routine practices into exciting and intellectually demanding ones. To this end, many argue for novel assessments that are tied both to new curriculum frameworks and to radically revised instructional materials. The combination is seen as a way to dramatically change learning and teaching. Would that happen? The studies discussed thus far have little to say on this point, for they all concern the present and past operations of schools and school systems. What do we know about how teachers might change in response to more consistent and ambitious guidance for their work?

Precious little, if we want a direct answer. We have found no studies of school systems that attempted to shift from local autonomy and traditional teaching to more centrally controlled and intellectually ambitious instruction. None of the national school systems that currently exhibit great consistency suddenly changed from fragmented to consistent operations. Some evolved over the course of several centuries, while others were hastily created in the wake of decolonization. But in neither case were teachers required to change from well-established traditional practice to novel and much more adventurous practice.

There have been some studies of efforts to turn teaching in a much more adventurous direction. Larry Cuban found that American classrooms remained traditional despite progressive reforms (Cuban 1984). He argued that teaching changes at a glacial pace and in fragmentary fashion. In most cases, teachers borrowed bits and pieces of progressive ideas and practices and integrated them into standard classroom formats. That conclusion fits with the work of other investigators in the United States and the United Kingdom who studied various efforts to push teaching in more ambitious and adventurous directions. All concluded that efforts to make teaching more ambitious produced change at the margins but little else (Goodlad, Klein, and Associates 1974; Popkewitz, Tabachnick, and Wehlage 1982; Stevens 1912).

It might be objected that progressivism was only a program. There were many ideas, books, articles, and pamphlets, some professors teaching courses, and even a few teacher education agencies devoted to the "new education." But there were no curricula, no assessments, and no instructional frameworks that might have helped teachers to learn a different pedagogy. From this perspective, the 1950s curriculum reforms were an improvement, for teachers had new texts as well as opportunities to learn about the new curricula. Some of the new texts were widely adopted, and many teachers took advantage of opportunities to learn. But reports of great change in teaching were few and far between. Some teachers seem to have dramatically changed their approach to instruction in the early years of reform, but many more struggled to understand and change (Sarason 1977). Most teachers seemed to make only marginal changes, grafting bits of reform ideas and practices onto established, traditional teaching. There is indirect evidence that these were major changes for the teachers involved (Cohen 1990b; Cohen and Ball 1991). But the difficulty of such change was not appreciated by most of those involved (Sarason 1977). Measures that might have supported more change thus were not contemplated, much less taken. And changed education priorities soon swept away opportunities for teachers to learn more. A subsequent NSF-sponsored study found few classroom traces of the curriculum reforms (Stake and Easley 1978).

Would not the recent reforms be much more potent? Instead of new texts and opportunities for further education, there would be an entire guidance system—new instructional frameworks that were reflected in novel sorts of assessment, in new curriculum materials, and in new approaches to teacher licensing and education. Would not "systemic reform"

(Smith and O'Day 1990) offer much more structure for teaching, much richer opportunities for teacher learning, and a chance for professional community in teaching? Would not more direction offer more support and pressure for change?

The idea has some appeal. But if greater structure and consistency would offer a more substantial basis for change in teaching, it does not follow that change would be easy or swift, for the greater structure would frame new and ambitious purposes, content, and methods. The agenda for teacher change would be vast, even with greater guidance. Consider, for example, studies of the "new math" in Europe. Some European school systems that adopted the new math had more consistent guidance for instruction than did others or the United States. But those differences did not seem to affect change in teaching. The research is spotty, but the most detailed study argued that the processes of reform were strikingly similar across systems with very different structures (Moon 1986). Reports about change in teaching also were quite homogeneous across systems. Participants and researchers reported that classroom practice changed only a little, and for the most part in fragmentary ways (Damerow 1980; Howson 1980; Moon 1986; Oldham 1980a, 1980b; Van der Blij, Hilding, and Weinzweig 1980). The new math seemed to fare little differently in the French system of consistent guidance structures than in the less consistent British or U.S. systems (Welch 1979).

We are inclined to think that some versions of systemic reform could offer more support for radical change in teaching than purely decentralized arrangements. But there is no evidence on the relative rates or depth of change under various organizational conditions. More important, there is growing evidence of several fundamental obstacles to the changes that reformers currently urge, none of which are structural in nature. One concerns teachers' knowledge. The recent reforms demand a depth and sophistication in teachers' grasp of academic subjects that is far beyond most public school teachers. For instance, while math is a leading area in the current reforms, most elementary school teachers have a very modest understanding of the mathematics they teach (Post, Taylor, Harel, Behr and Lesh 1988; Thompson 1984). They would need to learn a great deal more if the reforms were to have any chance of success. More important, teachers would have to shed established modes of understanding and adopt more modern, constructivist versions of knowledge. Such change is not just a matter of learning more—it could fairly be termed a revolution. Scholarship in several fields has shown that intellectual revolutions are very difficult to foment (Cohen 1990b; Cohen and Ball 1991; Fiske and Taylor 1984; Kuhn 1970; Markus and Zajonc 1985; Nisbett and Ross 1980).

Another obstacle lies in teaching. Even if teachers knew all that they needed, the reforms propose that students become active, engaged, and collaborative. If so, classroom roles would have to change radically. Teachers would have to rely on students to produce much more instruction, and students would have to think and act in ways they rarely do. Teachers would have to become coaches or conductors and abandon more familiar and didactic roles in which they "tell knowledge" to students (Lampert 1988; Newmann 1988; Roehler and Duffy 1988; Scardamalia, Bereiter, and Steinbach 1984; Sizer 1984). Researchers have studied only a few efforts at such change, but they report unusual difficulty, for teachers must manage very complex interactions about very complex ideas in rapid-fire fashion. The uncertainties of teaching multiply phenomenally, as does teachers' vulnerability (Cohen 1988; Cuban 1984; Lampert 1988; Newmann 1988; Roehler and Duffy 1988).

Since the recent reforms would require much teacher learning, they would require many changes in teachers' opportunities to learn. That is a third obstacle to change. Those who presently teach would need many educational opportunities on the job, as well as off it, in colleges, universities, and other agencies. Yet few schools now offer teachers many chances to learn on the job, and what they do offer is generally deemed weak at best. Most continuing education in universities has a dismal reputation among teachers and researchers. In addition, intending teachers would require fundamentally revamped undergraduate disciplinary and professional education. Few intending elementary teachers can major in an academic subject, and few intending teachers of any sort can learn new approaches to subject matter or pedagogy, since college and university educators rarely teach as reformers now intend (Boyer 1987; Cuban 1984; Cohen 1988; McKeatchie, Pintrich, Lin, and Smith 1986).

More consistent guidance for instruction could not solve these problems. Under some conditions, too complex to spell out here, such guidance might help to solve them. But fundamental change in teaching also would require fundamental reform of the education of intending and practicing teachers, and equally fundamental changes in schools and universities to support such learning. Even with those reforms, deep change in teaching probably would be slow and difficult.

Beyond Formal Structure

Guidance for instruction never stands alone. School systems consist not only in rules and formal structures, but also in beliefs about authority, habits of deference and resistance, and knowledge about how things work. Culture and social organization intertwine with formal structure in these systems. Many school systems that offer consistent guidance for instruction are situated in societies in which culture and other social circumstances seem to support academic effort. In contrast, U.S. society and culture seem to undermine academic effort. The success of school systems in Europe and Asia thus may owe more to the influences of culture and society than government or system structure. If so, the nearly exclusive attention to system structure in the current U.S. reform movement may be misplaced.

Social Circumstances of Schooling

Higher education and business firms are the two largest consumers of schooling in most societies. Hence their consumption patterns send signals concerning the qualities and accomplishments that they find desirable in students. The consumption patterns of American colleges and universities send mixed but generally weak signals about the importance of strong academic performance. Only a small group of highly selective colleges and universities has demanding admission standards. A much larger fraction has very modest requirements. Students need only a thin record of academic accomplishment in high school, often only a C or low B average, to be acceptable for admission. Only high school graduation is required for admission in still another large group of institutions. And not even high school graduation is required in another large group. There is something to celebrate in this, for many students can have a second or third chance to make good despite previous failures. But these arrangements also signal that high school students need not work hard in order to get into college or university (Bishop 1989; Powell et al. 1985; Trow 1961, 1988). It is thus irrational for most students who aspire to higher education to work very hard in high school, for only a few have a chance to enter a highly selective college or university. Their opportunities lie instead at less selective institutions, where much less high school work is required for admission (Powell et al. 1985; Trow 1988). It therefore is irrational for high school teachers to press those students to try hard and do their best work, for the students need not push themselves in order to push ahead.

A similar situation holds for the employment practices of most U.S. businesses. Few firms seem to ask for students' high school transcripts or references from teachers when considering them for employment. And even when firms do request transcripts, only a tiny fraction of schools supply them (Bishop 1989). The lack of employer interest deters students from thinking that grades, effort, or behavior count for jobs and deters teachers from thinking that their judgments about students can make a difference (Rosenbaum and Kariya 1989). Hence it would be irrational for students who intend leaving high school for work to do their best in school. Thinking deeply is difficult, and only a small fraction of students seem intrinsically motivated to do it. If students can get jobs without even presenting evidence about their grades, school behavior, and teachers' evaluation of their work, why should they work hard?

These patterns are unusual. Colleges and universities in Japan, France, and many other nations lay great weight on students' performance in high school or on high school leaving and university entrance exams. If students wish to enter university, it is essential to work hard in school and get good grades, prepare for the exams, or both (Rosenbaum and Kariya 1987). There are many troublesome features of such systems, including the exclusion of able students who do not do well on exams. But these systems leave no doubt about the importance of hard work and good school performance.

Employers in many nations also pay close attention to students' secondary school records in hiring decisions. This is true in Japan; New South Wales, Australia; Singapore; and West Germany (Bishop 1987, 1989; Clark 1985; Kariya and Rosenbaum 1989). Employers routinely review transcripts and teacher references when high school graduates or early school leavers apply for jobs. In some cases, schools and employers work closely in placing students in apprenticeship or regular work situations. Teachers know these things, as do students. It is understood that students who do not apply themselves and behave decently in school will have difficulty finding good jobs. There are important rewards for academic effort and good behavior, even for students who have no ambitions for further education.

Culture

Incentives are not the whole story. The values attached to learning and teaching differ among societies, as do attitudes toward authority and habits of child rearing. Such beliefs, values, and habits may support the guidance that issues from formal agencies in some cases and subvert it in others.

Americans have long been ambivalent about academic work. Anti-intellectualism is a prominent feature in American culture (Hofstadter 1963), and we are inclined to value experience over formal education. Americans also value practical rather than intellectual content within formal education (e.g., learning to "get along") and job-related knowledge and skills (Cusick 1983; Lynd and Lynd 1929; Powell et al. 1985). Eighty-one percent of the respondents in a Gallup poll said that the "chief reasons" people want their children to get a formal education are job opportunities, preparation for a better life, better-paying jobs, and financial security. Only 15 percent said that the chief reason was to become more knowledgeable or to learn to think and understand (Elam and Gallup 1989). Relatively few American mothers report working closely with their children on academic tasks or offering support for hard work and success in school (Stevenson et al. 1985; Stevenson, Lee, and Stigler 1986).

Intellectual work and academic accomplishment appear to be more highly regarded in other societies. In Japan and China, for instance, parents take education very seriously and hold teachers in high esteem. Investigators report that Japanese mothers play a central role in their children's academic success (Holloway, Kashiwagi, Hess, and Hiroshi 1986; Lebra 1976; Shimahara 1986; White 1987). They encourage children and work closely with them on assignments, creating an environment conducive to learning (Holloway et al. 1986; Stevenson et al. 1985; Stevenson and Lee 1990; White 1987). Similar practices are found among Chinese parents (Stevenson and Lee). Japanese and Chinese mothers also seem to hold higher standards for their children and to have more realistic evaluations of their achievement than American mothers (Stevenson and Lee).

Family life and values thus seem to support successful schooling in Japan while impeding it in the United States. One researcher noted that "it would be quite impossible to take account of Japanese formal education without recognising that—in many ways—it lives in close symbiosis with that culture" (King 1986, 75; see also White 1987). American commentators often have offered complementary explanations of weak work in school here (Coleman 1961; Cusick 1983; Lynd and Lynd 1929; Powell et al. 1985).

Habits of association and attitudes toward authority also may help to explain why formal guidance for instruction seems to be treated more seriously in some societies than in others. Since Alexis de Tocqueville, observers have noted Americans' distinctive individualism, their preoccupation with personal autonomy, and their focus on individual expression and development. These qualities often have been contrasted with more cooperative and deferential behavior in other societies, in which people seem more preoccupied with how they can fit in, work with others, and advance collective values.

For instance, Japanese teachers carefully foster cooperative work on common tasks, build habits of collaboration and conflict resolution, and teach accommodation to group preferences. They exercise great patience in encouraging students to work with groups, and use groups to regulate behavior, manage conflict, and support desired attitudes. In the process, Japanese teachers accommodate "discipline" problems that would be intolerable to most Americans. But they build many centers of support for the values and behavior they wish to inculcate rather than assuming the entire burden themselves. Many "discipline" problems are therefore managed by other students rather than the teacher alone (Boocock 1989; Peak 1989).

American teachers instead foster individual work on individual tasks. They cultivate little or no group activity and rarely build group strength. They do not support accommodation to group preferences but tend to impose their own preferences. They manage all discipline problems themselves and have little patience with misbehavior. American students learn little about alternative ways to manage conflict or about collaborative work.

Thomas Rohlen (1989) framed these comparisons in a broad analysis of differences in organizational life. He viewed Japanese classrooms as marked by more respect and deference than those in the United States but as less hierarchical and teacher centered. The Japanese emphasis on accommodation to group values and cooperative work helps to explain the coexistence of two things that strike Americans as inconsistent: deference to authority and enormous capacity for productive work in decentralized organizations. Rohlen notes that these qualities are found in all sorts of organizations, from primary classrooms to business and government:

> The result is an overall social structure that is in many respects centrifugal in terms of affiliation and the capacity to order events. Social contexts and organizations are built up from the bottom (or the outside), so to speak, in a way that invests the peripheral entities with great stability. The locus of social order is in the lower level, subordinate groupings. . . . These entities gain a degree of autonomy from the fact that internally they are strengthened by the pattern of attachment we are considering. (Rohlen 1989, 31–2)

Americans have few alternatives between individualism and imposed authority. We often fluctuate between centralized hierarchies and decentralization. The result makes it difficult for central authority to succeed, while also precluding the development of alternatives.

How does this bear on our analysis? The remarkable consistency in Japanese education may owe as much to deference to authority, habits of accommodation, and extraordinary pressures for cooperation at all levels as to formal guidance. Rohlen's account also suggests caution about the prospects for much more potent guidance for instruction in the United States, for it might be crippled by our habit of alternatively embracing central authority and fiercely resisting it.

Conclusion

Most schemes for fundamental change present a paradox. They offer appealing visions of a new order but therefore also contain a devastating critique of existing realities. If pursued, these critiques reveal the lack of many capacities that would be required to realize and sustain the new vision. Reformers can imagine a better world in which those capacities would be created, but their problem is more practical—how to create the new world when those capacities are lacking?

Recent reform proposals offer a version of this puzzle, for they entail two dramatic departures from American political and instructional practice. One is that schools should promote a new instructional order marked by deep comprehension of academic subjects, in which students are active learners rather than passive recipients and in which teachers practice a much more thoughtful and demanding pedagogy. The other departure is radical reform in school governance and instructional guidance to produce the desired changes in classrooms. These reforms include a national examination or testing system, national curricula, a national system of teacher certification, and many equally dramatic reforms at the state level. Although different in important ways, all of these plans and proposals move sharply toward greater state, national, or federal control of education. All seek to realize new and ambitious sorts of teaching and learning in ordinary classrooms. Hence all represent an effort to much more powerfully guide instructional practice with policy.

These are astonishing, even revolutionary, proposals and are appealing in many respects. But we have pointed to weak capacities for change in several crucial departments.

One is politics. Reformers seek much greater state, national, or federal control of education and a consequent tightening of the links between central policy and local practice. But the entire fragmented apparatus of American government weighs against such ventures. Past efforts at tightening the links between policy and instruction by increasing central control have met with extremely limited success and produced organizational side effects that have greatly complicated governance and administration. The reforms sketched above seem unlikely to succeed unless the governance and organization of U.S. education is either greatly streamlined or simply bypassed. Streamlining has much appeal, including relief from the burdens consequent upon past efforts to reform local practice with state or federal policy. But streamlining would entail an unprecedented reduction of existing policies and programs, and thus a reduction in existing governmental authorities at all levels. It would spell the end of many state and local government functions in education, even though it could ease

many administrative and organizational problems. What would induce local and state officials to accept the diminishment or demise of their
domains? Visions of a better school system? Barring fiscal catastrophe or
a sustained mass movement for fundamental change in education, we see
no sign of the requisite inducements.

Bypassing government appeals to many partly because the prospects
for streamlining seem so bleak. The creation of nongovernmental or quasi-
nongovernmental authorities that may design a national examination system already is under way. A similar course of action has been taken by
NBPTS in its efforts to create a national system of teacher examination
and certification. Such bypass operations have great short-run appeal, for
avoiding government sponsorship and operations could greatly ease the
work of designing and developing national education systems of one sort
or another. But the systems thus created would work in the medium and
long run only if government were streamlined, for national curricula, examinations, or teacher certification systems could operate efficiently only
if many extant policies and programs regarding testing, curriculum, instruction, and teacher licensing fell into disuse. Of course, that would
require many existing state and local government authorities to fade away
(i.e., streamlining), the difficulties of which we just touched upon.

Instructional practice is a second realm in which the capacity for change
is weak. Reformers seek much more thoughtful, adventurous, and demanding teaching and learning, and they envision new instructional guidance to produce it. But nearly the entire corpus of instructional practice
weighs against it. Teachers and students spend most of their time with
lectures, recitations, and worksheets. Intellectual demands generally are
modest, and a great deal of the work is dull. Only a modest fraction of
public school teachers have deep knowledge of any academic subject.
Research and experience both show that past efforts to fundamentally
change teaching have had modest effects at best. Most often, they have
resulted in fragmentary adoption of new practices, translation of new
practices into old ones, or both.

Solutions to these capacity problems would require fundamental redevelopment in education. An intellectually ambitious system of instructional guidance would be one key element, but few Americans have had
the education or experience that would prepare them to understand such
guidance or put it to appropriate use. To build new capacities for education would be to reeducate many Americans. That is obviously true for
teachers, but teachers' efforts would not prosper if parents and political
leaders did not understand and support their work. Additionally, few
teachers work in schools that could support radically different approaches
to instruction, let alone teachers' efforts to learn such things. Building

new capacity would require that schools become places in which teachers could learn and teach very differently.

Such redevelopment would be an immensely ambitious endeavor. The creation of new instructional guidance arrangements would be an extraordinary research and development task, surely the largest ever in U.S. education. For example, new examinations would have to be invented, to assess a broader range of academic knowledge and skills than conventional tests. The exams also would assess students' skill and knowledge in more diverse ways (e.g., writing essays in English, explaining and justifying answers in chemistry, and offering nonnumerical representations of mathematical problem solving). Because examinations of this sort would invite students to use and display a broad range of knowledge and skill (Nickerson 1989), the results would be difficult and time-consuming to evaluate, especially for a large and diverse population. Such things are possible, and approximations can be found here and there in the United States and some other nations (Resnick and Resnick 1989). But the approach has been little tried in the United States, and Americans have little experience with it. Specialists are just beginning to invent examples, and a few states are beginning to experiment with them (California State Department of Education 1985). A few problems with such exams have been suggested (Porter 1990), but many others are likely to appear if they actually are developed and widely used.

New curricula also would be needed for any guidance system keyed to deep understanding of academic subjects. Instructional frameworks would have to be devised, along with curriculum guides that focused attention on key elements of each academic subject. Texts and other materials that effectively opened access to those topics would have to be composed. These materials would have to be accessible to a large and diverse population of teachers and learners, and they would be most useful if designed in a way that teachers could learn from them while teaching, preparing to teach, and reconsidering their teaching. Such materials would be most helpful to teachers and students if subject coverage was integrated across the grades. Though such things seem possible, they are entirely unfamiliar in the United States. A few states are just beginning to develop more demanding and thoughtful curricula. It seems reasonable to expect that such a novel endeavor would take a long time to develop and longer to mature.

Neither new exams nor new curricula would work unless teachers understood them, and as things now stand, most teachers would not. This problem might be solved in part if teachers were extensively involved in building new frameworks, curricula, and assessments, and in grading students' work. Such activities could be extraordinarily educative if they were designed with that end in view, but to do so would greatly complicate the development tasks. Additionally, these activities would reach only a fraction of the teaching force, and would touch only part of the reeducation need. Teacher education itself would have to be greatly improved, which would require fundamental changes in college and university education. Both professional and subject-matter education would have to be deepened and focused much more closely on the content of schooling, and university teaching would have to radically improve. Such changes are daunting to contemplate, but they might be encouraged by the sort of examination system that the NBPTS has proposed. If intending teachers' grasp of subject matter and pedagogy could fairly be assessed, then the exams might offer college and university programs sensible targets for their educational efforts. If the targets were accepted, if teacher education programs were revised accordingly, and if school systems used the exam results as hiring criteria, the quality of teaching might be greatly improved. But note that such changes would be immense: the examinations do not now exist, and it would take colleges and universities at least a generation to make the required instructional reforms. NBPTS is just beginning to develop some exams, and current estimates are that it will take at least three years to produce an initial prototype in a single subject for a grade or two. The NBPTS staff hopes that a full set of examinations might be developed by the year 1997, though no one really knows how long it will take. Here too Americans are relatively inexperienced. Even if the exams were developed roughly on schedule, it would be prudent to assume that many adjustments would be required as the exams came into use. And only a handful of professors have given any thought to the reforms of higher education that might dramatically improve the education of intending teachers.

It would be no mean feat to solve any one of these research and development problems by itself. But the recent reforms are "systemic"; that is, they seek to link assessment of students' performance to the content and form of curriculum guides and course materials, and to tie both of them to teacher education. Hence the research and development tasks sketched above should be undertaken jointly. That would be an extraordinarily demanding and time-consuming effort. It is another reason we believe that devising a guidance system to support deep understanding of academic subjects would be a huge endeavor.

If changes in instructional guidance are crucial, they would not work all by themselves. Americans are well used to local control of education, and they have been less and less inclined to defer to teachers. Radical reform of instruction would be unlikely to get very far unless parents and political leaders supported it. Yet to do so these Americans would have to embrace very different conceptions of knowledge, teaching, learning, and schooling than they currently do. That is possible. For instance, administrators, political leaders, and parents could learn about new examinations by participating in their development, in field trials, and in revisions. Though such work probably would increase conflict in the short run, it might increase the long-run chances that the finished exams would be understood, accepted, and used appropriately. But the learning would be a great change for parents and political leaders, no less large or difficult than for teachers and students. And to give administrators, parents, and politicians opportunities to learn would complicate, slow down, and alter the development of new exams.

Finally, the reforms that we have been discussing would require changes in individual school operations and organization. One reason is that teachers and administrators would have a great deal to learn. It is unlikely they could offer the intellectually ambitious instruction that reformers seek unless they had ample time to learn on the job. Another reason is that the new instruction would be much more complex and demanding than the common fare in schools today. It is unlikely that teachers could do such work unless they had the autonomy to make complicated decisions, to work with colleagues, and to revise as they went. Still another reason is that teachers could hardly contribute to the development of a common instructional system unless they had much more time and opportunities to work with others in education beyond their school. These considerations suggest radical changes in schools and school operations, so that they offered more opportunities to learn on the job and greater autonomy for school professionals. But how could that be done in the context of reforms that entail much greater central authority and power? Not easily, unless the reforms were carefully designed to enhance such autonomy, and unless the capacities to exercise it were nurtured at all levels of education. Marshall Smith and Jennifer O'Day (1990) have sensibly argued that systemic reform would require a combination of "bottom-up" and "top-down" change. But given the present organization of U.S. schools and school governments, and the work habits of policymakers, teachers, and administrators, that would be a great change indeed.

These observations suggest that the recent reforms might have more chances of success if the entire venture were conceived and executed as a great education enterprise, one in which state and national leaders had as much to learn as teachers and students. That seems appropriate to a set of proposals that would require such radical change in individuals and institutions, and the cultivation of so many new capacities. But the recent reforms began to catch Americans' imagination just as economic and social problems began to further constrain the capacities for change. States and localities are struggling with a massive fiscal crisis, and many confront staggering social problems.

What happens when grand visions of change collide with limited capacities? The most common consequences are incremental alteration at the margin of institutions and practices, or self-defeating results, or both. For example, education reformers could relatively easily add streamlining mandates and a layer of streamlining agencies to the existing accumulation of mandates and organizations. But they would find it much more difficult and costly to replace the present cluttered and fragmented structure with one that was much simpler and more powerful. Similarly, bypass operations could easily add complexity rather than reducing it. For governments would not sit still. Experience suggests that they would respond by regulating the bypassing agencies, or by finding roles for themselves in interpreting and managing the functions generated by the bypassing agencies, or by taking over the bypassing agencies without closing down the authorities that were to have been bypassed, or some combination of the above. In this event efforts to increase simplicity and clarity might well further complicate and confuse matters.

Similarly, it would be relatively easy and cheap for reformers to add mandates for more thoughtful teaching and learning on top of extant mandates for teaching basic skills, informing students about drugs and AIDS, not to mention remedial education, bilingual education, and programs for cooperative learning and improving students' self-concepts. It would be much more difficult and costly to replace the present cluttered and fragmented accumulation of instructional guidance with a system that was simpler, more focused, and more powerful. It would be even more difficult to redevelop education in ways that would enable most educators to take good advantage of such changes.

But uncommon results are always possible. For instance, the recent reforms might succeed by a sort of osmosis. If reformers kept up the pressure for several decades, much more consistent and demanding instruction might result. Indeed, the extraordinary fragmentation of American institutions may create a porosity that permits such change. Something like that sort of osmosis seems to have occurred in the spread of basic skills instruction during the 1970s and 1980s. More time and pressure would be required for the more difficult reforms that we have discussed here, and most reform movements in education are notoriously brief, but the fragmentation of American government could open many opportunities to persistent reformers.

We also may underestimate the ingenuity of policymakers and educators. Perhaps they will seize on the growing social and financial crisis to turn schools in the direction that reformers wish. Streamlining, simpliplification, and consistency could be appealing slogans in an era of falling budgets and rising problems. Perhaps the crippling legacy of the Reagan years in public finance and the economy will become an opportunity to press ahead with its nationalizing legacy in education.

No one knows how the story will turn out. But in most cases, today is the best guide to tomorrow. If American politics and education run true to form, reformers will do better at addition than subtraction. They will introduce many different schemes to make education more consistent, but they will be less able to produce consistency among those schemes, to greatly reduce the clutter of previous programs and policies, or to fundamentally change teaching. If so, current efforts to reduce fragmentation would only add several new and unrelated layers of educational requirements and instructional refinements on top of many old and inconsistent layers. The new ideas would have their day, but only at the expense of further clutter and inconsistency.

References

Bankston, M. 1982. *Organizational Reporting in a School District: State and Federal Programs*. Stanford, Calif.: Institute for Finance and Governance, School of Education, Stanford University.

Bardach, E., and R. A. Kagan. 1982. *Going by the Book: The Problem of Regulatory Unreasonableness*. Philadelphia: Temple University Press.

Beauchamp, G., and K. Beauchamp. 1972. *Comparative Analysis of Curriculum Systems*. Wilmette, Ill.: The Kagg Press.

Berlak, A., and H. Berlak. 1981. *The Dilemmas of Schooling: Teaching and Social Change*. London: Methuen.

Berman, P., and M. McLaughlin. 1977. *Federal Programs Supporting Educational Change*. Santa Monica, Calif.: Rand.

Bishop, J. 1987. *Information Externalities and the Social Payoff to Academic Achievement*. Ithaca, N.Y.: Cornell University, Center for Advanced Human Resource Studies.

Bishop, J. 1989a. *Incentives for Learning: Why American High School Students Compare so Poorly to Their Counterparts Overseas*. Ithaca, N.Y.: Cornell University, Center for Advanced Human Resource Studies.

Bishop, J. 1989b. "Why the Apathy in American High Schools?" *Educational Researcher* 18: 6–10.

Boocock, S. 1989. "Controlled Diversity: An Overview of the Japanese Preschool System." *Journal of Japanese Studies* 15: 41–66.

Boyd, W., and D. Smart. 1987. *Educational Policy in Australia and America: Comparative Perspectives*. Philadelphia: Falmer.

Boyer, E. 1987. *The Undergraduate Experience in America*. New York: Harper and Row.

Broadfoot, P. 1983. "Assessment Constraints on Curriculum Practice: A Comparative Study." In M. Hammersley and A. Hargreaves, eds., *Curriculum Practice: Some Sociological Case Studies* (251–69). New York: Falmer.

Broadfoot, P. 1984. "From Public Examinations to Profile Assessment: The French Experience." In P. Broadfoot, ed., *Selection, Certification, and Control* (199–219). London and New York: Falmer.

Bryk, A., and M. Driscoll. 1988. *The High School as a Community: Contextual Influences and Consequences for Students and Teachers*. Madison, Wis.: National Center on Effective Secondary Schools.

Bryk, A., V. Lee, and J. Smith. 1990. "High School Organization and Its Effects on Teachers and Students: An Interpretive Summary of the Research." In W. Clune and J. Witte, Eds., *Choice and Control in American Education* (Vol. I, 135–226). New York: Falmer.

California State Department of Education. 1985. *Mathematics Framework*. Sacramento: California State Department of Education.

Cameron, J., R. Cowan, B. Holmes, P. Hurst, and M. McLean. eds., 1984a. *Australia* (International Handbook of Educational Systems). Chichester, England: Wiley.

Cameron, J., R. Cowan, B. Holmes, P. Hurst, and M. McLean. eds., 1984b. *France* (International Handbook of Educational Systems). Chichester, England: Wiley.

Cameron, J., R. Cowan, B. Holmes, P. Hurst, and M. McLean. eds., 1984c. *Japan* (International Handbook of Educational Systems). Chichester, England: Wiley.

Cameron, J., R. Cowan, B. Holmes, P. Hurst, and M. McLean. eds., 1984d. *Singapore* (International Handbook of Educational Systems). Chichester, England: Wiley.

Cantor, L. 1980. "The Growing Role of States in American Education." *Comparative Education* 16(1): 25–31.

Cheney, L. 1991. "National Tests: What Other Countries Expect Their Students to Know." Washington, D.C.: National Endowment for the Humanities.

Chubb, J., and T. Moe. 1990. *Politics, Markets, and American Schools*. Washington, D.C.: Brookings Institution.

Clark, B. 1965. "Interorganizational Patterns in Education." *Administrative Science Quarterly* 10: 224–37.

Clark, B. 1985. "The High School and the University: What Went Wrong in America, Part II." *Phi Delta Kappan* 66: 472–75.

Cohen, D. K. 1982. "Policy and Organization: The Impact of State and Federal Educational Policy on School Governance." *Harvard Educational Review* 32: 474–99.

Cohen, D. K. 1988. *Teaching Practice: Plus ça change*. East Lansing: National Center for Research on Teacher Education, Michigan State University.

Cohen, D. K. 1990a. "Governance and Instruction: the Promise of Decentralization and Choice." In W. Clune and J. Witte, eds., *Choice and Control in American Education* (Vol. I, 337–86). New York: Falmer.

Cohen, D. K. 1990b. "A Revolution in One Classroom: The Case of Mrs. Oublier." *Educational Evaluation and Policy Analysis* 12: 311–30.

Cohen, D. K., and D. Ball. 1991. "Relations Between Policy and Practice: A Commentary." *Educational Evaluation and Policy Analysis* 12: 331–38.

Coleman, J. 1961. *The Adolescent Society*. New York: Free Press.

Cuban, L. 1984. *How Teachers Taught*. New York: Longman.

Cusick, P. 1983. *The Egalitarian Ideal and the American High School*. New York: Longman.

Damerow, P. 1980. "Patterns of Geometry in German Textbooks." In H. G. Steiner, ed., *Comparative Studies of Mathematics Curricula—Change and Stability, 1960–1980* (281–303). Haus Ohrbeck: Institut für Didaktik der Mathematik der Universität Bielefeld.

Darling-Hammond, L. 1987. "The Over-Regulated Curriculum and the Press for Teacher Professionalism." *NASSP Bulletin*, 22–9.

Darling-Hammond, L., and A. E. Wise. 1985. "Beyond Standardization: State Standards and School Improvement." *Elementary School Journal* 85: 315–36.

Eckstein, M., and H. Noah. 1989. "Forms and Functions of Secondary School Leaving Examinations." *Comparative Education Review* 33: 295–316.

Elam, S. M., and A. M. Gallup. 1989. "The 21st Annual Gallup Poll of the Public Attitudes Toward the Public Schools." *Phi Delta Kappan* 71: 41–54.

Ellwein, M. C., G. V. Glass, and M. L. Smith. 1988. "Standards of Competence: Propositions on the Nature of Testing Reforms." *Educational Researcher* 17: 4–9.

Firestone, W. 1989. "Educational Policy as an Ecology of Games." *Educational Researcher* 18: 18–24.

Fiske, S., and S. Taylor. 1984. *Social Cognition*. Reading, Mass.: Addison-Wesley.

Floden, R. E., and C. Clark. 1988. "Preparing Teachers for Uncertainty." *Teachers College Record* 89: 505–24.

Floden, R., A. Porter, L. Alford, D. Freeman, S. Irwin, W. Schmidt, and J. Schwille. 1988. "Instructional Leadership at the District Level: A Closer Look at Autonomy and Control." *Educational Administration Quarterly* 24: 96–124.

Floden, R. E., A. C. Porter, W. H. Schmidt, and D. J. Freeman. 1978. *Don't They All Measure the Same Thing? Consequences of Selecting Standardized Tests* (Research Series No. 25). East Lansing, Mich.: Michigan State University, Institute for Research on Teaching.

Freeman, D., T. Kuhs, A. Porter, R. Floden, W. Schmidt, and J. Schwille. 1983. "Do Textbooks and Tests Define a National Curriculum in Elementary School Mathematics?" *Elementary School Journal* 83: 501–14.

Freeman, D. J., and A. C. Porter. 1989. "Do Textbooks Dictate the Content of Mathematics Instruction in Elementary Schools?" *American Educational Research Journal* 26: 403–21.

Fuhrman, S., W. Clune, and R. Elmore. 1988. "Research on Educational Reform: Lessons on the Implementation of Policy." *Teachers College Record* 90: 237–57.

Goodlad, J., M. Klein, and Associates. 1974. *Looking Behind the Classroom Door*. Worthington, Ohio: Charles Jones.

Haggstrom, G., L. Darling-Hammond, and D. Grissmer. 1988. *Assessing Teacher Supply and Demand*. Santa Monica, Calif.: Rand Corporation.

Hofstadter, R. 1963. *Anti-Intellectualism in American Life*. New York: Vintage Books.

Holloway, S., K. Kashiwagi, R. Hess, and A. Hiroshi. 1986. "Causal Attributions by Japanese and American Mothers and Children about Performance in Mathematics." *International Journal of Psychology* 21: 269–86.

Holmes, B. 1979. *International Guide to Education Systems*. Paris: UNESCO.

Horner, W. 1986. "Curriculum Research in France and Luxembourg." In U. Hameyer, K. Frey, H. Haft, and F. Kuebart, Eds., *Curriculum Research in Europe* (91–107). Strasbourg: Council of Europe.

Howson, A. 1980. "Some Remarks on the Case Studies." In H. G. Steiner, ed., *Comparative Studies of Mathematics Curricula—Change and Stability, 1960–1980* (502–08). Haus Ohrbeck: Institut für Didaktik der Mathematik der Universität Bielefeld.

Jackson, P. 1968. *Life in Classrooms*. New York: Holt, Rinehart, and Winston.

Kariya, T., and J. Rosenbaum. 1987. "Self-Selection in Japanese Junior High Schools: A Longitudinal Study of Students' Educational Plans." *American Journal of Sociology* 60: 168–80.

Kaufman, H. 1969. "Administrative Decentralization and Political Power." *Public Administration Review* 29: 3–15.

Kellaghan, T., and G. Madaus. 1991. *Proposals for a National American Test: Lessons from Europe*. Unpublished manuscript, Boston College.

Kida, H. 1986. "Educational Administration in Japan." *Comparative Education* 22: 7–12.

Kiesler, S., and L. Sproull. 1982. "Managerial Responses to Changing Environments: Perspectives on Problem Sensing from Social Cognition." *Administrative Science Quarterly* 27: 548–70.

Kimbrough, J., and P. Hill. 1981. *The Aggregate Effects of Federal Education Programs*. Santa Monica, Calif.: Rand.

King, E. 1986. "Japan's Education in Comparative Perspective." *Comparative Education* 22: 73–82.

Kirst, M. W. 1988. *Who Should Control Our Schools: Reassessing Current Policies*. Stanford, Calif.: Center for Education Research.

Kobayashi, V. 1984. "Japanese and U.S. Curricula Compared." In W. Cummings, E. Beauchamp, S. Ichikawa, V. Kobayashi, and M. Ushingi, eds., *Educational Policies in Crisis* (61–95). New York: Praeger.

Kreitzer, A. E., G. F. Madaus, and W. Haney. 1989. *Competency Testing and Dropouts*. Unpublished manuscript, Boston College.

Kuhn, T. 1970. *The Structure of Scientific Revolutions*. Chicago: University of Chicago Press.

Lampert, M. 1985. "How Do Teachers Manage to Teach? Perspectives on Problems in Practice." *Harvard Educational Review* 55: 178–94.

Lampert, M. 1988. *Teachers' Thinking about Students' Thinking about Geometry: The Effects of New Teaching Tools*. Cambridge, Mass.: Educational Technology Center.

Lawton, D., and P. Gordon. 1987. *The HMI*. London: Routledge.

Lebra, T. 1976. *Japanese Patterns of Behavior*. Honolulu: University Press of Hawaii.

Lee, V., and T. Bryk. 1989. "A Multilevel Model of the Social Distribution of High School Achievements." *Sociology of Education* 62: 172–92.

Lewis, H. 1985. *The French Education System*. London: Croom Helm.

Lewis, H. 1989. "Some Aspects of Education in France Relevant to Current Concerns in the U.K." *Comparative Education* 25: 369–78.

Lortie, D. 1975. *Schoolteacher: a Sociological Study*. Chicago: University of Chicago Press.

Lynd, R., and H. Lynd. 1929. *Middletown: A Study in Modern American Culture*. New York: Harcourt, Brace and World.

MacRury, K., P. Nagy, and R. E. Traub. 1987. *Reflections on Large-Scale Assessments of Study Achievement*. Toronto, Canada: Ontario Institute for Studies in Education.

Madaus, G. 1988. *The Influence of Testing on the Curriculum*. In L. Tanner, ed., *Critical Issues in Curriculum* (83–121). Chicago: University of Chicago Press.

Madaus, G. 1989. *The Distortion of Teaching and Testing: High-Stakes Testing and Instruction*. Unpublished manuscript, Boston College.

Madaus, G. 1991. *The Effects of Important Tests on Students: Implications for a National Examination or System of Examinations*. Paper presented at the American Educational Research Association Invitational Conference on Accountability as a State Reform Instrument: Impact on Teaching, Learning, Minority Issues and Incentives for Improvement, Washington, D.C.

Madaus, G., and T. Kellaghan. 1991. *America 2000's Proposal for American Achievement Tests: Unexamined Issues*. Unpublished manuscript.

Markus, H., and R. Zajonc. 1985. "The Cognitive Perspective in Social Psychology." In G. Lindzey and E. Aronson, eds., *Handbook of Social Psychology* (3rd ed., Vol. 1). Hillsdale, N.J.: Erlbaum.

McDonnell, L. M., and M. W. McLaughlin. 1982. *Education Policy and the Role of the States*. Santa Monica, Calif.: Rand.

McKeatchie, W., P. Pintrich, Y. Lin, and D. Smith. 1986. *Teaching and Learning in the College Classroom: A Review of the Research Literature*. Ann Arbor, Mich.: National Center to Improve Postsecondary Teaching and Learning.

McLaughlin, M. 1987. "Learning from Experience: Lessons from Policy Implementation." *Educational Evaluation and Policy Analysis* 9: 171–78.

Meyer, J. 1983. "Centralization of Funding and Control in Educational Governance." In J. W. Meyer and W. R. Scott, eds., *Organizational Environments: Ritual and Rationality* (179–98). Beverly Hills, Calif.: Sage.

Moon, B. 1986. *The New Math Curriculum Controversy: An International Story*. Philadelphia: Falmer.

Motone, J. 1991. *The Democratic Wish*. New York: Basic Books.

Murphy, J. 1974. *State Education Agencies and Discretionary Funds: Grease the Squeaky Wheel.*. Cambridge, Mass.: Heath.

Newmann, F. M. 1988. "Higher-Order Thinking in the High School Curriculum." *NASSP Bulletin* 72: 58–64.

Nickerson, R. 1989. "New Directions in Educational Assessment." *Educational Researcher* 18: 3–7.

Nisbett, R., and L. Ross. 1980. *Human Inference: Strategies and Shortcomings of Social Judgment*. Englewood Cliffs, N.J.: Prentice-Hall.

Noah, H., and M. Eckstein. 1989. "Tradeoffs in Examination Policies: An International Comparative Perspective." *Oxford Review of Education* 15: 17–27.

Office of Educational Research and Improvement State Accountability Study Group. 1988. *Creating Responsible and Responsive Accountability Systems*. Washington, D.C.: U.S. Department of Education.

Ohta, T. 1986. "Problems and Perspectives in Japanese Education." *Comparative Education* 22: 27–30.

Oldham, E. 1980a. "Case Studies in Geometry Education: Ireland." In H. G. Steiner, ed., *Comparative Studies of Mathematics Curricula—Change and Stability, 1960–1980* (326–346). Haus Ohrbeck: Institut für Didaktik der Mathematik der Universität Bielefeld.

Oldham, E. 1980b. "Case Studies in Algebra Education: Ireland." In H. G. Steiner, ed., *Comparative Studies of Mathematics Curricula—Change and Stability, 1960–1980* (395–425). Haus Ohrbeck: Institut für Didaktik der Mathematik der Universität Bielefeld.

Orfield, G. 1969. *The Reconstruction of Southern Education*. New York: Wiley.

Organization for Economic Cooperation and Development. 1971. *Reviews of National Policies for Education: Japan*. Paris: Organization for Economic Cooperation and Development.

Organization for Economic Cooperation and Development. 1973. *Educational Policy and Planning: Japan*. Paris: Organization for Economic Cooperation and Development.

Peak, L. 1989. "Learning to Become Part of the Group: The Japanese Child's Transition to Preschool Life. *Journal of Japanese Studies* 15: 93–124.

Peterson, P. 1981. *City Limits*. Chicago: University of Chicago Press.

Peterson, P., B. Rabe, and K. Wong. 1986. *When Federalism Works*. Washington, D.C.: Brookings Institution.

Popkewitz, T., H. Tabachnick, and G. Wehlage. 1982. *The Myth of Educational Reform: A Study of School Responses*. Madison, Wis.: University of Wisconsin Press.

Porter, A. 1990. *Assessing National Goals: Some Measurement Dilemmas*. Paper presented at the 1990 Educational Testing Service Invitational Conference, The Assessment of National Education Goals, New York.

Porter, A., R. Floden, D. Freeman, W. Schmidt, and J. Schwille. 1988. "Content Determinants in Elementary School Mathematics." In D. A. Grouws, T. J. Cooney, and D. Jones, eds., *Effective Mathematics Teaching* (96–113). Reston, Va.: National Council of Teachers of Mathematics.

Post, T., B. R. Taylor, G. Harel, M. Behr, and R. Lesh. 1988. *Intermediate Teachers' Knowledge of Rational Number Concepts*. Unpublished manuscript, University of Wisconsin.

Postlethwaite, T. N., ed. 1988. *The Encyclopedia of Comparative Education and National Systems of Education* (Vol. C). Oxford, England: Pergamon Press.

Powell, A. 1991. *Private Schools*. Unpublished draft essay, Cambridge, Mass.

Powell, A., E. Farrar, and D. K. Cohen. 1985. *The Shopping Mall High School*. Boston: Houghton Mifflin.

Purkey, S., and M. Smith. 1983. "Effective Schools: A Review." *Elementary School Journal* 83: 428–52.

Putnam, R. T., R. Heaton, R. Prawat, and J. Remillard. In press. "Teaching Mathematics for Understanding: Discussing Case Studies of Four Fifth-Grade Teachers." *Elementary School Journal.*

Ramirez, F., and J. Boli. 1987. "The Political Construction of Mass Schooling: European Origins and Worldwide Institutionalization." *Sociology of Education* 60: 2–11.

Ramirez, F., and R. Rubison. 1979. "Creating Members: The Political Incorporation and Expansion of Public Education." In J. W. Meyer and M. Hannan, eds., *National Development and the World System* (72–82). Chicago: University of Chicago Press.

Resnick, D. P., and L. B. Resnick. 1985. "Standards, Curriculum, and Performance: A Historical and Comparative Perspective." *Educational Researcher* 14: 5–20.

Resnick, L. B., and D. P. Resnick. 1989. *Assessing the Thinking Curriculum: New Tools for Educational Reform.* Pittsburgh, Pa.: Learning Research and Development Center.

Roehler, L., and G. Duffy. 1988. "Teachers' Instructional Actions." In R. Barr, M. Kamil, P. Mosenthal, and P. Pearson, eds., *Handbook of Reading Research* (Vol. 2, 861–84). New York: Longman.

Rogers, D., and D. Whetten. 1982. *Interorganizational Coordination.* Ames, Ia.: Iowa State University.

Rohlen, T. 1989. "Order in Japanese Society: Attachment, Authority and Routine." *Journal of Japanese Studies* 15: 5–40.

Romberg, T. A., E. A. Zarinnia, and S. R. Williams. 1989. *The Influence of Mandated Testing on Mathematics Instruction: Grade 8 Teachers' Perceptions.* Unpublished manuscript, University of Wisconsin—Madison.

Rosenbaum, J., and T. Kariya. 1987. "Self-Selection in Japanese Junior High Schools: A Longitudinal Study of Students' Educational Plans." *Sociology of Education* 60: 168–80.

Rosenbaum, J., and T. Kariya. 1989. "From High School to Work: Market and Institutional Mechanisms in Japan." *American Journal of Sociology* 94: 1334–65.

Rowan, B. 1982. "Organizational Structure and the Institutional Environment: The Case of Public Schools." *Administrative Science Quarterly* 27: 259–79.

Rowan, B. 1983. "Instructional Management in Historical Perspective: Evidence on Differentiation in School Districts." *Educational Administration Quarterly* 18: 43–59.

Rowan, B. 1990. "Commitment and Control: Alternative Strategies for the Organizational Design of Schools." In C. Cazden, ed., *Review of Research in Education* (Vol. 16, 353–89). Washington, D.C.: American Educational Research Association.

Ruddell, R. B. 1985. "Knowledge and Attitude Toward Testing: Educators and Legislators." *The Reading Teacher* 38: 538–43.

Salmon-Cox, L. 1981. "Teachers and Standardized Achievement Tests: What's Really Happening?" *Phi Delta Kappan* 62: 631–33.

Sarason, S. 1977. *The Culture of the School and the Problem of Change.* Boston: Allyn & Bacon.

Scardamalia, M., C. Bereiter, and R. Steinbach. 1984. "Teachability of Reflective Processes in Written Composition." *Cognitive Science* 8: 173–90.

Schwille, J., A. Porter, L. Alford, R. Floden, D. Freeman, S. Irwin, and W. Schmidt. 1986. *State Policy and the Control of Curriculum Decisions.* East Lansing, Mich.: Institute for Research in Teaching, Michigan State University.

Schwille, J., A. Porter, R. Floden, D. Freeman, L. Knappen, T. Kuhs, and W. Schmidt. 1983. "Teachers as Policybrokers in the Content of Elementary School Mathematics." In L. Shulman and G. Sykes, eds., *Handbook of Teaching and Policy* (370–91). New York: Longman.

Scott, R., and J. Meyer. 1983. "The Organization of Societal Sectors." In J. W. Meyer and W. R. Scott, eds., *Organizational Environments: Ritual and Rationality* (129–54). Beverly Hills, Calif.: Sage.

Sedlak, M., C. Wheeler, D. Pullin, and P. Cusick. 1986. *Selling Students Short: Classroom Bargains and Academic Reform in American High Schools*. New York: Teachers College Press.

Shanker, A. 1989. *Asking the Right Questions*. Washington, D.C.: American Federation of Teachers.

Shimahara, N. 1986. "The Cultural Basis of Students' Achievement in Japan." *Comparative Education* 22: 285–303.

Sizer, T. 1984. *Horace's Compromise*. Boston: Houghton Mifflin.

Smith, M., and J. O'Day. 1990. "Systemic School Reform." In S. Fuhrman and B. Malen, eds., *The Politics of Curriculum and Testing* (233–67). Philadelphia: Falmer.

Sproull, L., and D. Zubrow. 1981. "Standardized Testing from the Administrative Perspective." *Phi Delta Kappan* 62: 628–30.

Stackhouse, E. 1982. *The Effects of State Centralization on Administrative Structure*. Unpublished doctoral dissertation, Stanford University.

Stake, R., and J. Easley. 1978. *Case Studies in Science Education, Vol I. The Case Reports* (Stock No. 038-000-00377-1). Washington, D.C.: U.S. Government Printing Office.

Stevens, R. 1912. *The Question as a Measure of Efficiency in Instruction*. New York: Teachers College.

Stevenson, D., and D. Baker. 1991. "State Control of the Curriculum and Classroom Instruction." *Sociology of Education* 64: 1–10.

Stevenson, H., and S. Lee. 1990. "Contexts of Achievement: A Study of American, Chinese and Japanese Children." *Monographs of the Society for Research in Child Development* 55(1–2) (Serial No. 221).

Stevenson, H., S-Y. Lee, and J. Stigler. 1986. "Mathematics Achievement of Chinese, Japanese, and American Children." *Science* 231: 693–99.

Stevenson, H., J. Stigler, S. Lee, G. Lucker, S. Kitamura, and C. Hsu. 1985. "Cognitive Performance and Academic Achievement of Japanese, Chinese and American Children." *Child Development* 56: 718–34.

Thompson, A. 1984. "The Relationships of Teachers' Conceptions of Mathematics and Mathematics Teaching to Instructional Practice." *Educational Studies in Mathematics* 15: 105–27.

Travers, K., and I. Westbury. 1989. *The IEA Study of Mathematics I: Analysis of Mathematics Curricula*. New York: Pergamon.

Trow, M. 1961. "The Second Transformation of American Secondary Education." *International Journal of Comparative Sociology* 2: 144–66.

Trow, M. 1988. "American Higher Education: Past, Present, and Future." *Educational Researcher* 17: 13–23.

Tyson-Bernstein, H. 1988. "The Academy's Contribution to the Impoverishment of America's Textbooks." *Phi Delta Kappan* 70: 194–98.

U.S. Bureau of the Census. 1989. *Statistical Abstract of the United States, 1988*. Washington, D.C.: U.S. Department of Commerce.

Van der Blij, F., S. Hilding, and A. Weinzweig. 1980. "A Synthesis of National Reports on Changes in Curricula." In H. G. Steiner, ed., *Comparative Studies of Mathematics Curricula—Change and Stability, 1960–1980*. Haus Ohrbeck: Institut für Didaktik der Mathematik der Universität Bielefeld.

Welch, W. W. 1979. "Twenty Years of Science Curriculum Development: A Look Back." In *Review of Research in Education*, Vol. 7. Washington, D.C.: American Educational Research Association.

Westbury, I. 1980. Conclusion to Conference Proceedings: "Reflection on Case Studies." In H. G. Steiner, ed., *Comparative Studies of Mathematics Curricula—Change and Stability,*

1960–1980 (509–22). Haus Ohrbeck: Institut für Didaktik der Mathematik der Universität Bielefeld.

White, M. 1987. *The Japanese Educational Challenge.* New York: Free Press.

Wirt, F., and M. Kirst. 1982. *The Politics of Education: Schools in Conflict.* Berkeley, Calif.: McCutchan.

Wise, A. 1979. *Legislated Learning.* Berkeley, Calif.: University of California.

Witte, J. F. 1989. *Choice and Control in American Education: An Analytic Overview.* Madison, Wis.: University of Wisconsin—Madison.

Witte, J. 1990. *Understanding High School Achievement.* Paper presented at the meeting of the Political Science Association, San Francisco.

9

Goals 2000 and a Reauthorized ESEA: National Standards and Accompanying Controversies

MICHAEL W. KIRST

Stanford University

JAMES W. GUTHRIE

University of California–Berkeley

Introduction

Clinton administration Goals 2000 legislation envisions national education curriculum and student performance standards. The Clinton strategy further anticipates meshing these standards with ESEA Chapter I compliance measures. If successful, this will represent a substantial departure from ESEA's 25-year operational pattern. This section summarizes Clinton administration national education standards provisions and explains their proposed interaction with ESEA Chapter I implementation strategies. The section also analyzes the philosophic, political, and practical consequences and controversies that assuredly will accompany efforts to enact and implement these precedent-shattering ideas.

In the autumn of 1989, then-President Bush and the governors of all 50 states adopted a set of six national education goals. Since this unprecedented pronouncement, substantial attention has been given to related and equally sweeping education reform ideas such as national curriculum standards, national achievement testing, and national performance standards for students.

Until recently, while these bold proposals have been discussed intensely by national and state education policymakers, for most practicing educators in the United States, nationalizing notions were only rhetoric. If you were a teacher or school principal, "national this" and "national that" might be fit topics for discussion in the teachers' lounge, but they were not part of workaday reality.

Today, these proposals to nationalize education seem less remote. The Clinton administration, in its Goals 2000 legislation, suggests that states "voluntarily" establish curriculum and performance standards. However, that is not the main news. The blockbuster headline is that administration policy wonks have also invented a means for gaining powerful federal government leverage in the education reform movement.

The lever to enforce state and local school district compliance with national standards is embedded in proposed amendments to the Elementary and Secondary Education Act (ESEA) Chapter I. States that are either unable or unwilling to adopt curricular and performance standards will risk losing their Chapter I funding.

ESEA has existed for almost three decades. During this time, its proponents have tenaciously fended off all but the most minor alterations to the act. Now, through its Goals 2000 legislation and plans for reauthorizing ESEA, the administration is proposing a sweeping change. If successful, the Clinton plan will alter Chapter I, minimizing its long-standing regulatory and fiscal accounting outlook and transforming it into a powerful administrative instrument for fundamentally changing the U.S. public school system.

By refusing to approve a state's Chapter I operating plans unless they ensure acceptable curriculum and performance standards, the U.S. Department of Education could possibly have a mechanism for making virtually all of U.S. education "standards" oriented. If such a plan went into effect, the public schools could be expected to offer a relatively uniform core curriculum and students could be expected to display related knowledge and skill at a specified minimum level.

Aside from value judgments about how good, bad, right, wrong, productive, or unproductive such monumental alterations in the once decentralized education system would or could be, the entire nationalization prospect raises many practical questions. Should standards be voluntary or mandatory, "national" or "federal"? Who or what agencies would establish standards for or within states? What is the role to be played by professional education organizations and subject-matter associations? What is a subject-matter community? What is the balance of influence among public representatives, professional educators, academic specialists, and others in developing standards? What criteria should the U.S. secretary of education employ to judge a state's proposed standards? How much research and development time would states be given to construct standards? From where will the resources come to support such efforts? What tests will be used to appraise progress in meeting standards? Will the establishment of national standards erode the time-honored purposes of ESEA Chapter I? Is there more at risk here than there is to be gained?

The list of questions could continue, but the point remains the same. However exciting or demoralizing the Clinton administration's national standards proposals are taken to be, there are many controversial and practical issues to be resolved before the ideas can be implemented.

This section deliberately offers no solutions to the above problems. Whatever the final answers, they should stem from a full discussion among professional educators, academic experts, and representatives of the public.

The Evolving Call for National Standards

The current nationwide education standards movement is a result of policymakers' perceptions of fundamental problems in K through 12 education that began in the 1980s with the publication of *A Nation at Risk* (National Commission on Excellence in Education 1983). A flurry of national reports and commentaries alleged that U.S. education standards were too low and that drastic steps needed to be taken (Finn 1991). The general feeling was that some kind of national intervention was needed. Former President Bush spearheaded the movement by leading an education summit in Charlottesville, Virginia, in 1989 that resulted in a statement of national education goals. In 1990 the president proposed world-class content standards and a set of achievement tests in five core subjects (U.S. Department of Education 1991). Bill Clinton, then governor of Arkansas, was the key liaison between the National Governors Association and President Bush for planning and follow-up to the education summit of 1989.

The arguments put forward in support of these national standards can be summarized under four main points:

Lack of Adequate Local Standards.   Critics assert that state and local standards for student achievement and teacher performance are lacking in rigor and do not provide uniform student outcome data useful for interstate or school-by-school comparisons. National intervention is required if local standards are to be raised to meet the world standards of our major economic competitors.

Standardized Multiple-Choice Tests Evaluate Low-Level Skills.   Widely used multiple-choice tests are said to focus on low-level basic skills that emphasize single correct answers. School districts tend to use commercial tests that do not adequately emphasize analysis, statistical inference, mathematical problem solving, hands-on science, synthesis, expository writing, and complex reading. Many current tests, such as the California Test of Basic Skills and the Stanford or Metropolitan Achievement Tests, are not geared to the high curricular standards characteristic of education in Europe and Asia (Smith and O'Day 1991). Only national policies can push the education system to criterion-referenced assessments similar to the 1 to 6 subjective performance ratings given to Olympic ice skaters.

Misleading Results. Parents and the general public may be hearing a phony story from the commonly used standardized multiple-choice tests. Test results exaggerate what U.S. students know and can do, and few districts report that they are below average (Cannell 1987). Local districts can cite old norms or not hold to a specific standard, but merely make public where they stand on a bell-shaped curve.

Lack of Incentives. U.S. tests and examinations rarely contain high stakes for students who take them. Few employers examine the transcripts of high school graduates, and state assessments are seldom considered for college entrance. The SAT is not aligned with the high school curriculum and does not measure achievement in subjects such as history and science (Bishop 1990). Critics argue that student scores based on high national standards need to be linked to decisions in employment and college admission.

Responding to assertions such as these, a coalition of national leaders, including President Bush and President Clinton, governors, and some professional experts in the academic disciplines, have advocated the need for national subject-matter curricular standards that meet world-class benchmarks and a related set of voluntary state assessments (National Council on Education Standards and Testing 1991). Examples of state tests that embody high standards are the California Learning Assessment Program and the Connecticut Mastery Tests. The coalition believes that examination results should be reported for individual students and that high stakes decisions, such as college admission and employment, should be based largely on student performance.

The political momentum behind these national efforts is impressive and growing. The pressure for education reform is not solely top-down, but rather is coming from all directions, including political leaders, business, professional associations, universities, and school districts. Political support for national standards rests not just in the Clinton administration; it includes a significant number of Republican governors and legislators as well as former President Bush. Both teachers unions (NEA and AFT), the

National School Boards Association, the Council of Chief State School Officers, and the National Governors Association supported the recommendations made in January 1992, for national standards and examinations (National Council on Education Standards and Testing 1991). By the 1980s, some state policymakers had begun to specify standards in core curriculum subjects and to create new examinations. For example, the California State Board of Education approved curricular standards in mathematics based in part on the recommendations of the National Council of Teachers of Mathematics. California then developed a state assessment system that was aligned with these mathematics standards.

Evolution of ESEA Chapter I

While the national standards debate proceeded, the largest federal education program, Chapter I, continued to rely on low-level standardized tests and a curriculum that was not acceptable to the national standards alliance. How could Chapter I be so deeply rooted in past practice and seemingly so inattentive to present developments? A bit of history is in order.

Throughout their history, Chapter I programs have been directed primarily toward elementary reading and math and have emphasized remedial approaches (Smith and O'Day 1991). When enacted in 1965, the program was the centerpiece of an equal opportunity policy and assumed that state and local educators could not be trusted to target scarce federal dollars to disadvantaged students. The federal management approach reflected a fear that local political concerns would divert Chapter I funds to less-needy children. Therefore, the principal delivery mode relied on detailed federal financial flow regulation reinforced by field audits. There was little federal concern about curriculum content, but a great deal of attention to which schools and students received federal money.

There evolved a deep fear, lasting from 1965 to 1986, that Title I[1] money might spill over to non-Title I students in the school or classroom. Consequently, a separate administrative apparatus was created and sustained, composed of state and local Chapter I coordinators whose allegiance was different from, and sometimes counter to, that of supporters of a district-wide or statewide core curriculum. These Chapter I coordinators created their own professional association and often met separately from regular classroom teachers at state and national education conventions. Technical assistance and provision of services, such as curricular models, was

---

[1]The legislation was referred to as Chapter I and Title I at different times.

abandoned by the late 1960s. From then until now, program managers and auditors have been the key federal Chapter I players and curriculum or teaching experts have been shunted to other federal divisions. Federal research efforts have concentrated on program regulation and fiscal compliance, with scant attention to the commonplaces of education—teaching, curriculum, and learning strategies. In effect, Chapter I developed an accounting, rather than an instructional, mentality as it grew from $1 billion in 1965 to $7 billion in 1994.

This regulatory focus and distinctly identifiable federal role in categorical programs has long been reinforced by a view that Chapter I is effective and, thus, it would be unwise and risky to alter it. It was assumed that acceptable levels of compliance with Chapter I financial targeting and special service requirements were linked to achievement gains in the early grades among Southern blacks. Indeed, a careful administrator could listen carefully to the federal rhetoric surrounding Chapter I in the 1970–85 period and hear almost nothing about curricular content or how to teach. There was an assumption that something educationally different needed to be done through Chapter I, but the federal government transmitted no clear message about what or how.

Instructional issues began to surface in the debate about the 1988 congressional reauthorization of Chapter I. Education experts in the 1980s returned to a concern about instruction. The U.S. Department of Education commissioned a series of papers from education researchers. One, written by Robert Calfee (1986), asserted, "Tracking, pullout programs, and reliance on paraprofessionals [in Chapter I] to monitor remedial learning serve as barriers rather than facilitators to improving the curriculum of literacy for youngsters at risk."

Calfee and other reformers contended that Chapter I should be aimed at improving whole schools as education organizations instead of focusing on programs targeted to individual students within schools. For instance, low-income students receive Chapter I services that differ from the regular curriculum and are less likely to promote literacy. Chapter I reading teachers stress decoding at the expense of comprehension and rarely require expository essays.

There are weak links between the remedial reading specialists who tutor Chapter I students and regular classroom teachers. This does not mean that all pullout programs are bad or that such a strategy cannot be improved. Until regular classroom teachers are retrained, there may remain a need for pullout remedial strategies. The Clinton administration's point is that both pullout and regular teachers need a new vision of Chapter I's curriculum content and improved instructional techniques based on national standards.

Bill Honig (1986), California's former chief state school officer, expressed the federal administrative issues surrounding this reconceptualized learning approach as follows:

> Chapter I is often operated as a separate remedial program, substituting a narrow, repetitious curriculum for a well-balanced core curriculum. There is a need for some development work in this area to train teachers to help eligible students to master the base curriculum and to provide integrated learning experiences.

Henry M. Levin (1986) noted that even in the regular class, the traditional notion is that "educationally needy students should be placed in slow, repetitive, remedial programs. Not only do these programs bore students, but they reinforce students' negative self-images." A federal presence that focuses on these types of instructional issues is quite different from one that is keyed to fiscal audit trails. Chapter I should encourage faster-paced core curriculum instruction.

What disadvantaged students are missing is first-class, rapid-paced instruction from teachers who have confidence that such students can learn. This cannot be provided by simply reorganizing classroom structures or exhortation from the federal bully pulpit. Jane David (1981) has analyzed the current dilemma of how to deregulate Chapter I fiscal targeting while at the same time improving instructional content and methods:

> We need teachers who have high expectations, excellent diagnostic skills, and enough understanding of the knowledge and experience. . . . But abandoning all targeting and fiscal controls, especially in today's social and political climate, would translate into general aid, and lose the whole point of the program.

These criticisms preceded the 1988 reauthorization but they were not heeded by Congress, which apparently remained satisfied with Chapter I results. Moreover, the Democratic-dominated Congress was suspicious of the Reagan administration's motives in revamping Chapter I.

A Closer Examination of Current Proposals

The advent of the Clinton administration placed in power a number of Democrats critical of Chapter I policies and results. Much current thinking about instruction reflects the 1989 education summit and the 1994 statement of national goals. National content standards in Goals 2000 are merged with the current administration's thinking on "systemic reform." The key themes of this new amalgam are policy coherence, alignment, and linkage to high content standards.

Categorical programs, such as Chapter I, bilingual education, and special education, have come to be viewed as major contributors to incoherent policy. Current Chapter I programs rely on low-level standardized tests to demonstrate accountability because federal legislation requires that national norms be used to judge local Chapter I programs. This approach, in turn, encourages schools and teachers to utilize a "pullout drill-and-kill workbook curriculum."

Newly proposed ESEA and Goals 2000 legislation links Chapter I to a new instructional approach. States will be expected to develop content standards and submit them for certification by the National Education Goals Panel (NEGP). State student performance assessment practices are to be revised and aligned with these nationally approved content standards. Local Chapter I programs would then be based on these state content standards and assessments. The Clinton administration's bill explains it this way (U.S. Department of Education 1993):

> Paragraph (3) would replace all current testing requirements in Chapter I which, evidence suggests, have held back efforts to enrich the curriculum with more challenging material. In their place would be a state-level set of high-quality, yearly student assessments. These assessments would be comprised of multiple, up-to-date measures of student performance, and be used as the primary means of determining whether LEAs [local education agencies] and schools are, in fact, making adequate yearly progress.

The Clinton administration proposes to deregulate the instructional approaches used to meet high standards. This means more use of schoolwide approaches and fewer fiscal incentives to use pullout programs. The new legislation requires intensive and sustained staff development oriented to high national content standards.

Local incentives to meet national standards are also included in the administration's bill, which explicitly links Chapter I to a coherent and systemic strategy oriented to national and state content standards. Presumably, the administration will audit SEAs (state education authorities) to make sure that local Chapter I programs are based on state content standards and assessments that are compatible with the national standards approved by NEGP under the 1994 Goals 2000 statute. Since opportunity-to-learn standards are *not* to be set at the national level, federal oversight of Chapter I on this issue probably will be minimal.

The federal role in promoting national standards will be reinforced by a widespread technical assistance program providing consultants to SEAs and LEAs. These technical assistance providers will be expected to be experts in curricular content as well as teaching methods. They would be employed in 10 new regional centers and would include Chapter I programs as a priority. Federal grants could be given to SEAs to develop better technical assistance capacity for instructional leadership. Such arrangements would resemble a return to the pre-1965 role of U.S. Office of Education (USOE) subject-matter specialists who were national leaders in their curricular and instructional fields. These new technical assistance units would create locally based networks, coordinate field services, and produce curriculum reform ideas for local consideration. Forty-nine federal categorical program centers would be consolidated into 10 comprehensive ESEA-Technical Assistance centers under the proposed reauthorization of ESEA.

Still another proposed Clinton reform would promote Chapter I SEA program review strategies that carefully link federal categorical aid in Chapter I and bilingual education with academic content and instructional strategies within regular classes and core curricula. The federal government would design model Chapter I schoolwide improvement plans. Federal policy would fund a major staff development effort by merging Eisenhower and Chapter II funds to help classroom teachers improve instructional techniques for the disadvantaged, rather than leaving teachers to rely on pullout remedial specialists.

The Clinton plan relies on restructuring the existing federal role rather than increasing federal funds. It is ambitious and assumes new state curriculum frameworks and assessment systems can be devised within three years. States such as Kentucky and California have taken much longer to create even partial state assessment systems based on performance and portfolios. Moreover, President Clinton's bill proposes that Limited English Proficiency (LEP) programs be integrated with Chapter I in terms of both program operation and assessment. Federal and state language emphasizes "change at the local level." The bill is replete with federal and state approval criteria and actions the LEAs "must" take *before* approval of funding. One criterion aims to ensure a better transition from preschool and Headstart to K through 3.

In effect, the objectives of Goals 2000 are enforced through ESEA requirements for alignment with national standards. For example, SEAs are required by the federal government to specify whether local Title I plans for staff development are "intensive, sustained, and oriented to national and state standards." Presumably, the new federal regulations will specify what these terms mean. The administration's package of Chapter II plus

Eisenhower program funds proposes an $800 million staff-development fund to implement national standards.

State and Local Responses

Can states accommodate to these rigorous and fast-paced requirements? What experiences have states had with performance standards to date? California, Florida, and New Hampshire provide contrasting examples.

The California curricular framework will be aligned to the national content standards. Each subject will embody common themes. Chapter I is part of the statewide reform initiative (California Department of Education 1990) requiring that students—including students at risk—must be successful in the district-adopted curriculum that is based on the state framework.

California will submit its state framework to the NEGP under Goals 2000 and will have a new assessment system in place in 1995 based on the state framework. This state assessment system will be used to judge LEA annual student improvement under Chapter I. If NESIC (National Education Standards and Improvement Council) and NEGP approve California's new curriculum framework and assessment system (called CLAS—California Learning Assessment System), then the federal impact on California's Chapter I program will be minimal. CLAS is designed to test all students, so Chapter I students would be held to the same high standards as other students. Moreover, California plans to translate CLAS into Spanish and use it for the assessment of improvement in bilingual education.

The impact of Chapter I changes on Florida, however, would be quite different. Florida has deemphasized its state-centralized policies and now encourages flexible school-site improvement plans. Consequently, Florida abolished its state assessment test initially administered in the mid-1970s. Florida has no precise timetable for creating a new state assessment system, but has selected some LEAs to develop the general design. Florida must accelerate development if the state is to be eligible for Chapter I funds under the new standards agenda. Moreover, Florida's curriculum framework is not nearly as fully developed and specific as California's. Florida may have to completely overhaul the state curriculum framework it designed in the mid-1980s. Another alternative would be to let each LEA (67 counties) deal directly with the federal government concerning what standards would be acceptable in order to receive Chapter I funds.

New Hampshire provides an interesting case because of its long history of strong local control in education. The localist political culture limits the state role and has precluded the development of any state standards. The New Hampshire State Education Department does not have the legitimacy or probably the capacity to develop an elaborate state system like the one in California. New Hampshire provides less than 10 percent of state funding for education while California state authorities control 88 percent of total school spending. Unlike Florida, New Hampshire is organized around small local districts that would have great difficulty creating standards simply to satisfy Chapter I requirements. How can the federal government expect New Hampshire to meet national education standards when the concept is alien to the political tradition of the state? New Hampshire's motto, "Live Free or Die," symbolizes the Granite State's resistance to centralized standards.

If the U.S. Department of Education makes an exception for New Hampshire, then other states may protest. It will be difficult to design Chapter I standards policies that take into account the diversity of the 50 states.

Additional Controversies Not Yet Resolved

The national standards proposals are triggering much discussion and substantial controversy among ESEA supporters, professional educators, and government officials. Aligning Chapter I with curricular and performance standards will alter more than 25 years of instructional procedures, administrative activities, and accounting mind-sets. It is not clear that the transition to a dramatically new system can be accomplished quickly, if at all. Controversy is likely to center around four principal issues: (1) philosophic or governance issues, (2) practical problems of implementation, (3) legal liability, and (4) political inertia.

Philosophic Issues. Controversy continues concerning the matter of decision-making authority. The prospect of national curriculum and performance standards alters the status quo so dramatically that the legitimacy of the existing authority structure is being questioned. National standards trigger many questions about who should have the authority to decide what. The controversy covers virtually every facet of the education reform movement from questions of should this be done? and should we participate? to who should set the standards?

Are the newly proposed standards to be truly voluntary? Goals 2000 specifies that they are. However, linking the standards concept to Chapter I argues to the contrary. Chapter I funding flows to all 50 states. The amounts of money involved, soon to be increased, are considerable, $8 or $9 billion. States questioning the utility or appropriateness of national standards will nevertheless have grave practical difficulty forgoing Chapter I funding. Arizona provides a good example. Arizona government objected philosophically to many provisions of the Education for All Handicapped Children Act and decided, at the cost of forgoing federal funds for special education, to disregard crucial provisions of the new statute. Eventually, the state succumbed to both the siren song of added resources and the entreaties of advocates for the handicapped within its borders. Would not Chapter I national standards requirements establish a similar dynamic in which a state, realistically, would have little choice but to sign up with the plan? Not to do so would simply be too costly. How voluntary is this?

Questions of authority are raised by the standards-setting process itself. Who or what agency or agencies should be authorized to establish standards for a state and for the nation? How will the secretary of education know whether or not a state's proposed set of standards should be approved? By what guidelines can the secretary act? Are national curriculum and student performance standards similar to air quality, toxic waste disposal, air safety, highway construction, student loan eligibility, school bus construction, stock and bond issuance, beef and chicken cleanliness, and a host of other national activities regulated by the Interstate Commerce Act for which reasonably scientific standards have been established?

If poultry contain an excessive bacterial count, dressed chickens can be removed from supermarket shelves. The health regulators are reasonably sure that the consuming public is at risk under such conditions. Now, let us examine the counterpart for schooling. It is one thing to assert that Johnny needs to know how to read, write, and count. It is quite another matter to specify the required level of proficiency. At what point is Johnny's reading level too low to meet national standards? How will we know that Johnny's reading level places Johnny or the public at risk? Who should determine acceptable reading levels? Is this a scientific or political question? Whatever the answer, it is unlikely to be quick or easy in coming. *Practical Problems of Implementation.* Even if one assumes that such questions concerning the legitimacy of national standards setting are resolved, immense practical problems remain. Developing details of a new curriculum, retraining the nation's teachers, reconstructing a system of performance appraisal, and reorienting a massive federal government enforcement structure will all be necessary.

Clinton administration officials and other supporters of national standards contend that the United States already has a national curriculum—one that is implicit, not explicit. Relatively invisible interactions of textbook publishers, test manufacturers, national professional associations, college entrance requirements, and nationwide professional publications all redound to a national curriculum. The current problem, administration officials assert, is that the public is the only principal actor that does not realize there is a national curriculum, and if the public were aware, it would want the standards set at a higher level. Consequently what Goals 2000 is attempting to do is make the current system explicit and the standards high.

Those assertions may be accurate. However, the very reason that such a subterranean national curriculum can exist is because it is implicit. Efforts to make it explicit will assuredly trigger conflict and take a long time to resolve. State textbook adoption provides an analog. In states in which the board of education adopts textbooks for statewide use, controversies over selection can be intense. Many of the books that trigger conflict when subjected to the intense scrutiny of public examination can be privately purchased by school districts with hardly a scintilla of conflict. Creationists, representatives of ethnic and racial groups, and members of various religions may perceive their interests threatened by a particular curriculum component or textbook. Whatever the reality of the situation, it will take time to resolve such issues.

Test construction is another time-consuming component of a national standards strategy. One should never underestimate the time and effort necessary to construct even a new version of an old examination. Altering the test paradigm substantially, such as by moving away from multiple-choice, norm-referenced tests to criterion-referenced examinations, and linking performance criteria to a national curriculum, will take a long time and involve vast amounts of additional development resources.

California and Kentucky are examples of states moving in this direction. Each has been engaged for almost a decade and still has not constructed a complete examination system.

Reorienting the compliance mentality of federal, state, and local officials will be another major implementation hurdle. Thousands of individuals are well trained in monitoring the existing pullout, clean-audit-trail model. To erase this mentality and substitute a model focused on curriculum and technical assistance for instruction will not be easy or quickly accomplished. Many of the existing state and local Chapter I coordinators will have to be retrained or replaced.

Legal Liability. Build a curriculum ballpark and the lawyers will come. Whatever the other merits or demerits of national curriculum and performance standards, they assuredly will serve as anchor points against which to judge the adequacy and equity of a state's education system. If a state adopts a performance standard and Johnny's reading does not achieve that standard, is the state at risk of malpractice? If it can be shown that Johnny is mentally retarded, absent most of the time, or simply did not turn in homework assignments, the school system may sidestep such charges. However, curriculum standards pose a further question. If the state submits a standardized curriculum package to the U.S. secretary of education, which is then approved, every school or school district in the state better ensure that it offers such courses and experiences. Otherwise Johnny has a strong equal protection case.

Advocates for national standards are quickly realizing that such standards offer leverage for upgrading the education of historically neglected or low-achieving groups of students. Indeed, such standards might provide far more powerful legal leverage to ensure better education for such students than any of the Chapter I compliance standards. However, standards opponents may also recognize the implicit power of such legal exposure and move to dilute the threat by watering down the standards. Johnny, no matter how poorly he performs, may still meet the standard if the "bar" is set low enough.

Political Inertia. Many national, state, and local educators and government officials have a strong vested interest in maintaining Chapter I as it is now and has been for a long time. More is at stake than simply having to learn new rules. Chapter I currently pays the salaries of thousands of school district, state, and federal employees. National standards imply an entirely different set of skills that emphasize curriculum and instructional knowledge, rather than compliance monitoring. It may be that many current Chapter I employees will be quite capable of acquiring the new skills, but certainly many will not. Moreover, even those who can may not be eager to expend the effort necessary. Consequently, there is substantial inertia that may block any transition to a standards orientation (Kirst 1988).

So what? Chapter I politics are dominated by Chapter I employees. The Bush administration backed off its 1988 efforts to radically alter Chapter I through the use of a modified voucher system. Former President Reagan proposed that Chapter I should offer grants to pupils rather than to schools. An early 1981 Reagan proposal attempted to combine Chapter I with many other already existing authorities into a huge federal block grant program. It did not take Reagan administration officials long to see that the entire plan was jeopardized by the inclusion of Chapter I. All the other vested interests could be overcome and finessed. Indeed, they eventually were and the current version of ESEA Chapter II is a massive block-grant program. However, Chapter I was withdrawn as a proposed component simply because its political defenders were too strong to overcome without the expenditure of more presidential energy than then appeared justified. Is the Clinton administration committed to making such an effort?

Conclusion

Clinton administration standards proposals are intended to alter several fundamental and long-standing components of U.S. education. Local control, however much it has been eroded over the last century, is still a branch of theology in many political circles. Establishing national curriculum and performance standards would dramatically counter the long tradition of decentralized decision making. National, state, and local education policymakers will have to accommodate fundamental changes if the Clinton proposals are enacted. Given the amount of effort that such change will entail, finding solutions to issues such as those described above appears to be the crucial next step.

Too often this country has engaged in "either/or" curriculum policy. Curricular discussions in the United States have had a disturbing tendency to oscillate between polar extremes. At one point we create new math and then we revert to rote drill and practice. For a time there is a push for open classrooms and then the idea disappears from the policy agenda almost entirely. High schools are urged to become shopping malls with broad curricula and many options, only to be turned around again into offering a required core of traditional subjects. This time, with a change as massive as national standards, it is important to be sure of our intended outcomes and equally sure that the policy strategies will achieve them.

Our major conclusion is that policy analysts and educators should understand the close link between two Clinton administration initiatives—Goals 2000 and the revision of ESEA. Goals 2000 may amount to $900 million, but ESEA will approach $7.5 billion. If federal and state approval of local ESEA Chapter I applications for the disadvantaged depends upon the development and implementation of national content and assessment standards, the impact of Goals 2000 will be multiplied dramatically. Such a change would reorient the entire Chapter I conceptual and administrative approach that evolved from 1965 to 1994. But this Chapter I administrative apparatus is entrenched deeply in the political and organizational cultures of state and local education agencies. Change will not be easy or rapid.

References

Bishop, John. 1990. "Incentives for Learning." *Research in Labor Economics* (Vol. II, 17–51) JAI Press.

Calfee, Robert. 1986. "Reinventing Chapter I." In B. I. Williams, ed., *Designs for Compensatory Education* (250). Washington, D.C.: ERIC 293901.

California Department of Education. 1990. *Every Student Succeeds.* Sacramento, Calif.: California Department of Education.

Cannell, John Jacob. 1987. *Nationally Normed Referenced Testing in American Schools. How All Fifty States Are above the National Average.* Daniels, West Virginia: Friends for Education.

David, Jane. 1981. Letter to Michael W. Kirst. August 18.

Finn, Chester. 1991. *We Must Take Charge*. New York: Macmillan.

Honig, Bill. 1986. Letter to Secretary of Education William Bennett. August 5.

Kirst, Michael W. 1988. "The Federal Role and Chapter I." In Dennis Boyle and Bruce Cooper, eds., *Federal Aid to the Disadvantaged*, (97–118). Philadelphia: Falmer.

Levin, Henry. 1986. Interview on accelerated schools with Stanford Daily. October 3, 1.

National Commission on Excellence in Education. 1983. *A Nation at Risk*. Washington, D.C.: U.S. Department of Education.

National Council on Education Standards and Testing. 1991. *Raising Standards for American Education*. Washington, D.C.: National Education Goals Panel.

Smith, Marshall, and Jennifer O'Day. 1991. "Systemic School Reform." In Susan Fuhrman and Betty Malen, eds., *The Politics of Curriculum and Testing* (233–68). New York: Falmer.

U.S. Department of Education. 1991. *America 2000: A Sourcebook*. Washington, D.C.: U.S. Department of Education.

U.S. Department of Education. 1993. *Improving American Schools Act of 1993*. Washington, D.C.: U.S. Department of Education.

**PART
V**

STANDARDS AND THE PROFESSIONAL LIVES OF TEACHERS

10

Teachers' Professional Development: Critical Colleagueship and the Role of Professional Communities

BRIAN LORD

Education Development Center, Newton, Mass.

Introduction

In his 1990 essay "A Revolution in One Classroom: The Case of Mrs. Oublier," David Cohen investigated how one teacher altered her classroom practice to reflect the new directions outlined in the California Mathematics Framework (Cohen 1990, 311–29). The essay, part of a larger study of the "relationship between instructional policy and teaching practice," detailed Mrs. Oublier's efforts to make sense of the new policy and to integrate innovative approaches into her instructional routines. The framework is a bold attempt by the state education agency in California to introduce nontraditional, constructivist approaches to teaching and learning into the state's mathematics classrooms. As is true with many of the national content standards efforts and other state subject-area frameworks, the aim is to increase students' understanding of subject matter and to diminish the repetitive, mechanical, and routine character of "school knowledge" (McNeil 1988).

Cohen's message in this essay is extremely important for any consideration of teachers' professional development in the context of broader content standards. In order to set the stage and raise some crucial questions, I include two lengthy, though telling, excerpts from Cohen's paper:

175

Baratta-Lorton's book *Math Their Way*[1] thus enabled Mrs. O to wholeheart-
edly embrace teaching math for understanding, without considering or reconsidering her views of mathematical knowledge. She was very keen that
children should understand math, and worked hard at helping them. However, she placed nearly the entire weight of this effort on concrete materials
and activities. The ways that she used these materials—insisting, for instance, that all the children actually feel them, and perform the same prescribed physical operations with them—suggested that she endowed the
materials with enormous, even magical instructional powers. The lack of
any other ways of making sense of mathematics in her lesson was no oversight. She simply saw no need for anything else.

In what sense was Mrs. O teaching for understanding? The question opens
up a great puzzle. Her classes excluded traditional conceptions of
mathematical knowledge, and were organized as though explanation and
discussion were irrelevant to mathematics. Yet she had changed her math
teaching quite dramatically. She now used a new curriculum specially designed to promote students' understanding of mathematics. And her students' lessons were very different than they had been. (Cohen 1990, 318)

And several pages later:

[One] reason for Mrs. O's smooth lessons[2] has to do with her knowledge of
mathematics. Though she plainly wanted her students to understand this
subject, her grasp of mathematics restricted her notion of mathematical understanding, and of what it took to produce it. She did not know mathematics deeply or extensively. She had taken one or two courses in college, and
reported that she had liked them; but she had not pursued the subject further. Lacking deep knowledge, Mrs. O was simply unaware of much
mathematical content and many ramifications of the material she taught.
Many paths to understanding were not taken in her lessons ... but she
seemed entirely unaware of them. Many misunderstandings or inventive ideas
that her students might have had would have made no sense to Mrs. O,
because her grip on mathematics was so modest. In these ways and many
others, her relatively superficial knowledge of this subject insulated her from
even a glimpse of many things she might have done to deepen students'
understanding.

Additionally, however much mathematics she knew, Mrs. O knew it as a
fixed body of truths, rather than as a particular way of framing and solving
problems. ... Lacking a sense of the importance of explanation, justification, and argument in mathematics, she simply slipped over many opportunities to elicit them, unaware that they existed.

These limitations on her knowledge meant that Mrs. O could teach for

[1]*Math Their Way* presents an instructional system for primary grades mathematics that
promotes understanding of mathematical patterns through the use of concrete materials.
[2]Cohen perceives this smoothness as concealing certain instructional tensions.

> understanding, with little sense of how much remained to be understood, how much she might incompletely or naively understand, and how much might still remain to be taught. She is a thoughtful and committed teacher, but working as she did near the surface of this subject, many elements of understanding and many pedagogical possibilities remained invisible. Mathematically, she was on thin ice. Because she did not know it, she skated smoothly on with great confidence. (Cohen 1990, 322–23]

As the education community moves with startling speed toward a standards-driven approach to curriculum, instruction, and assessment, there is good reason to ask whether the nation's teachers will be proceeding on thin ice. The images of teaching and learning contained in standards documents (those completed as well as those still in draft) call for dramatic changes, and, unlike the first wave of reform in the early 1980s, this wave will succeed, if it succeeds at all, *in the classroom and among teachers*. What Cohen so aptly highlights is the struggle that veteran teachers face in fully grasping the nature of these changes and in reframing the ways they work with students.

Cohen's images of Mrs. O raise several questions for those who are concerned about teachers' professional development: In what ways might professional development contribute to a more reflective stance toward instruction? How will teachers be helped to move beyond "relatively superficial" interpretations of national content standards? From whom might Mrs. O get critical feedback on her teaching, and how might constructive criticism be built into the very fabric of professional development? Are there forums within which she might become more comfortable with the uncertainty and rough edges inherent in constructivist approaches to teaching and learning? What kind of professional development could help Mrs. O (and thousands of other Mrs. O's) acquire (or deepen) subject-matter knowledge and what Shulman (1987) calls "pedagogical content knowledge" to prepare for or to improve standards-based curriculum and instruction?

National Content Standards: New Images of Teaching and Learning

Taken individually and collectively, the various standards-setting efforts[3] have portrayed a new picture of "what students should know and be able

[3]Completed or in various stages of development are National Standards for Education in the Arts (Consortium of National Arts Education Associations—Dance, Music, Theater, Visual Arts); National Standards in Civics Education (Center for Civic Education); National

to do" as a consequence of K through 12 subject-matter instruction. The emerging standards, both finished text and ongoing dialogue, reflect common themes as well as broad consensus on the kind of instruction that students must receive if they are to be knowledgeable, active, and productive citizens in the twenty-first century. In the early years of the national content standards discussion, many of the major subject-matter groups were convened under the umbrella of the national Curriculum Congress (since incorporated as the Alliance for Curriculum Reform) to chart this common ground. In less than a day, they compiled a list that included the following objectives:

- higher expectations and standards for all students, not just the college-bound;
- more challenging and interesting content for everyone, based on the assumption that all students can learn whatever they are motivated to learn and when they are given adequate opportunities to learn;
- more heterogeneous grouping of students and less "ability grouping" or tracking;
- more responsiveness to the diverse needs of an increasingly diverse student body;
- more active learning for students and less passivity; more hands-on, direct opportunities to "make meaning" with language, science, mathematics, writing, the arts, etc.; fewer remote, irrelevant, or concocted educational experiences, including textbooks; more primary sources, original documents, and "real-life" contexts;
- more small group learning for students and less isolated learning; more time spent working together cooperatively, as people do in real work and civic situations, and less time spent in competitive learning environments;
- more performance assessment of students and less emphasis on

Standards in Economics Education (National Council for Economics Education); National Standards for English Education (National Council of Teachers of English [NCTE], International Reading Association, and the Center for the Study of Reading); National Standards for Foreign Languages Education (American Council of Teachers of Foreign Languages [ACTFL] and associations for teachers of French, German, Spanish, and Portuguese); National Standards in Geography Education (National Council for Geographic Education); National Standards in History Education (National Center for History in the Schools); Curriculum and Evaluation Standards for School Mathematics, Professional Standards for Teaching Mathematics, and Assessment Standards for Mathematics (National Council of Teachers of Mathematics [NCTM]); National Standards for Physical Education (National Association of Sport and Physical Education [NASPE]); National Science Education Standards (National Research Council [NRC]); and Curriculum Standards for the Social Studies (National Council for the Social Studies [NCSS]).

multiple-choice, norm-referenced testing; more accountability for robust learning experiences and less for test scores;

- more critical and creative thinking and problem solving for students and less emphasis on rote knowledge, drill, and memorization;
- more learning for understanding and less learning for grades or scores; more learning how to learn throughout life;
- more opportunities for teachers to select or tailor learning so students learn a few essential things thoroughly, instead of merely "covering" a large number of things;
- more organization of time around student learning and less organization of time around adult or bureaucratic needs; and
- more diverse kinds of teaching and learning opportunities to accomplish the above goals; new kinds of pre-service and in-service professional development programs to strengthen the capacity of the teaching force to carry out such an agenda; greater involvement of teachers in designing curriculum and assessments (Lord, et al. 1992).

These are not insignificant grounds of agreement; they represent a new vision of teaching and learning and a tall order for teachers' professional development. The conditions, goals, and prescriptions for improvement outlined here are prevalent in the national content standards and reflect the extent of the struggle facing Mrs. O.

A sampling of some of the standards documents and drafts themselves gives a feel for the substance of the new reforms. For example:

National Standards for Arts Education

The Standards ask that students should know and be able to do the following by the time they have completed secondary school:

They should be able to communicate at a basic level in the four arts disciplines—dance, music, theater, and the visual arts. This includes knowledge and skills in the use of the basic vocabularies, materials, tools, techniques, and the intellectual methods of each arts discipline.

They should be able to communicate proficiently in at least one art form, including the ability to define and solve artistic problems with insight, reason, and technical proficiency.

They should be able to develop and present basic analyses of works of art from structural, historical, and cultural perspectives, and from combinations of those perspectives. This includes the ability to understand and evaluate work in the various arts disciplines.

They should have an informed acquaintance with exemplary works of art from a variety of world cultures and historical periods, and a basic understanding of historical development in the arts disciplines, across the arts as a whole, and within cultures.

They should be able to relate various types of arts knowledge and skills within and across the arts disciplines. This includes mixing and matching competencies and understandings in art-making, history and culture, and analysis in any arts-related project. (Consortium of National Arts Education Associations 1994, 18–19)

NCTM Curriculum and Evaluation Standards for School Mathematics

Curriculum Standards for Grades K through 4:

Standard 2: Mathematics as Communication
In grades K through 4, the study of mathematics should include numerous opportunities for communication so that students can:
- relate physical materials, pictures, and diagrams to mathematical ideas;
- reflect on and clarify their thinking about mathematical ideas and situations;
- relate their everyday language to mathematical language and symbols;
- realize that representing, discussing, reading, writing, and listening to mathematics are a vital part of learning and using mathematics.
(National Council of Teachers of Mathematics 1989, 26)
Standard 9: Geometry and Spatial Sense
In grades K through 4, the mathematics curriculum should include two- and three-dimensional geometry so that students can:
- describe, model, draw, and classify shapes;
- investigate and predict the results of combining, subdividing, and changing shapes;
- develop spatial sense;
- relate geometric ideas to number and measurement ideas;
- recognize and appreciate geometry in their world.
(National Council of Teachers of Mathematics 1989, 48)

Curriculum Standards for the Social Studies

Theme: Culture Level: Middle Grades

Standard: Social studies programs should include experiences which provide for the study of culture and cultural diversity, so that the learner can:
a. describe commonalities and differences among cultures;
b. show how information and experiences may be interpreted by people from diverse cultural perspectives and frames of reference;
c. describe how the elements of a culture, such as traditions, beliefs, and values, behavior patterns, and artifacts relate to an integrated whole;

    d. describe and analyze alternatives within and across cultures for dealing with social tensions and issues;

    e. explain why individuals and groups respond to change as they do, given shared assumptions, values, and beliefs;

    f. demonstrate the value of cultural diversity, as well as cohesion, within and across groups.

    (National Council for the Social Studies Task Force 1993, 36, draft quoted with permission)

Curriculum and instruction that embraces standards such as these will confront teachers with the need for a much more comprehensive knowledge base (at each grade level), new models of pedagogical reasoning (Shulman 1987, 14), new instructional strategies, and restructured professional relationships among teachers and between teachers and students (Lord 1992, 5). The challenge for each of the Mrs. O's in each of the subject areas is how best to acquire and share this knowledge, develop new reasoning skills, augment the repertoire of instructional strategies, and build these new relationships. Teachers' work, as presently organized (Elmore 1990; Fullan 1991; Gideonse 1990; Lortie 1975), provides few opportunities and little incentive to tackle these problems head-on. Nor are these problems ameliorated by the penchant of national, state, and local policymakers to restate them as straightforward matters of implementation or systemic alignment. In their landmark study in 1975, Berman and McLaughlin left little room for doubt that traditional models of policy implementation were liable to fail in the complex world of school and classroom. This point was reinforced in Elmore and McLaughlin's 1988 study *Steady Work: Policy Practice and the Reform of American Education.* Attempts to solve Mrs. O's problems by mandate, or worse yet, simply to bypass them by decentralizing responsibility and "holding teachers accountable" will yield the same remarkably unsuccessful outcomes as a long list of reforms dedicated to what Timar and Kirp (1988) termed the "management of educational excellence." Inside the black box of standards-based change lie the knowledge, skill, and judgment of teachers and a set of individual and collective commitments to professional development.

Challenges to the "Dominant Paradigm"

Professional development that is conceptually and practically rooted in what Little calls the "dominant paradigm" (1989) or the "training paradigm" (1993) has little chance of achieving the broader transformations in teaching that are implied (or, in some cases, prescribed) in these evolving standards documents. The principal features of this paradigm, as Little (1989) describes them, are

1. A nearly exclusive focus on the individual as classroom teacher, but in a narrowly conceived way;
2. Centralization of resources and activity;
3. A service delivery mode that is market oriented and menu driven;
4. Low individual or collective opportunity to learn; and
5. Absence of professional development policy (3–4).

Instead of centralized in-service activities emphasizing generic skills development, however, teachers like Mrs. O will need a host of new supports to accelerate and deepen their learning and to guide them through experimentation and the real struggles that accompany change in the classroom. While the more routine forms of staff development have had substantial utility for what teachers need to accomplish in classrooms as they are presently organized and for effectively transmitting the "school knowledge" (McNeil 1988) that is often viewed as obligatory by teachers and students alike, these strategies are in conflict with the challenges of new structure and new knowledge:

> The training-and-coaching strategy that dominates local professional development has much to recommend it when considered as a balanced part of a larger configuration, and when linked to those aspects of teaching that are properly rendered as transferable skills. But the training model is problematic. The content of much training communicates a view of teaching and learning that is at odds with present reform initiatives. (Little 1993, 144)

In short, even at its best, teacher training relies on too small a toolbox for the renovations that the curriculum standards community demands. The desired changes in teaching require greater conceptual sophistication and a set of highly polished pedagogical skills that are only rarely rewarded in today's schools. The tendency, reinforced by current professional development practices, has been to think of teaching in reductionist terms, as a set of behaviors, skills, and items of knowledge to be routinely "applied" in classroom settings. Here, one thinks of the programs that fall under the heading of Competency-Based Teacher Education and Effective Teaching (Richardson 1990). This image of teaching, however, fails to capture what is most crucial to this "uncertain craft" (McDonald 1992), the complex relationships and enduring questions that require the exercise of sound professional judgment. Teachers work in fluid situations, organizing classroom activities and discourse in ways that help students extend their understanding and make connections with concepts already in their grasp. As most teachers are aware, teaching itself can be, and often is, unpredictable. The circumstances in which professional knowledge becomes relevant are difficult to anticipate, but if teachers lack crucial knowledge (as did Mrs. O) they are likely to miss opportunities to advance student learning. This is precisely why teaching demands professionals whose knowledge of subject matter, instruction, and student learning is both broad and deep. It is also why the kind of professional development available to teachers needs to move beyond the dominant modes described by Little (1989, 1993). To become more proficient at "teaching for understanding" (Cohen, McLaughlin, and Talbert 1993), teachers need opportunities to voice and share doubts and frustrations as well as successes and exemplars. They need to ask questions about their own teaching and about their colleagues' teaching. They need to recognize that these questions and how they and their colleagues go about raising them, addressing them, and on occasion even answering them constitute the major focus of professional development.

Teachers' Questions

Consider the kinds of questions that teachers raise, consider the genuine concerns they have about how best to reach their students—this is the grist for professional development experiences. Even teachers like Mrs. O, whose limited knowledge of subject-matter precludes raising certain kinds of questions, are prepared to inquire about their teaching:

> How shall I teach this middle grades unit on gasses and airs when I have had little training in science? Will the hands-on experiments I have planned help clarify or confuse matters? Where do I turn to get guidance on the curriculum? The district no longer has a science supervisor, and the only certified science teacher in the school is committed to paper-and-pencil approaches and a textbook published in 1964.

> Should I have introduced this concept on geometric shape before these students had an opportunity to explore other ideas about measurement? The kids' questions seemed to take us there and they seemed genuinely excited about the material. But do they really have the skills to develop these ideas? How does this affect lesson plans for tomorrow or the rest of the week? I took the chance, took the detour, but now we're a bit behind. I really don't want to leave them hanging on some of these ideas; I need to cover so much material before the achievement tests.

Some of the kids in my tenth-grade class are reading fiction by Dickens and Austen and even Calvino; others have trouble with short passages in the anthology that the department authorized. How do I structure classroom discussions and small group interactions that account for these differences but avoid the kind of tracking that shunts some kids into a dead-end curriculum? I think some of the kids are embarrassed about their reading levels and I don't think I've done a very good job at helping them share their ideas with me or their classmates. I need to do better; I just need some time to think it through, a chance to talk to some other teachers who have more experience than I have, but I have so many papers to grade and I just lost my classroom aide.

The principal just distributed copies of the new . . . Standards; he says we're going to "implement" them over the next three years. I've been teaching 24 years and I have real questions whether these inquiry-based learning and problem-solving approaches are going to work. I'm skeptical that it's going to make much difference for the kids in my classroom, and I'm not ready to throw my work and experience out the window. Where am I going to get the time to experiment with these new approaches? No one else in this school is teaching this way, and the one teacher [who] did try it a couple [of] years ago didn't last six months. I want to see how this is going to work before I jump on board.

These are the kinds of questions and worries, enduring questions and worries, that are part of the fabric of teaching.

Key features of professional development, in the light of national content standards, are to support teachers in their efforts to bring to the surface these questions and concerns, to help teachers expose their classroom practices to other teachers and educators, and to enable teachers to learn from constructive criticism. This is what I term "critical colleagueship." It holds an important place in many other professions and arts (e.g., medicine, scientific research, visual and performing arts) but runs counter to the "norms of privacy" (Little and McLaughlin 1991) that are pervasive in the teaching community. The point is to ask increasingly more powerful and revealing questions about the practice of teaching, especially about those facets of teaching that are influenced by the constructivist approaches so richly described in standards documents and the research literature. This kind of professional development provides support for greater reflectiveness and sustained learning. It invites teachers to think more deeply and experiment more thoroughly with what, for many, are altogether novel ways of teaching. Through exchanges that support the description and redescription of teaching practices, it substitutes a more complex phenomenology of teaching for commonplace instrumentalist accounts. While recognizing the value of technical training, it places that training in a wider context of teachers' questions and strategies. And it stands in opposition to piecemeal approaches that look to staff development as discrete opportunities for skills transmission and acquisition.

This kind of collegiality cannot be fostered in environments of professional isolation. Teachers need to hear other points of view, need to air their own ideas among colleagues whom they trust and respect. Yet the willingness of teachers to serve as commentators and critics of their own or other teachers' practices is dependent, in part, on perceived reciprocity—on the likelihood that other members of a department, a faculty, or the profession more generally, will participate fully. If this reciprocity is in doubt or if the professional community is too small or insular or inexperienced to meet legitimate expectations for new knowledge and productive insights, then teachers may well choose the privacy and security of their own classrooms (as many teachers currently do) and take private paths to professional development. If too many members of the community cannot or will not make meaningful contributions to critical understanding, then teachers will guard their best knowledge and disguise their real doubts about teaching. In other words, there must be a reasonable expectation that a professional community has access to the right kind of resources, that participants share relevant interests and experience, and that collaboration will be real before individual teachers will begin exposing their practice to critical review.

I will return to the concepts of critical colleagueship and professional communities in the subsequent discussion. But first, what are the realities for teachers' professional development today? Do they provide a basis for engaging teachers, especially teachers like Mrs. O, in the kind of learning and professional growth that sit comfortably alongside national content standards?

Current Configurations of Professional Development

What are the principal configurations of professional development that are available to teachers through their schools, districts, professional associations, and other public and private agencies? What kinds of activities or programs are most common? What are the principal costs of these programs? What are teachers' views about participating? While, on the whole, there are very few studies that address these questions in a systematic way, three have provided a preliminary account. Moore and Hyde (1981)—*Making Sense of Staff Development: An Analysis of Staff Development Programs and Their Costs in Three Urban School Districts*, Little et al. (1987)—*Staff Development in California*, and Miller, Lord, and Dorney (1994)—*Staff Development: A Study of Costs and Configurations in Four School Districts* provide some detail on the state of staff development programs, activities, responsibilities, and spending in the K through 12 system. Other studies focusing on the broader context of teaching and its implications for professional development have been conducted by McLaughlin, Talbert, and their colleagues at the Teacher Context Center at Stanford University (McLaughlin 1993; Talbert and McLaughlin in press). While the literature is replete with reports on specific staff development programs and projects, research on broader reform initiatives of which professional development may be a significant part, and discussion of more overarching theoretical issues, there are few comprehensive studies of current practices. Given the weight of reform that rests on the possibilities for change among the nation's corps of veteran teachers, the fact that the larger picture of teachers' professional development has been so little studied is both surprising and worrisome.

The research findings from the three major studies cited above help frame a common picture. The major features are:

1. Teachers rely on district-sponsored staff development programs and activities for the larger part of their professional development;
2. These programs and teachers' experiences of them tend to be fragmented; responsibilities for staff development are spread across a multiplicity of district offices and seldom does the district have a unifying vision or strategy that links these efforts.
3. District staff often serve as staff development providers or coordinators, although, as most districts experience budget cutbacks, these positions are being eliminated or consolidated with other projects or positions that have responsibilities other than staff development.[4]
4. Central office staff continue to rely on one-shot activities that emphasize technical skills development and have limited follow-up, and often turn to large-group sessions in order to "reach" more teachers.
5. Few staff development activities provide teachers with opportunities for extended cooperative work, for experimentation, risk-taking, or

---

[4]In a few districts, central office staff have begun to serve less as providers or regulators of staff development and more as co-collaborators or supporters of school- or teacher-designed activities. The transition from regulatory role to technical assistance role is an enormous challenge for district bureaucracies; an atmosphere of residual distrust often affects these relationships.

inquiry that requires thoughtful critique of one's own work and that of others.

6. The principal cost of teachers' professional development is the salaries of staff development providers and participants.[5] There is comparatively little money devoted to collegial activities such as teacher networks, institute participation, or conference attendance. Support for these activities, where it exists, often comes from federal or private sources, although some states have funded professional development networks. Teachers' travel is especially constrained during tight fiscal times, and coupled with teachers' limited access to telephone or other forms of electronic communication, teachers' professional contact with colleagues is severely limited.

7. Few teachers are satisfied with the nature or extent of district-sponsored staff development efforts, and only a small number participate in more intensive or sustained professional development programs;

8. Teachers are seldom expected to assume additional responsibilities as a consequence of their professional development. In other words, schools and districts seldom capitalize on their investment in teachers' learning. With the exception of small numbers of "mentor teachers" or "career teachers," few teachers assume new roles vis-à-vis their colleagues or new instructional assignments that would take advantage of acquired knowledge or skills. The expectation is that students will reap the return on investment, although there is seldom any sustained evaluation or review of programs to determine whether students benefit.

9. Staff development often serves as a political football. Central office staff and school administrators use staff development as a public response to the "problem of the day." "Our teachers have been (are being) trained to do *x*" (where *x* is a variable covering anything from multiculturalism and race sensitivity to performance assessment or effective schools practices) is a refrain that provides political cover.

Beneath the Surface of Current Practice

The image of teachers' professional development that emerges from these studies stands in stark contrast to the images and expectations of teach-

---

[5]Moore and Hyde (1981) and Little (1989) include the present value of teachers' future salary increases as a major cost of staff development. Miller, Lord, and Dorney (1994) do not. Even without the addition of future salary increases, however, provider and participant salary costs are the highest costs for district-sponsored staff development. This is not surprising, given the labor-intensive character of professional development work.

ing that are implicit in national content and teaching standards. It is fair to ask why professional development has taken this shape; the answers may provide some direction for what we might do differently, or, at the very least, for thinking more clearly about staff development practices.

First, staff development traditionally has been valued for its *instrumental* significance. In this view, teachers' sole responsibility is the education of students and, consequently, any activities that do not contribute directly to student achievement or welfare are not part of the teacher's job. Teachers are the instruments through which knowledge is transmitted to students, and the place where this happens is in classrooms. "Teaching" is something one does exclusively in the presence of students. This view is broadly shared in the education community, even, or perhaps especially, among teachers. They often voice a reluctance to leave the classroom or desert their students in order to pursue their own professional development. Many will argue that they have too little time with students as it is without these additional absences. Another consequence of instrumentalist reasoning is that absences for professional development purposes can be justified only insofar as the staff development experience provides direct (and preferably measurable) benefits to students, e.g., new approaches to using materials or technology or new techniques for working with students in cooperative groups. In short, while many teachers often express a desire for professional development that is intellectually challenging, others prefer programs with immediate payoff, something that will improve opportunities for their students and thus serve as a warrant for time away from the classroom.

Second, the *dominant epistemology* governing staff development work continues to be *reductionistic and positivistic*. It is assumed that knowledge about curriculum, instruction, and assessment *can* be broken down into discrete elements (neatly packaged in one-shot workshops), noncontroversial (free of conflict, criticism, or real debate), context-independent, and empirically verifiable or replicable. Knowledge that fits this description can be transmitted by telling and is not subject to continual revision and renewal. Pervasive in district staff development programs is the view that "one size fits all," and that change in practice follows directly on change in knowledge. Teachers' questions, doubts, skepticism, and uncertainty are seldom addressed in staff development workshops or in-service activities; instead, technical knowledge is offered as a practical solution to the question of what teachers need to know. It is not surprising that this epistemology reinforces and even fosters anti-intellectualism in the teaching community. Knowledge is constructed and imported from outside the community of practicing teachers, and little credence is given to perceptions, experiences, and ideas that have their origins inside the classroom. Teachers often discount and distrust outsiders' knowledge, and this clearly impedes the effectiveness of staff development activities and programs.

Third, prevailing forms of staff development for teachers are *bureaucratically manageable, measurable*, and, in a limited way, *equitable*. District-sponsored professional development draws on public funds and thus is subject to public accountability. Mandated workshops or in-service days can be centrally organized and empirically shown to reach a large number of teachers. Administrators can construct a per teacher cost and thus better argue for the cost-effectiveness of their programs. Of course, little is known about the success of these programs in enriching teachers' understanding or deepening their knowledge, nor is much effort made to design links among different activities that might expand the overall power of a learning experience. In contrast, it is difficult to achieve high levels of accountability with what Little (1993) calls the "messier" types of professional development. It presents a challenge, for example, to determine how many teachers participate (or how often they participate) in staff development activities such as collegial study groups or teacher collaboratives or to identify what it is that these teachers actually do when they work together.

Often not far beneath the surface of district-sponsored staff development programs is a very admirable impulse to provide equal opportunity or equal access to professional development experiences for all teachers in a district. Where resources are extremely limited, fair-minded administrators organize programs to ensure broad and equitable access under conditions of scarcity. The upshot of this approach is that many, most, or even all teachers receive the same treatment despite significant differences in what, where, whom, and how they teach. Instead of programs that emphasize opportunities to experiment, raise hard questions, or explore in depth, staff development is reduced to discrete experiences that do little more than introduce a topic or technique. Like some early reform efforts that centered on equal educational opportunity, this impulse toward equity in staff development concentrates too little on the quality, relevance, and appropriateness of the opportunities themselves.

Alongside these issues of equity and managerial and fiscal accountability for staff development stands the district's political accountability for education change and responsiveness. Demands for reform cover a wide spectrum of education philosophies and political constituencies, e.g., demands for multiculturalism, demands for basic education, demands for constructivist teaching and learning, demands for integrated curricula, and demands for integration of educational and social services. These demands require district response and, in politically charged times, one of the principal salves at the disposal of the central office is the banner of staff development. Teacher training is a politically viable and visible response to complex issues surrounding education change and improvement.

Contradictions in Current Practice

What are the internal contradictions embodied in the training model, and how do these contradictions sow the seeds for a different approach?

Contradiction 1. Many teachers need and demand short-term results from staff development work. Short-term results, however, seldom add up to substantial change, and staff development that emphasizes such results contributes to the perception, if not the reality, of a "deskilled" occupation (Apple 1988). Teachers are left hungry for more substantial professional development experiences and for more control over what counts as substance. The urgent need for additional support, given increasingly complex curricular, demographic, and social issues, pushes teachers and staff developers toward quick-fix solutions that often only compound problems and leave both participants and providers frustrated by the lack of progress. Teachers' initial impulse is to insist that the new information, skills, and techniques acquired result in demonstrable outcomes and observable classroom utility. This promise of immediate utility serves as a magnet for attracting teachers into staff development programs and as a means for overcoming teachers' a priori objections to leaving the classroom for purposes of continued learning. Districtwide efforts to supply this kind of narrow, instrumental staff development seldom meet the needs of more than a few teachers, however, and leave a legacy of unmet needs and professional frustration.

Contradiction 2. The effort to reach all teachers in a district in order to achieve widespread results leads to a precariously thin staff development program and little real change. The intensity or intensiveness of such experiences is so weak that they fail to have a deep or lasting effect on any teacher despite having reached every teacher. Although teachers sit together during large-group sessions, they seldom engage in protracted dialogue and learn little about one another's work. This artificial collegiality drives teachers to seek other avenues of professional interaction or to seek other rewards in teaching.

Contradiction 3. The goal of providing skills training for individual practitioners (with limited follow-up or feedback) leads to isolated efforts at implementation of innovations or to pro forma compliance with curricular and instructional policies. It limits critical review of teachers' efforts to change their practices and denies the profession a cumulative record of the effectiveness of new ways of teaching. It leads to highly differentiated implementation, a "melange of traditional and novel approaches" (Cohen 1990, 312), as teachers try to patch together a coherent instructional program out of disparate policies and other external influences. Teachers' efforts to adapt new ideas to current practices and to develop connections between disjointed staff development experiences become invisible. *Contradiction 4.* Most district-sponsored staff development takes the form of telling or telling combined with superficial discussion sessions or workshop practice. The national content standards, however, emphasize broader conceptual understanding and the exercise of teachers' judgment. The standards suggest that teachers should facilitate student learning by helping them construct meaning through problem solving and inquiry. Staff development in the transmission model provides little opportunity for teachers to enlarge their subject-matter knowledge or experiment with altogether new instructional strategies. Teachers are denied the opportunities for inquiry-based learning, though policymakers and staff-development providers insist that these same teachers embrace this new approach in their classroom instruction.

Rethinking Professional Development

The dismal state of most district-sponsored staff development, the conceptual impoverishment of many activities and programs, and the internal contradictions that decrease the effectiveness of staff development experiences while increasing professional isolation and frustration suggest that we approach teachers' professional development from a different angle. We know little about Mrs. O's staff development experiences. Cohen observes that neither she nor other educators or policymakers had asked "how she saw her math teaching in light of the Framework" (1990, 325). Beyond this, we know little about the nature or extent of the support she received. But it is important to consider what might help her, and others like her, to gain a better grasp of subject matter and become more comfortable with new approaches to teaching and learning. What are some of the crucial factors that might improve Mrs. O's prospects for substantive change? In the remainder of this section, I consider two interrelated approaches that might prove fruitful for invigorating teachers' professional development. The first of these is critical colleagueship, the second resource-rich professional communities. My remarks on each of these topics are preliminary and speculative. There is not a large base of empirical evidence to support a call for professional development that reflects the particular virtues, capacities, or professional relationships that I describe below, but, nonetheless, by beginning to redescribe the process of professional development itself, we may be able to lay the ground for further research and development.

Critical Colleagueship

In the past decade much has been written about the virtues and challenges of collegiality and collaboration in helping teachers improve their practice. (See, for example, Fullan 1991; Lieberman, Saxl, and Miles 1988; Little 1990a, 1990b; Little and McLaughlin 1991; Lord 1992; McLaughlin and Yee 1988.) While the positive influences of greater collegiality are not automatic (Little and McLaughlin 1991), there is a substantial body of research pointing to a range of benefits for teachers. Among these are greater openness regarding classroom practice, mutual obligation to share knowledge, collective planning and design of curriculum and instruction, and opportunities for exercising leadership. These benefits alone, however, will provide, at best, a limited foundation for standards-based teaching. For a broader transformation, collegiality will need to support a critical stance toward teaching. This means more than simply sharing ideas or supporting one's colleagues in the change process. It means confronting traditional practice—the teacher's own and that of his or her colleagues—with an eye toward wholesale revision.

Among the elements of critical colleagueship are the following:

1. Creating and sustaining productive disequilibrium through self-reflection, collegial dialogue, and on-going critique.
2. Embracing fundamental intellectual virtues. Among these are openness to new ideas, willingness to reject weak practices or flimsy reasoning when faced with countervailing evidence and sound arguments, accepting responsibility for acquiring and using relevant information in the construction of technical arguments, willingness to seek out the best ideas or the best knowledge from within the subject-matter communities, greater reliance on organized and deliberate investigations rather than learning by accident, and assuming collective responsibility for creating a professional record of teachers' research and experimentation.
3. Increasing the capacity for empathetic understanding (placing oneself in a colleague's shoes). That is, understanding a colleague's dilemma in the terms in which he or she understands it.
4. Developing and honing the skills and attributes associated with negotiation, improved communication, and the resolution of competing interests.

5. Increasing teachers' comfort with high levels of ambiguity and uncertainty, which will be regular features of teaching for understanding.
6. Achieving collective generativity—"Knowing how to go on" (Wittgenstein 1958)—as a goal of successful inquiry and practice.

These are virtues and capacities that, if well practiced and deeply held, would help teachers like Mrs. O make the transition from traditional models of curriculum and instruction to the constructivist, inquiry-based approaches favored in the national content standards. In fact, they are virtues that are constitutive of standards-based instruction itself. The claim here is that teachers' professional development that has as its aim the transformation of teaching can be *identified* with the growth of these attributes.

Unfortunately, most teachers simply do not have the tools, background, preparation, or appropriate opportunities for developing or exercising the traits of critical colleagueship. At few points in their professional preparation and seldom in their classroom work do teachers have opportunities to observe other teachers teach, to be observed as they teach, to engage in open and constructively critical discussions about what they observe and what they do, or to reflect on new ideas, practices, and policies that influence teaching. The fragmented and discontinuous learning experiences that Goodlad and his colleagues (1990, 27–34) describe as ubiquitous in teacher education institutions do little to prepare teachers for engaging actively with their colleagues to discuss key issues of professional practice:

> There is a renewing kind of "tension" between the frontiers of what is known and the frontline implementing of day-to-day practice that [is] present in medicine and law but absent in education. (Robert Levin in Goodlad, Soder, and Sirotkin 1990, 61)

Engagement with the frontier of knowledge in the context of ongoing classroom practice is foreign to most teachers, even those prepared in state flagship or research universities. There is little common ground for discussion about what constitutes good practice (teachers' training experiences are likely to be quite diverse and not deeply rooted in a common canon of pedagogy and content) and little commitment to subjecting any teacher's views, opinions, or claims of knowledge to critical review. Time for reflection is limited by the many demands on teachers' time, and teachers often respond to new classroom challenges or demands by turning to the most reliable routines. This was clearly Mrs. O's response to some of the subtleties of the California Mathematics Framework.

These shortcomings in teacher preparation and development are compounded by the random or accidental character of teachers' efforts to acquire new knowledge and skills. Veteran teachers often hear about new ideas, methods, and strategies from the colleague next door, from a grade-level leader or department chair, or from an eclectic army of materials that sift down through the central office, academic department, or resource teacher. These new influences are seldom a consequence of a concerted and sustained program of investigation undertaken by the teacher or his or her colleagues. Neither the teaching profession nor district bureaucracies have provided appropriate incentives or adequate support for teachers to undertake organized research.

Whereas traditional models of staff development are predicated on sameness and the functionalist purposes of training, critical colleagueship depends on difference and conflict as driving forces. This is what is meant by "productive disequilibrium." Instead of relying on routine dissemination of information and techniques to inspire new practices, critical colleagueship turns to increased reflection, informed debate, honest disagreement, and constructive conflict as tools of change. The kinds of changes that the education community is asking Mrs. O to make have not been well charted. There is ample room for challenging, rethinking, or even rejecting some dimensions of this new approach. Despite its privileged position in recent cognitive theory and its favorable treatment in standards documents, constructivism, for all practical purposes, remains a collection of unrealized images and "promissory notes" (Wolf 1994). Teachers will need to evaluate and translate the central concepts of constructivism into tangible and coherent classroom practice. In part, this means that Mrs. O must develop those dispositions or habits of mind that provoke self-examination of classroom practices. It means she must probe deeper and ask better questions about the nature of curriculum, instruction, and student learning. It means inviting collegial observation and critique of her own teaching and engaging in critical review of the teaching of others, whether that of her colleagues or that represented through sufficiently rich case studies. Standards-based instruction requires that teachers abandon some of the comfort of routine and look beyond the initial attempts to implement a policy or program. For example, Mrs. O needs to ask better questions about her use of manipulatives with students; she needs to work with colleagues to help her formulate these questions and the search for answers; and she needs to seek out informed critique of these and other elements of her practice. This invites conflict, discomfort, and dissonance, but these are the prices for a more than superficial response to content standards or frameworks. Mrs. O may feel strongly that her approach to teaching mathematics contributes to greater understanding than another teacher's inquiry-based approach, and these differences could precipitate lively argument and disagreement about how to proceed. But bringing this disagreement to the surface and openly challenging the culture of noninterference (Pellegrin 1976) that has become so deeply entrenched in the world of teaching are crucial components of self-renewing change. Professional development that is tied to standards-based reform will reflect this critical stance. It will emphasize negotiation and debate among colleagues and place significant weight on teachers' self-directed inquiries as they actively seek resolution of their differences.

Reframing and redescribing the everyday activities of teaching in ways that promote new insight into subject matter and student learning are crucial to the success of critical colleagueship. Professional development in the context of national standards is not about solving the problem of the day or about introducing a new trick of the trade, but rather about seeing or "reading" teaching in novel ways, in ways that provide productive or pregnant insights into an exchange with a student, the shape of a lesson, the organization of the curriculum, or the strength or weakness of a particular text. Review, reflection, and critique are essential to effective teaching because teaching itself so often relies on "knowledge-in-action" (Schon 1983) or "personal knowledge" (Polanyi 1958), an implicit understanding of actions, decisions, and classroom discourse that may prove difficult to characterize, describe, or analyze. One of the defining objectives of critical colleagueship, then, is to provide opportunities for teachers to talk about their teaching, to understand the value and the power of their own descriptions.

At the core of increased reflectiveness is learning to question current concepts about subject matter and other elements of instruction and student learning. By holding up to examination taken-for-granted assumptions and everyday concepts and beliefs, teachers are able to build a more coherent conceptual foundation to support practice. This is especially important in the case of staff development programs and activities that support standards-based reforms. At present, few teachers share the concepts related to subject-matter content and instruction that standards documents take as fundamental and that serve as a point of departure for constructivist teaching and learning. In order to integrate these concepts into a meaningful and consistent picture of highly accomplished teaching (National Board for Professional Teaching Standards 1993), teachers must first question the concepts (assumptions, images, pictures) that currently drive their practice. The futility of trying to lay a complex, constructivist epistemology on top of more behaviorist, competency-based approaches to teaching has been pointed out in recent research (Cohen 1990; Cohen and Spillane 1992; Darling-Hammond 1993). The aim of professional development must be to expose assumptions about teaching (some of which are archaic and even damaging to students) and to produce what I have called productive disequilibrium in traditional concepts and daily routines. This approach is not, as any administrator or policymaker would acknowledge, an easy sell. When the consequence of staff development activities or involvements is professional discomfort or conflict, it is difficult to see an immediate benefit for students and thus to rationalize this use of teacher time.

What kinds of professional development promote these elements of critical colleagueship? They include, but are not limited to, informal study groups, peer observation and critique, case studies and case construction (see, for example, Barnett 1992; Barnett and Sather 1992); action research (Watt 1993); journal writing and analysis (Duckworth 1987); multimedia reconstruction of classroom experiences (Ball, Lampert, and Rosenberg 1993); story construction that relates teachers' struggles, not merely teachers' successes (Driscoll, Miller, and Dorney 1992); teacher leadership programs (Driscoll and Miller 1993); grant writing, proposal review, and project management (e.g., the small grants program implemented by the *Local Education Funds*); curriculum development and field testing; conference presentations; publication in professional journals; and review of national content standards. This is clearly a different picture of professional development from the training or peer coaching models that absorb the time and resources of most school districts today. It suggests a different set of responsibilities and obligations for teachers, but also provides a set of opportunities for strengthening the profession.

Expanding a Resource-Rich Professional Community

Critical colleagueship is, in many respects, a local activity. Small groups of teachers form communities of interest around matters related to their teaching. They tackle projects together, they review cases together, they develop curriculum together, they work, in general, toward improving their teaching. Predicated on openness and trust, these communities require face-to-face communication and frequent opportunities to strengthen professional relationships. The questions that teachers raise in these local communities are first and foremost, questions that emerge from their classrooms or in local context. This connection to the classroom is one of the factors contributing to greater authenticity of professional development. But there are very real problems with this strongly localistic cast to collegial work. First, it is fair to ask whether the questions that teachers pose in these local settings are well framed, for example, whether they take account of national content standards or whether they build on similar questions being asked by teachers in the next school or the next district. Second, do local forms of colleagueship, inspired by national content standards and/or state curriculum frameworks, create a set of programs or activities that, taken together, make sense for the district, its schools and students? In short, how can local efforts to develop critical colleagueship avoid parochialism and ensure some coherence in the professional development program?

These questions become particularly acute in the face of efforts by many districts to decentralize and restructure roles and responsibilities for all facets of school policy, including professional development. The focus of these efforts has been largely on helping schools and school systems function more effectively in the face of overwhelming change (Schlechty 1990); it has dealt less with how teachers within these schools and school systems acquire, use, and share new knowledge about academic content, instruction, and student learning. This is not meant as a criticism of school restructuring; for critical colleagueship to flourish in schools, the conditions of teachers' work will need to change dramatically, and this means reinventing the organization of school itself. It is to say, however, that turning too much attention inward, drawing only or largely on the intellectual and material resources within the school, is dangerously limiting. While improving school culture or school climate can improve educational opportunities for our K through 12 students, it may still leave unaddressed the question of how teachers will come by the knowledge that they need in order to transform teaching in and across the subject areas.

One of the criticisms frequently leveled at the national content standards movement is that it tears the curriculum standards discussion out of the hands of local practitioners and turns it over to a community of policy-makers, legislators, and curriculum professionals. In the place of standards-driven reform, some critics urge personalization and responsiveness to students in educational programs and practice. The danger in this focus, I believe, is that teachers are invited, indeed encouraged, to initiate change based on their best knowledge *within the classroom or within the four walls of the school*. Lord et al.'s (1992) argument that small groups of teachers in isolation and with only their independent experiences of curriculum and instruction to guide them can, individually or collectively, create a restructured education environment in which students will have access to a comprehensive, balanced, and challenging curriculum seems fundamentally flawed. The point of the movement toward the professionalization of teaching and toward the wider influence of national content standards is that teachers need and should turn to a broader community of educators and education resources to inform local judgments. Compare the case of medicine. We expect when we enter a hospital in Kansas or Louisiana or Michigan that the doctors who provide treatment and the institution itself have a shared standard of practice for performing a coronary bypass—not identical practice, but practice that is well-informed, current, and subject to outside review. We might also expect that when we enter a school in Kansas or Louisiana or Michigan that teachers and schools have a shared standard of practice for offering instruction in human biology or U.S. history or mathematical probability—again, not identical practice, but practice that is well-informed, current, and subject to outside review. Only rarely and in a small number of schools will teachers be sufficiently well-informed about new models of teaching and learning to ensure a shared high standard of practice. This suggests that the principal goal of staff development reform should be to expand the community within which teachers focus exclusively on their own work or draw on whatever knowledge is readily at hand.

To overcome the insularity of teaching and to bolster the knowledge base within the profession, teachers need access to resource-rich professional communities. There is no one right model for these communities; indeed, we are just beginning to collect evidence on what they are and how they engage teachers in innovation and mutual support. (See, for example, Jennings 1993; Little and McLaughlin 1991; Lord 1992; Talbert and McLaughlin in press.) They include teacher networks like Collaboratives for Humanities and Arts Teaching (CHART) and Urban Mathematics Collaboratives (UMC), the Bay Area Writing Project, the California Subject-Matter Projects, a number of university/school partnerships and collaborations, cross-school or cross-district visitation teams, and increasingly, the activities of the major subject-matter associations, e.g., NCTM, National Science Teachers Association (NSTA), NCSS, NCTE, and others. Among the characteristics that account for the family resemblance across these professional communities are

1. Teacher ownership or, at the very least, increased partnership for teachers in decisions regarding professional development activities.
2. A collective commitment to acquiring and using new knowledge in the subject areas, especially knowledge that could be characterized as "cutting edge" (Little and McLaughlin 1991).
3. A reliable connection to resource-rich institutions, organizations, or associations independent of the school or school district, e.g., university education, liberal arts, and science departments, as well as

      libraries, museums, theaters, businesses and industries, and civic agencies.

4. Intensive, and in some cases long-term, professional relationships among participants.
5. A perspective on the profession of teaching that extends beyond the four walls of the school and beyond the duration of individual teachers' careers.
6. A greater commitment to "lateral accountability" (Wolf 1994) within the teaching profession, i.e., the critical review of teachers' practices by other teachers.
7. High levels of teacher involvement in the reform of systemwide structures.

Not all resource-rich professional communities have the same features: teacher networks may emphasize teacher ownership of professional development activities; partnerships with industry may emphasize access to professionals in fields other than education; subject-matter associations may emphasize a perspective that is national in scope and help to build cross-district professional relationships. All, however, set the stage for critical colleagueship and serve as a safeguard against parochialism in teachers' professional development.

    Much has been written recently about the role of subject-area networks and alliances in teachers' professional development, but less has been said about the role of subject-matter associations in fostering programs or activities that lead to more profound engagement among colleagues and deeper knowledge of the field. Indeed, some have commented on the invisibility of the major associations in the professional development arena. For example, Little maintains:

> The place of teachers' professional associations remains nearly invisible in the mainstream professional development literature. We know little about the role played by the largest and most prominent subject matter associations (NCTE, NCTM, NSTA, and others) in the professional lives of teachers or in shaping teachers' disposition toward particular reforms. Although it is clear that the subject associations are exerting an increasingly powerful influence in the articulation of subject curriculum and assessment standards, we have virtually no record of the specific nature or extent of discussion and debate over subject matter reform. (1993, 135)

While Little is correct that the research literature provides few clues on the role of subject-matter associations in teachers' professional development, there is, nonetheless, ample evidence of their involvement, if not of their overall impact in this arena.

Although subject-matter associations are not closely allied with district-sponsored staff development and may not view their primary mission as teachers' professional development, many of their programs and activities support critical colleagueship as defined here. They are among the resource-rich professional communities that engage teachers around subject-matter knowledge and that provide teachers with access to a wider network of education professionals—researchers, curriculum developers and, most important, other teachers. In many respects, the subject-matter associations are stage-setters for new models of professional development. For example, the associations support:

- standards-setting efforts that involve teachers in formulation, review, and critique, not simply in implementation;
- national and regional conferences whose sessions increasingly reflect both the debate over standards and the process of shifting instruction to more student-centered, constructivist approaches. (See the NCTM 1994 annual meeting program and the NCSS seventy-third annual meeting program.) These conferences provide opportunities for teachers to hear and participate in a national dialogue, to interact with colleagues beyond the boundaries of a district, and to glimpse possibilities that may not be part of accepted practice at the local level;
- publications that provide some voice for accomplished teachers and a vehicle to ensure at least some cumulation of knowledge in the field. These include anthologies, yearbooks, journals, magazines, newsletters, and updates aimed at practicing teachers; and
- supporting materials (text, video, CD-ROM—the NCTM Addenda Series is an example) that help give shape to standards-based teaching and reform and further teachers' efforts to develop a critical stance toward their teaching.

Of course, the impact of these efforts is diminished by the distance of subject-matter associations from factors that affect teachers' professional lives. Historically these associations have not had control over teachers' entry into the profession or over advancement throughout a career. State and local education agencies have laid claim to these occupational levers and, thus, distanced teachers' associations from effective authority over the norms of professional development. Increasing their influence may require nontraditional approaches to professional development such as:

- technical assistance teams and monetary subsidies to support local collaboratives, networks, and alliances engaged in active inquiry about subject matter and instruction;

- leadership institutes that help teachers acquire the communication and negotiation skills that are necessary for systemwide change;
- establishing or expanding electronic networks that support "structured conversations" among teachers throughout the nation;
- expanding local, regional, and national teachers' academies in the subject areas;
- establishing or expanding small grants programs that support innovative teaching in the subject areas; and
- approaching national standards as "living documents," the basis for ongoing discussions and debate among teachers.

Collaboratives, teacher networks, partnerships, and alliances have fared little better than subject-matter associations in exerting influence over the direction and control of teachers' professional development writ large. For the most part, these groups have operated at the margins of local school district life (Lord 1992) and with weak or peripheral connections to the mainstream staff-development initiatives offered by central office staff. This isn't surprising, since part of the attraction of collaboratives and teacher networks is their independence from large, impersonal bureaucracies and their critical stance toward current classroom practices. It does present a problem, however, for efforts to embed teachers' professional development in larger efforts to reform systemwide structures.

The challenge for resource-rich professional communities, whether subject-matter associations, teacher networks, collaboratives, or other teachers' groups, is to create professional development opportunities that are intellectually vigorous, self-renewing, and more rewarding for participants than the limited menu of district-sponsored programs. Ideally, these communities would become a viable option to narrowly conceived inservice activities and a model for professional growth that could be incorporated in district policies and practice.

Conclusion

National content standards require of most teachers a "revolution" in their teaching. The changes they are being asked to make go to the heart of professional practice—to closely held views about what counts as knowledge, to the organization of instruction, and to working relationships with colleagues. This kind of transformation comes from the inside; it will do little good to "train" teachers or "tell" teachers how it's done. Professional development that upholds this revolution will stay close to teachers' questions and concerns, reflect the intellectual virtues of serious inquiry, and recognize the place of critical colleagueship in self-renewing change. While not a panacea, it is one strategy for helping Mrs. O find her way off thin ice and back onto solid ground.

References

Apple, Michael W. 1988. *Teachers and Texts: A Political Economy of Class and Gender Relations in Education.* New York: Routledge.

Ball, Deborah, Magdalene Lampert, and Mark Rosenberg. 1993. "Using Multimedia Technology to Support a New Pedagogy of Teacher Education." Invited demonstration, American Educational Research Association annual meeting, Atlanta, Ga., April.

Barnett, Carne. 1992. "Building a Case-Based Curriculum to Enhance the Pedagogical Content Knowledge of Mathematics Teachers." *Journal of Teacher Education* 42.

Barnett, Carne, and Susan Sather. 1992. "Using Case Discussions to Promote Changes in Beliefs among Mathematics Teachers." Presentation at the annual meeting of the American Educational Research Association, San Francisco, April.

Berman, Paul, and Milbrey W. McLaughlin. 1975. *Federal Programs Supporting Educational Change. Vol. IV: The Findings in Review.* Santa Monica, Calif.: Rand Corporation, R/1589-4, April.

Cohen, David K. 1990. "A Revolution in One Classroom: The Case of Mrs. Oublier." *Educational Evaluation and Policy Analysis* 12.

Cohen, David K., Milbrey W. McLaughlin, and Joan E. Talbert, eds. 1993. *Teaching for Understanding.* San Francisco: Jossey Bass.

Consortium of National Arts Education Associations. 1994. *National Standards for Arts Education.* Reston, Va.: Music Educators National Conference.

Darling-Hammond, Linda. 1993. "Reframing the School Reform Agenda: Developing Capacity for School Transformation." *Phi Delta Kappan* 74.

Driscoll, Mark, Barbara Miller, and Judith Dorney. 1992. Unpublished proposal. Education Development Center.

Driscoll, Mark, and Barbara Miller. 1993. Unpublished proposal. Education Development Center.

Duckworth, Eleanor. 1987. *The Having of Wonderful Ideas.* New York: Teachers College Press.

Elmore, Richard F. 1990. "Introduction: On Changing the Structure of Public Schools." In *Restructuring Schools: The Next Generation of Reform*, ed. Richard Elmore and Associates. San Francisco: Jossey Bass.

Fullan, Michael G. 1991. *The New Meaning of Educational Change.* New York: Teachers College Press.

Gideonse, Hendrik D. 1990. "Organizing Schools to Encourage Teacher Inquiry." In *Restructuring Schools: The Next Generation of Reform*, ed. Richard Elmore and Associates. San Francisco: Jossey Bass.

Goodlad, John I., Roger Soder, and Kenneth Sirotkin, eds. 1990. *Places Where Teachers are Taught.* San Francisco: Jossey Bass.

Jennings, Randolph. 1993. *Fire in the Eyes of Youth: The Humanities in American Education.* Philadelphia: Collaboratives for Humanities and Arts Teaching.

Levin, Robert A. 1990. "Recurring Themes and Variations." In *Places Where Teachers are Taught*, eds. John I. Goodlad, Roger Soder, and Kenneth Sirotkin. San Francisco: Jossey Bass.

Lieberman, Ann, Ellen R. Saxl, and Matthew B. Miles. 1988. "Teacher Leadership: Ideology and Practice." In *Building a Professional Culture in Schools*, ed. Ann Lieberman. New York: Teachers College Press.

Little, Judith W. 1989. Untitled paper prepared for the Teacher Networks Group Seminar on Staff Development, June.

Little, Judith W. 1990a. "Conditions of Professional Development in Secondary Schools." In *The Contexts of Teaching in Secondary Schools*, eds. Milbrey McLaughlin, Joan Talbert, and Nina Bascia. New York: Teachers College Press.

Little, Judith W. 1990b. "Teachers as Colleagues." In *Schools as Collaborative Cultures: Creating the Future Now*, ed. Ann Lieberman. New York: Falmer Press.

Little, Judith W. 1993. "Teachers' Professional Development in a Climate of Educational Reform." *Educational Evaluation and Policy Analysis* 15.

Little, Judith W., William H. Gerritz, David S. Stern, James W. Guthrie, Michael W. Kirst, and David D. Marsh. 1987. *Staff Development in California*. San Francisco: Far West Lab and PACE.

Little, Judith W., and Milbrey W. McLaughlin. 1991. "Urban Math Collaboratives: As the Teachers Tell It." Stanford, Calif.: Center for Research on the Context of Secondary Teaching, April.

Lord, Brian T. 1992. *Subject-Area Collaboratives, Teacher Professionalism, and Staff Development*. Newton, Mass.: Education Development Center, Reports and Papers in Progress.

Lord, Brian T., Barbara Miller, and the Alliance for Curriculum Reform Working Groups. 1992. *New Directions in Curriculum Change*. Paper prepared for the Alliance for Curriculum Reform, April.

Lortie, Dan C. 1975. *Schoolteacher: A Sociological Study*. Chicago: University of Chicago Press.

McDonald, Joseph P. 1992. *Teaching: Making Sense of an Uncertain Craft*. New York: Teachers College Press.

McLaughlin, Milbrey W. 1993. "What Matters Most in Teachers' Workplace Context?" In *Teachers' Work: Individuals, Colleagues, and Contexts*, eds. Judith Little and Milbrey McLaughlin. New York: Teachers College Press.

McLaughlin, Milbrey W., and Sylvia Mei-ling Yee. 1988. "School as a Place to Have a Career." In *Building a Professional Culture in Schools*, ed. Ann Lieberman. New York: Teachers College Press.

McNeil, Linda M. 1988. *Contradictions of Control: School Structure and School Knowledge*. New York: Routledge.

Miller, Barbara, Brian Lord, and Judith Dorney. 1994. *Staff Development: A Study of Costs and Configurations in Four School Districts*. Newton, Mass.: Education Development Center, Reports and Papers in Progress.

Moore, Donald R., and Arthur A. Hyde. 1981. *Making Sense of Staff Development: An Analysis of Staff Development Programs and their Costs in Three Urban School Districts*. Chicago: Designs for Change, April.

National Board for Professional Teaching Standards. 1993. Letter from David Mandel. October 25.

National Council for the Social Studies Task Force. 1993. *Curriculum Standards for the Social Studies*. Draft, April.

National Council of Teachers of Mathematics. 1989. *Curriculum and Evaluation Standards for School Mathematics*. March.

Pellegrin, R. J. 1976. "Schools as Work Settings." In *Handbook of Work, Organization, and Society*, ed. Robert Dubin. Skokie, Ill.: Rand McNally.

Polanyi, Michael. 1958. *Personal Knowledge*. Chicago: University of Chicago Press.

Richardson, Virginia. 1990. "The Evolution of Reflective Teaching and Teacher Education." In *Encouraging Reflective Practice in Education*, eds. Renee Clift, W. Robert Houston, and Marleen Pugach. New York: Teachers College Press.

Schlechty, Philip C. 1990. *Schools for the 21st Century.* San Francisco: Jossey Bass.

Schon, Donald A. 1983. *The Reflective Practitioner.* New York: Basic Books.

Shulman, Lee S. 1987. "Knowledge and Teaching: Foundations of the New Reform." *Harvard Educational Review* 57.

Talbert, Joan E., and Milbrey W. McLaughlin. In press. "Teacher Professionalism in Local School Contexts." *American Journal of Education.*

Timar, Thomas B., and David L. Kirp. 1988. *Managing Educational Excellence.* New York: Falmer.

Watt, Molly. 1993. Unpublished concept paper for a National Action Research Network. Education Development Center.

Wittgenstein, Ludwig. 1958. *The Blue and Brown Books.* New York: Harper and Row.

Wolf, Dennie Palmer. 1994. Personal communication. March 13.

11

Teachers Regulating Themselves: Teachers Owning Their Standards

PHILIP A. CUSICK

Professor, Department of Educational Administration,
Michigan State University

Introduction

Professionalism is difficult to discuss because it has so many meanings, some of which refer to the individual professional, some to the collective profession. I will disaggregate the term and treat its dual meanings separately. Torres described professionalism as follows:

> At base, professionalism involves the transference of *policymaking authority* from the state to an occupation. . . . *Self-regulation* is considered necessary in professions because the *special expertise* and training that professionals possess makes others unable to *evaluate performance* or *determine the best policies* for such occupations. . . . Because of the relative *autonomy* that professions have, they have been said to hold *monopolies* over certain services. . . . A professed *commitment to service* to clients and to a *code of ethics* are personal assurances that professional powers will not be misused, while *state boards of practice, comprised of colleagues*, serve as formal *policing* and *sanctioning* bodies. (1988 382, emphasis added)

Torres identified the key concepts basic to any discussion of professionalism: policymaking, self-regulation, specialized training, evaluation, policy setting, autonomy, monopoly, commitment to service, a code of ethics, and collegial policing and sanctioning. This section examines how these concepts relate to teaching as a profession and to teachers as professional practitioners. It also describes current and proposed changes in education standards and concludes with an assessment of how these changes will affect teachers' professionalism.

My argument is that heretofore teachers have exercised a high degree of control over those elements of the profession that relate to them as individuals, but little control over those elements that relate to them collectively. Schools have been organized and run in ways that give the teacher great autonomy. Descriptive studies of classrooms have consistently shown that as individuals teachers are quite free to set the agendas of their classes, interpret the curriculum as they choose, and evaluate their own efforts. On the other hand, teachers have generally failed to have influence on those elements of the profession that relate to the collective. Teachers, as a group, have not exercised power over education policy, they do not have a strong ethical code, and they do not exercise control over their members through policing and sanctioning bodies. But the situation is now being reversed. Proponents of education reform regard teachers as isolated, idiosyncratic, self-referenced, and solipsistic, and they are impatient with teachers, whom they see as blocking change at the classroom door. The reformers[1] are advocating, and urging states to implement, policies that diminish an individual teacher's control over the classroom and subject matter. Proposed reforms will subject teachers to increased scrutiny and control and leave them with much less autonomy. But education reform cannot succeed without the support of teachers, and reformers are inviting teachers to join their efforts to set standards and influence policy. The weakening of individual professionalism can be offset by strengthening professionalism collectively.

The U. S. Educational System

People in the United States have great faith in education and demonstrate that faith by their willingness to build and support a system of schools within every community, require attendance of every child for at least 10 years, spend approximately $5,400 per annum on every child's education, and send 60 percent of their offspring to some kind of education beyond high school. The education they support is a system, and if the conditions and methods of teachers' work change, several of the system's other elements will also have to change. We begin by describing the education

---

[1]The term *reformer* encompasses a broad range of philosophies and opinions.

system, paying particular attention to current and proposed changes that may affect teachers' professionalism.

"A system is a set of collectivities, side-by-side and overlapping" (Parsons 1949, 101). The formal organization of education is often referred to as a system. Within the formal organization, at the national level there is a secretary appointed by the president and a department of education. There are 50 state superintendents, state boards, and state departments of education. There are more than 15,000 local school districts, each with an elected board, superintendent, assistants, coordinators, principals, and teachers. Finally, there are more than 40 million students, ranging from preschool to late teens, divided according to age, ability, and sometimes interests. The sum of these individuals and their organizational links compose the formal system of education in the United States. Publicly funded by a combination of taxes, guided by state legislatures and local boards, the system determines funding, curriculum, requirements, credits, programs, attendance, and discipline.

The system's formal side is a bureaucracy with specialists, rules, and regulations, and even in this most personal endeavor, the separation of person from role. The bureaucracy keeps track of people and events, allocates resources in a somewhat equitable manner, and assures the public that the doors will be open and the lights on; that teachers will be certified, present, and prepared; that cafeterias and buses will be clean and running. It is true that the bureaucratic goals can conflict with education goals, and the bureaucracy is often blamed for absorbing energy that should go into teaching and learning. It is also true that bureaucracy has high transaction costs, requiring a great deal of effort and energy just to keep it running, independent of what it is designed to accomplish. But the bureaucracy is what gives schools the orderly appearance they need to maintain public confidence. It connects people and roles to activities and outcomes. It adds an element of rationality to an undertaking that sometimes defies precise definition. At the same time, we must admit that there are not a lot of ways to run a large collective endeavor full of children. Bureaucracy—with its rules, regulations, procedures, and predictable routines—is the most sensible alternative.

The formal organization is not the whole education system. In addition to those individuals with formal roles in the bureaucracy, the system includes all those who take an interest in schools and who make it their business to see that at least one aspect of the endeavor is run as they would like. Thus the system includes collectivities such as teachers unions; subject matter associations such as the National Council of Teachers of English; Theodore Sizer's Coalition of Essential Schools; the Education Commission of the States; the College Board; the New American Schools

Development Corporation; the local Concerned-Citizens-in-Favor-of-Tax-Relief; national and state associations of principals, teachers, guidance counselors, and coaches; and the innumerable clubs formed to support the band, football team, orchestra, and library. The system also includes authors and publishers of textbooks, foundations, and surveillance groups that monitor textbooks. It includes national, state, and local associations for impaired children, and universities and employers that tell schools what they expect of graduates. It includes creationists who want their views to prevail in science class and home-schoolers who don't want their children in science class at all. It includes all those with definite ideas about education—their own, their child's, some other child's—who do not hesitate to let the schools know what they want and who, if they do not get what they want, create or join organizations to accomplish their goals.

There are other types of collectivities that influence schools—less visible, less organized, without dues and membership, without headquarters and lobbyists, but equally powerful. Consider the case of honors or Advanced Placement courses in high school. There are good reasons for the existence of such classes, but there are also good reasons for their elimination, since they tend to serve children from more affluent families. One can argue against such offerings in favor of a structure that does not group students along ability lines. On the other hand, the argument for quality can be turned into an argument for equality: A school's high-ability students deserve the same opportunities afforded their counterparts in other schools. Arguing either or both ways, the coalition of interests supporting such classes may be composed of parents who want their children to take tougher classes, colleges that are looking for evidence of effort and quality, administrators who want to advertise their schools as offering a quality education, and teachers who like to teach high-ability students. Such coalitions are usually invisible unless their interests are threatened, and then they coalesce, show up at board meetings, head for the state legislatures, or take their children out of the school.

To explain a system with such diverse associations and interests that are not under control of the formal organization but overlap and augment it is complicated. But to explain the system without these associations and interests, in terms of its formal organization alone, makes no sense and tells no one how education works in the United States. In fact, the education system works very much like the rest of public life, where the forming of associations that press for or against action is the norm:

> Americans of all ages, all stations in life, and all types of dispositions are forever forming associations. There are not only commercial and industrial

associations in which all take part, but others of a thousand different types—religious, moral, serious, futile, very general and very limited, immensely large and very minute. Americans combine to give fetes, found seminaries, build churches, distribute books, and send missionaries to the antipodes. Hospitals, prisons, and schools take shape this way. (de Tocqueville [1839/] 1969, 513)

Affecting the System

The topic of this section is teachers' professionalism, and the extent to which teachers can define the methods and conditions of their work. No one denies the importance of teachers or the power they exert in delivering instruction, which is the system's core function. But in a system that includes almost everyone and is constructed in a way that encourages participation by everyone, the power of one group to control the central function is limited by the desire and right of many others who want their views included and who will organize to achieve this.

The system encourages such organizing. It is open and accessible. U. S. freedom of conscience and choice and the right to associate with others on behalf of similar causes encourages participation. The fact that the formal organization is somewhat jerry-built with its 50 state systems, more than 15,000 local districts, and overlapping and often inconsistent authority lines also encourages participation. The inconsistency created by the sometimes conflicting goals of quality and equality also encourage participation. Any and all may assert that their own children, or some category of children, are not getting a quality education or are being treated unequally, accusations that have to be taken seriously by educators. Not only are there many opportunities to get involved, there are an equal number of reasons.

Finally, and most important, is the fact that while education is a public good, it is also a private good. We trust the schools to turn out a cohort of engineers. But we do not trust the local high school to see that our daughter is among them. So by ourselves or with other parents, we pressure the local school to offer a curriculum that will give students, among them our daughter, a chance to enter a university engineering program. That a single person and millions like him find ways to actively participate in a child's education both characterizes the system and differentiates it from systems that are more hierarchical, closed, and, from the client's point of view, inaccessible. While the notion of a more organized, planned, and coordinated system is conceptually appealing, the fact is that while we have great faith in education, we have little faith in educators and demonstrate a consistent unwillingness to turn decisions concerning our own children, or children we care about, over to educators.

Several critics advocate improving U. S. education by creating a more centralized, coherent decision-making apparatus. Smith and O'Day (1990) are among those who would like to see more "system" in the system. They suggest that states design and implement a "coherent instructional guidance system [consisting of] challenging and progressive curriculum frameworks, a supportive organizational environment and instructional content directed toward complex thinking and problem solving" (245). However, it is precisely the fragmented nature of the system that allows and encourages participation by so many varied groups. A more rational and hierarchical system would not allow parents a voice in textbook selection. A more rational system would have the English 9 curriculum determined at the national or state level by appointed experts and implemented by professional teachers rather than by a loose confederation that includes students, teachers, state guidelines, the National Council of Teachers of English, the principal and the school board, textbook authors and publishers, parents, advocates of one or several ideologies, and the colleges to which the students aspire.

Reformers and critics of education—almost to a person—speak of education only as a public good, as a way to increase economic competitiveness and ensure equality. Their suggestions for strengthening teachers' professionalism emphasize increasing teachers' power relative to that of other groups in order to attain some public good. That is all very well but it ignores the fact that education is also a private good and that millions of people insist on participating in the education system. If strengthening teachers' professionalism means weakening the power held by other collectivities, it will be resisted throughout the system.

Current Reform Efforts and the Teacher

Education reform draws a variety of sometimes unlikely parties together. One of the more interesting and successful reforms was instigated by Theodore Sizer, former professor and dean of the School of Education at Harvard. He concluded that too much energy in secondary schools was wasted on the bureaucracy, that educating students was superseded by moving them around and keeping them in order, and that students' intellectual development was being ignored. Sizer analyzed these problems and proposed some solutions in *Horace's Compromise* (1984) and later founded the Coalition of Essential Schools to implement his ideas.

The Coalition was initially funded by private donors, later by the Exxon

Foundation and Southwest Bell. Sizer was also assisted by Brown University, where he set up offices and served as professor and chair of the Department of Education. In 1984, Sizer identified 14 high schools—some private, some public—in which the staff, or some of the staff, was willing to try out his ideas. The number of schools, the Coalition staff, and the funding base expanded rapidly. In 1989 the Education Commission of the States (ECS), a quasi-private association of state departments of education that was looking for a secondary school reform model to take nationwide, settled on Sizer's Coalition. At present, the Coalition has a substantial staff, more than 700 associated schools putting its ideas into practice, with ECS's Relearn project expanding that number in several states. The Coalition just received $50 million from the Annenberg Foundation to continue its work. Thus one individual mobilized a set of public and private schools and associations to take his vision into schools. The Coalition's development suggests that change is more likely to come from outside the formal education system than from within.

As another example, consider the efforts of the National Council of Teachers of English (NCTE), a general-interest association of English teachers, supervisors, curriculum directors, teacher educators, and others involved in the language arts. As explained by Executive Director Miles Myers, a subunit of that organization—the English Coalition—was formed to promote the view "that English . . . instruction should expand from emphasis on talking and writing for communication to talking and writing for discovering new ideas and thinking through problems" (Myers 1994, 2).

The NCTE obtained federal funding from the Department of Education. In partnership with the International Reading Association and the Center for the Study of Reading at the University of Illinois, it formed an additional group—the Standards Project for English Language Arts—to study and develop new standards to be presented to the membership of those organizations. Thus, a subunit of a general-interest association joined with subunits of other coalitions to pursue a specific venture. The newly formed group obtained its own funding (often federal), worked out its agenda, and took recommendations back into the parent organizations.

Yet another example comes from the National Science Teachers Association (NSTA), an organization of science education professionals that has as its purpose the stimulation, improvement, and coordination of science teaching and learning. NSTA has initiated a reform project (SSRC) in which it is argued that there is a finite number of mathematics and science principles that schools should teach and students should learn. The goal of the project is to provide students with "hands-on experience, sequencing over time at successively higher levels of abstraction, and taking

account of student preconceptions" (Aldridge 1992, 13). The project believes that too many teachers teach facts, memorization, and individual
competition, which state-mandated tests and colleges encourage. It also
believes that the present approach to teaching science hardens achievement differences along class lines because middle-class students know
that memorized facts can be exchanged for places in preferred colleges
and so will put up with rote learning. Economically disadvantaged students are not similarly socialized and are thus quicker to reject this type
of instruction.

The first step in the development of this project was a planning meeting, sponsored by the National Science Foundation and ". . . attended by
some 110 scientists and science educators; participants included a Nobel
Laureate in physics, association representatives in math, technology, and
other subject-matter educators, teacher educators, science teachers, science educators, and even a vice president of the Academy of Sciences of
the USSR" (Aldridge 1992, 18).

A "scope, sequence, and coordination project" emerged from that
meeting, funded with $13 million from the Department of Education and
the National Science Foundation for the middle level. For the high school
project, there are centers in California, Texas, Iowa, North Carolina, Alaska,
and Puerto Rico, with 200 schools in California and 34 in Houston, Texas,
currently involved. In the centers, teachers, scientists, and teacher educators take their ideas into the local secondary schools to prove their
worth.

A similar effort has been mounted by the National Council of Teachers
of Mathematics (NCTM), a 112,000-member organization composed of
mathematics teachers, mathematics teacher educators, mathematicians,
and state and district coordinators and mathematics supervisors. As explained by Glenda Lappan of Michigan State University (a former board
member and president of the organization, as well as a present member
of the Standards Coordinating Committee), in the early 1980s, when the
association had 60,000 members, mathematics teachers were "bombed
out by the new math and eager to respond to the new politicized and
policy-oriented environment." Thanks to a grant funded by the National
Science Foundation through the National Academy, the NCTM has worked
to set up a nationwide support system for mathematics teachers. Working
groups developed a set of standards describing mathematical tasks, discourse, clientele, analysis, reflection, preparation, reasoning, connections, and problem solving. One objective was to develop a set of curricular materials that was accessible, up-to-date, and integrated, and
emphasized solving problems rather than doing calculations. The goal was
not a single curriculum, but rather checkpoints in key early, middle, and

high school years where students will be asked to demonstrate competence. The NCTM has provided guidelines to be used in raising standards at district levels and in influencing universities that prepare teachers.

There are patterns to education reform. First, it is usually not those teachers and administrators already ensconced in the schools who initiate reform. Running the 40-million-student system and coping with ever increasing demands absorb their time and effort. Rather, reform is more often initiated by the quasi-private associations that focus on schools. Second, those with the ideas obtain some money (often federal), hold a conference with national experts, and publish a set of recommendations with parallel criticisms of extant practice ("we should be doing this but instead we are doing that"). Third, the efforts are taken into some states and districts and finally into schools and classes where the new ideas are tried out. Fourth, the goal is to take the worked-over plan into state legislatures, where the proven reforms will be turned into mandates that teachers will be required to follow.

As to the reformers' more specific ideas, what bothers them most is that classrooms are generally prosaic. They want to see some emotional excitement, some joy in learning, some intellectual curiosity. They want discourse, interaction, student involvement, problem solving, application, integrated curricula, and reflective thinking. Instead, they see teachers lecturing about disconnected facts and encouraging rote memorization, passive students, short-answer tests, and an absence of ideas. Much of the blame falls on the school bureaucracy. Reformers argue that schools tend to bureaucratize instruction into a series of minor and mind-numbing tasks. They disparage the bureaucracy with its artificial specializations and emphasis on order that exaggerate socioeconomic differences. And they disparage the system that allows teachers to remain isolated in their classrooms behind closed doors, immune to the influence of reform efforts. Finally, reformers want to make the education system more rational.

The Role of Teachers in Reform

After students, teachers are the most important group in the education system. Teachers play a role in reform efforts, but their collective role is limited by their weak affiliations. Rather than participating as teachers qua teachers, they participate as individuals affiliated with more focused interests, disciplines, and ideologies. Any successful reform group must include teachers, but it also has to include representatives from universities, state departments of education, federal and state agencies, districts, and the like. Education policy and reform are not single-interest games; they are coalition games and should include all with an interest in the endeavor.

That Bronxville High or Brighton High in New York joined the Coalition of Essential Schools did not mean that every teacher in those schools joined, or even that a majority joined. Teachers could join or not, whole- or half-heartedly. If the group of supporting teachers decided to leave the Coalition, as they did at Brighton, then the effort was terminated. If the principal who initiated the Coalition left, as she did at Bronxville, then the effort also ended. But at Central Park East in New York City, another Coalition school, the reform effort was organized so that if one teacher did not wish to participate, that teacher did not join the staff. In most of the Coalition schools, however, each teacher decided whether she or he wished to join and how much effort to devote.

Early proponents of the Coalition effort hoped that teachers would embrace the reformist logic and join the effort. But teachers seldom find reformist logic as compelling as reformers think it is. Muncey and McQuillan (1993), two anthropologists who studied the Coalition for five years, reported that in some schools, nonparticipating teachers felt that the Coalition teachers received too many of the schools' limited resources, and so actively worked against the effort. These authors found that the individual teacher was the deciding element in the success or failure of the reform effort.

McLaughlin, who studied policy implementation in education, suggested that such individual decision making is typical in the education enterprise: "A ... lesson from detailed studies of implementation ... is that change ultimately is a problem of the smallest unit. At each point in the policy process, a policy is transformed as individuals interpret and respond to it. What actually is delivered or provided under the aegis of a policy depends finally on the individual at the end of the line" (1987, 174).

Each teacher should be free to judge the worth of a reform endeavor and then to join or not join. If teachers do not join, they should still be able to say that they are doing their job, teaching their subject, and educating their students. In a sense, teaching is like belonging to the Franciscans, where one's allegiance is owed primarily to one's personal interpretation of the teaching of Saint Francis and only secondarily to the way the extant Franciscan order interprets those teachings.

This matter of personal interpretation and choice is central to teachers' professionalism. As individuals, teachers are professionals. As evidence we cite their freedom to behave as they wish in the classroom and to judge the worth of reform efforts. In the present system, reform can be derailed by noncooperating teachers who argue that they know just as much as the reformers and that the reform efforts are wrong, naive, or more trouble than they are worth. Teachers—as a collective—are not the most important unit in the education system as currently organized. The single teacher is the important unit. But reformers are not very tolerant of individual choice. Centrist-minded reformers, dismayed that teachers have closed their classroom doors to previous reform efforts, would like to have their ideas mandated by legislatures and forced on teachers. The present system allows teachers to remain uninvolved; the reformed system would collectivize teachers and allow them much less individual freedom.

There are advantages for teachers who join reform efforts. If teachers in Lansing's Otto Middle School join Michigan's New Partnership for Education (MNPE) and work to improve their methods, they will receive a $250 stipend each semester, the opportunity to work with colleagues and with staff from Michigan State University, and the chance to attend the two-week summer institutes on Mackinac Island. One might say that the 45 who have joined after four years are expressing their professional prerogative. One might say that the 35 who have not joined are also expressing their professional prerogative and have demonstrated that by keeping their distance.

At Plainview Elementary School in Saginaw, Michigan, the district curriculum director and the principal, drawing on ideas that Glaser laid out in *The Quality School* (1992), are working with teachers to (1) manage without coercion; (2) teach and talk about quality; (3) have students evaluate themselves; and (4) avoid useless work. For the teachers in that school who support the effort, it means reading and discussing Glaser's book, perhaps going to California for a week to attend a Glaser workshop, and taking his ideas into the classroom. Seventy-five percent of the school's teachers are participating. The principal, Ms. Jane Van Steenis, says she will "work with" those who have not committed themselves. She admits that the latter are good and qualified teachers and that she has neither the intention nor the means to force them to participate. Thus does reform play by the system's rules. It opens opportunities for some, without demanding compliance by all. For teachers who join in there are increased opportunities. They get out of the classroom, meet other professionals, work on interesting projects, and network with a larger community of educators from universities, state education departments, and foundations. Those who do not join are allowed to continue in their comfort zone.

Future Reform Efforts and the Teaching Profession

Each of these reform efforts centers on teachers and includes teachers. The participation of teachers is necessary, but not sufficient. Reform efforts also need the support of teacher educators, state education department personnel, subject experts, and university educators. For example, in the National Council for the Social Studies (NCSS) project to develop curriculum standards for the early grades, middle grades, and high school, the working group consists of four professors, two curriculum directors from public schools, an official from a state education department, two supervisors of social studies, and two teachers. And William Aldridge, the executive director of the National Council of Science Teachers, describes himself as "a 20-year science teacher." Glenda Lappan, cited earlier, says, "To be credible, you have to stay close to the classroom." Even the home-schoolers—at least in Michigan—find public school teachers who join and support their efforts.

Reform opens opportunities for teachers to exert influence. But as education concerns take center stage, reform efforts increase and policymakers and legislators become less patient with teachers' freedom to negate those efforts. Reformers want teachers to use their collective power, not to argue for increased individual rights and privileges, but to reform teaching and improve learning. The reformers don't want what they see as obstructionist politics and they are encouraged by what they see as a backlash against teacher unions (*Forbes*, September 20, 1993). At present teachers are being asked, invited, and solicited to join reform efforts. In the future, they may have no choice. Reformers are going to try to force compliance via legislated mandates. Teachers' right to refuse to join in a reform effort may be abrogated.

There are two views about the future direction of education reform efforts. In one view, while at present the education policymaking arena is characterized by a plethora of competing interests, in the future a more rational, planned, and centralized policy will emerge. Participants will be compelled to comply with well-thought-out reforms and the vision espoused by Smith and O'Day (1990) will become reality. There is a power vacuum in schools, one that policymakers and legislators will fill with mandates and regulations. The fact that teachers can close their doors and do whatever they want frustrates reformers who are tired of seeing teachers sidetrack reform efforts. Reformers are trying to take power away from individual teachers. If they are successful, teachers will have much less influence in their own classrooms. But they may be on their way to having more influence in larger policy matters.

This view that schools are becoming more rational and organized is supported by reference to the way organizations and fields of organizations develop. Consider education reform efforts not in isolation but as a group, as a field of similar and overlapping efforts. These separate efforts are becoming more similar in structure, language, personnel, goals, and in the ways they try to influence policymakers. They are becoming isomorphic. That organizations from the same field tend toward isomorphism, and that the entire field goes through *structuration* (becoming a single structure rather than a group of competing organizations) is a well-documented phenomenon. That this has occurred in schools and school districts is also well documented (DiMaggio and Powell, 1983). The conditions that make organizations in a particular field isomorphic and the conditions that drive isomorphic organizations into structuration are at work among the coalitions of individuals interested in education reform. A major condition for organizations to become isomorphic is the predominance of the state. And in education, not only does the state (or states) have the power, it is convinced it has to use it if the education system is to be reformed: "Wherever you look, in continental Europe, in East Asia, even in the United States, governments are busy refashioning their educational systems, improving their schools, expanding their universities. They are all convinced that tomorrow's jobs will go to the brainy rather than the brawny" (*The Economist*, November 20, 1994, 62). Individual states are exercising more power, so influencing state policy is the major goal of reformers. They adopt similar strategies, emulate the more successful among themselves, and the field becomes more isomorphic. Therefore, while past reform efforts have been fragmented, the next generation of reforms may be supported by a more unified field. Individual teachers can resist a series of disaggregated reforms; they may not be able to resist a cohesive field of reforms.

In the other view of education reform efforts, increasing numbers of competing interests mean less centralized control. As an example, consider the 1960s when federal aid to education dramatically increased. It was feared at the time that federal aid would result in a more centralized system with less individual freedom. But as Cohen pointed out, the expansion of funding for education resulted in less, not more, control and centralization:

> The expansion of state and federal policy has stimulated growth in the organization and often in the power of education agencies at all levels of government. . . . The growth of public policy has enhanced power and expanded organization for many private agencies concerned with education governance . . . power and organization often have grown in tandem rather than growing in one place at the expense of another. (1982, 476)

Further, as centers of power and influence grow at state and federal levels, they grow correspondingly at local levels. For the last 30 years, the more money that flowed into education, the greater the number of interests that arose to take part in overseeing the expenditure of that money. Federal aid increased the amount of money, increased the number of concerns, and increased the number of participants and the opportunities to participate. But more money, more issues, more importance attached to the endeavor resulted in less—not more—centralized control. "The number of interests restrain[s] the unbalanced concentration of power in any particular agency" (Cohen 1982, 485). He explained:

> In the education of disadvantaged children, for example, diverse specialties developed in teaching, administration, testing, and research. Specialized agencies were drawn into education curriculum development, evaluation, and the provision of services. New child and parent advocate groups sprang up. Few of these interests were organized 20 years ago, but now each has distinctive issues of special concern, and distinctive perspectives on the issues. . . . Each new policy increases the organized interests and these interests open up new facets of issues. (1982, 485)

Cohen argued that the system works against the kind of centralized control that reformers such as Smith and O'Day (1990) call for.

For an up-to-date example of Cohen's argument, consider Kon's (1993) account of textbook development in California. When that state was putting together a new social studies text, several interests jumped into the debate. African Americans, Hispanics, women, native Americans, and immigrants, among other groups, argued that in a multicultural nation, the social studies curriculum should be multicultural. Consensus was achieved and the elementary social studies text that emerged covered all points of view. When the book came to the teachers, who had no hope of covering everything and no direction about which elements to choose, they did what they always do: They selected what was familiar and friendly. The question is whether Cohen's argument—that the system is becoming not more, but less, controlled—will hold up in a time when the coalitions attempting to influence state education policies are coalescing into a single structure.

We have described the present education system and illustrated how it works with reference to some current reform efforts. We have also enumerated the rules by which the system operates and by which even the reformers have to play. Multiple and competing groups influence the way the formal organization is constructed and the way it does business. The system allows a great deal of individual freedom and, as we will argue in the following discussion, that freedom extends particularly to teachers who manage what goes on in their classrooms.

The Current Character of Teachers' Professionalism

Teachers are quasi-autonomous individuals operating inside their own classrooms. They are independent and self-reliant; they regulate and evaluate themselves; they set their own policy. But the reform efforts that we have described are aimed at reducing the control teachers have over their students and their classrooms. Reformers want to take the control of content and delivery away from individual teachers and lodge it in a larger collective that would include teachers but would also include other interests. The great majority of teachers enjoy more individual professional freedom than they are likely to have if the proposed reforms succeed.

Currently, education is carried on and schools are organized by assigning teacher specialists to instruct batches of students for fixed periods each day. "The task of universal elementary public education is still usually being conducted by a woman alone in a little room, presiding over a youthful distillate of a town or city" (Kidder 1989, 53).

In elementary schools, students are divided by age and, to a lesser extent, by ability. In secondary schools, students are divided by age and interest and, to a lesser extent, ability. Teachers spend almost all of their working time with students and apart from one another. Although this arrangement is decried by reformers and blamed for a host of problems, from teacher dissatisfaction to lack of change to inequality to teachers' resistance to reform, it is highly functional. It provides order, always a first priority for parents and necessary in a place full of children. And as Kidder points out, it is a form of damage control: "each teacher to her own room and her own duties ... makes teachers conveniently interchangeable. ... and also gives an institution a ready-made system of damage control. ... When problems arise, they are isolated from the start in individual rooms. The doors of the rooms of incompetent and inadequately trained teachers can always be closed" (1989, 51–2).

To Lortie, the isolation of teachers is a defining characteristic of the profession. It is also teaching's main attraction because teachers obtain their greatest satisfaction from working with students. They create collegial affiliations to the extent that they want them: "teachers ... work largely alone; there is little indication that they share a common technical culture. Yet we have observed that they turn to one another for assistance and consider peer help their most important source of assistance" (1975, 76). Working alone, calling on colleagues for assistance when they need it, making their own decisions, exercising discretion over what and how they teach and how they relate to students, is the way teaching is carried out at present.

We cannot discuss teachers' professionalism without considering the issue of control in the classroom. Control is, as any school teacher knows, a primary concern. It is an issue about which reformers are astonishingly cavalier. Reformers go on and on about "higher-order thinking skills" but pay no attention to the problem of getting and keeping the attention of 25 children for sustained periods of time on matters that are not, to the majority, inherently interesting. Control is a central issue in any classroom. Teachers handle it in varied ways, but all have to handle it and are judged— by administrators, colleagues, students, and parents—on how they do it and how well they do it. Several researchers, among them Gold and Miles (1981) and Smith and Keith (1971), studied schools under changing conditions and described what happened when control was slipping or when some teachers and parents *thought* control was slipping. Acrimonious public meetings were held, principals were fired, superintendents retreated from innovation, teachers left the school, innovations were abandoned.

The school must at all times give the apprearance of knowing what it is doing with the citizenry's children. We may call control an unworthy goal, a misplaced goal, or a goal forced on teachers by the school bureaucracy. But to work in a public school, teachers have to be able to exercise authority relative to students. Teachers who cannot control the students are released; principals who cannot control their schools are fired. There is no tolerance for those who fail here. Waller argues that orderly behavior among students is always a problem: "The teacher-pupil relationship is a form of institutionalized dominance and subordination. Teacher and pupil confront each other in the school with an original conflict of desires and however much that conflict may be reduced in amount or however much it may be hidden, it still remains" (1932, 195).

For evidence of how teachers integrate control into their lessons and of how much freedom they have to operate the way they want, consider 25 years of descriptive studies of classrooms, beginning with Jackson's (1968) *Life in Classrooms* and extending to Kidder's *Among Schoolchildren* (1989). The evidence is consistent: Teachers close their doors; they give their own cast to the curriculum; they deal with administrators to the extent that they want to do so; they make their own decisions about how to teach. Each maintains control of the class. Each is different from the rest. Consider Mrs. Caplan as described by Moore:

> "What number would you try for the problem 5 into 185?" "Suppose there are 96 children and you want to divide them into 4 equal teams?" "Will 4 go into 16 again?" "What is a shorter method of adding?" "How many of you feel this is right?" To the students' correct answers she gives a steady stream of affirmative and complimentary responses. "Some of you are getting very good." "Yes, it [a whole number] can be anything. Can it also be

money?" To a student with an almost correct answer, "Think a moment, George. Is this correct?" The students are quiet, orderly, wait anxiously to participate. And it is not that she has the best students. Juan was a problem child in early years, but presents no problem of discipline to Mrs. Caplan. (1967, 100–101)

Or consider Moore's characterization of Mrs. Rosencranz, from the same school:

"Take your things and go over there where Rose used to sit. For once I would like to see your own work, not Helen's." To another child . . . "Where are the questions? Where are you looking? Will you find it out the window? Turn around and get to work." (1967, 125)

"Billy, what are you doing?" "I'm doing it over." "You're not doing anything over." "Close your books and get back to your own seats. . . . Stand. Get into a line in the front of the room . . . get quiet. . . . I won't say it a third time. . . . Aren't you listening? What did I say?" . . . [to another teacher] "Would you like to throw two of your boys out? Particularly that bigmouth over there?" (1967, 126–29)

For another example, look at how Mr. Baxter handles the less interested students, who are more likely to exhibit control problems, as described by Powell, Farrar, and Cohen:

Baxter's "worksheet routine" was standard procedure in many other classes. The motives behind the treaty were clear: "Because if you look at kids and say, 'They are out to get me' and if I keep them very busy, if I pass them a worksheet every five minutes . . . then you have very busy, very quiet kids." The administrator concluded in frustration that "interpretation, analysis, inference, main ideas are really not part of our educational curriculum." (1985, 199)

Another way to deal with difficult students is to create an interesting experience and form an alliance with more compliant students. Consider how Mr. D handled his Law and Society class, a popular elective for lower achievers, as described by Cusick and Wheeler. The teacher set up a mock trial. While preparing the students for their roles, he interjected comments and opinions. Explaining the idea of expert witness:

"Dr. Verkampen, tell me about your credentials." "Vell, I have 17 Ph.D.'s. I've written three books, I've taught at the University of Paris, now the University of California at Berkeley." See class, he's got the credentials. "May we enter this person as an expert witness? Yes, of course." "Dr. V, tell me,

do you think John Hinckley is insane?" "Absolutely, he's loonier than a loon."
Now you ask some guy on the street, "Do you think Hinckley is crazy? He
shot the President." "Hell no, he took his gun out and aimed it" or "Hell
no, it's about time somebody shot him." But these people don't have the
credentials to be expert witnesses. (1987, 69–70)

While the trial was proceeding, Mr. D continued in his central role,
standing slightly off to the left, calling back students who were drifting
off, correcting mistakes, and looking sharply at the few talking among
themselves. Trusted students had key roles. With their cooperation, he
suppressed disruption from less interested students. Even those who were
not prepared were scrambling to do a decent job on the witness stand.
It was a great class. It was also the creation of a single teacher who was
operating in a social studies department that for several years had been
working on a common curriculum. The department effort was regarded
as successful. But collegial efforts never intruded on how each teacher
prepared and carried out his or her class.

On the other hand, there are teachers who do literally nothing. They
may be few, but then no one knows how many there are because classroom
doors are closed, and observations are few and mostly prearranged. Cusick (1973, 1983) found several such teachers in his studies. He described
one, Mr. P, a social studies teacher who used class time to make small
talk, give students random advice, and recollect on his own past. He often
left the room, and:

One day he started on railroad mileage. Another teacher walked in. "Hey,
I fixed your TV." "Oh, excuse me," said Mr. P and walked out. Twenty minutes
later he returned and he told us that he wanted to talk about the increase
in railroad mileage between 1830 and 1940 and while he was reading the
graph from the book, not one student was paying a bit of attention. (Cusick
1983, 54)

The teachers described above have some things in common. They are
all experienced, most are tenured, salaried, and probably members of the
union. They show up, teach the approved curriculum, or in the case of
Mr. P do not teach the approved curriculum, and run their classes the
way they want. Each exercises wide discretion; each is to a considerable
degree autonomous and self-regulating; each polices himself or herself.
No one would mistake Mr. Baxter for Mrs. Caplan or Mr. P.

The rhetoric of reform often describes teachers as if they were low-
level employees ordered about and closely supervised. But that view does
not jibe with 25 years of descriptive studies showing teachers as operating
with a considerable measure of the independence of action that

characterizes professionalism. The depressed, downtrodden, and depersonalized teacher that the "teacher empowerment" advocates were describing in the early 1980s is absent from the descriptive studies, even from studies that describe female teachers in early rural Vermont (Goodson 1992).

Instead, the descriptive studies show teachers focused on their classes, displaying a great deal of indifference to events outside the classroom, and not very affected by administrators. Mrs. Zajac interacts with her colleagues on a need basis. She calls teacher friends to "discuss ways of handling Clarence"; she confers with Debbie, the reading specialist; she works with Pam, her student teacher. She seeks out the principal when she wants a particular teaching resource. She sees the vice-principal when she wants to talk about a particular student. She lunches in the teachers' room where "banter and complaints were more common than shop talk" and where the teachers talked about "wakes and weddings, sales and husbands." But those interactions are peripheral to her central concerns— her classroom and her students—that consume her emotion, time, and energy (Kidder 1989).

Similar autonomy and independence were described by McNeil, even at Nelson High, a school that made an effort to integrate the social studies curriculum and where: "The staff was organized from the start to consider the content behind course titles and credits; this consideration belonged to principal and teacher alike, in concert with each other" (1986, 136).

Nelson High's faculty had adopted a curriculum that "brought together concepts and methods of inquiry from varied social studies disciplines."

> Ninth-grade focused on world backgrounds up to 1500 . . . tenth grade . . . covered the years 1500–1870 . . . world conflicts in contemporary history from 1870 formed the eleventh-grade course . . . the senior course was contemporary issues [with emphasis on] each individual developing as a thinker, individual, and citizen." (McNeil 1986, 130)

However much the staff had cooperated to develop an integrated curriculum, in practice, each retained a unique approach to instruction:

> Within the department . . . all teaching styles are different. . . . Mr. Lancaster's curiosity knew no limits; his course content was constantly changing in its particulars. He continually sought new information, read scholarly papers and news publications, and brought his findings into his classroom. . . . Mr. Hobbs . . . read widely and gathered material for his classes from many sources. Unlike Mr. Lancaster, he was more organized and demanded more concrete involvement from his students. His course was centered on text-

book assignments, with added lectures and films and considerable class discussion based on Socratic-style questions. (McNeil 1986, 140–51)

Mr. Guthrie, the department chair:

> Based much of his economic content on his personal experience and on his
> expectations for the students' future. Since most of them were middle class
> and lower-middle class, he assumed that their adult lives would follow at
> least a pattern of trade school or university, steady jobs, and modest in-
> vestments. In his economic units, he combined printed handouts, in abun-
> dance, with speakers from the community. (McNeil 1986, 146)

These social studies teachers were free to select favored material, develop their own style, and close the door against collegial advice and
intrusion. They were even free to proceed from their own assumptions
about their students' futures.

There is no space in this brief section to review the evidence documenting the argument that teachers make policy, regulate themselves,
evaluate their efforts, and do their policing, not as a group, but as individuals, each to himself or herself. It is often asserted that teachers resist
external control. But descriptive studies show not so much that they resist control, as that they make their own decisions about how to exercise
control over content and students.

Administrators don't tell teachers what to do. No one much tells teachers what to do. That is, according to Lortie (1975), one of the appeals of
teaching. Indeed the descriptive studies demonstrate that administrators
play a very limited role in what teachers do. At Westhaven Elementary,
where Johnson (1985) spent a year in classes and with teachers, the principal was not only absent from classrooms, he was rarely mentioned and
then not even referred to by name. To teachers, it was "the administration
feels," or "the administration thinks." It is not that teachers and
administrators don't get along. They just don't encounter each other often,
and when they do, the conversation is about scheduling and staffing the
school's multiple and overlapping events.

Administrators have their own concerns. They spend their time in the
halls, in the cafeteria, in the office with parents and students, or in the
parking lot discouraging disruptive behavior. Turning again to descriptive
studies—this time of administrators—Kemetz and Willower reported that
the elementary principals they studied had up to 40 unscheduled meetings a day, "with a mean duration of 4.4 minutes. Eighty-six percent of
the principals' activities (70 percent of their time) involved face-to-face
contact with one or more persons, and another 8 percent was spent on

the telephone. The remainder was spent writing notes, completing reports, and processing correspondence, or doing similar tasks." The authors concluded that the job of building administrator is characterized by a "high volume of work completed at an unrelenting pace." The work is characterized by "variety, brevity and fragmentation of tasks, and preferences for verbal media and live action" (1982, 72).

Martin and Willower (1981) found that secondary school principals exhibited the same "busy person" syndrome as elementary principals. They spent 16 percent of their time on desk work. An additional 45 percent was spent on meetings, scheduled and unscheduled. Exchanges, sometimes on the phone, sometimes in person, amounted to 19 percent. The remainder of the time was spent being in charge and being "available"—touring, observing, monitoring, and supervising. In the latter situations, principals positioned themselves visibly so as to invite further interaction. Principals' days are characterized by multiple and brief verbal interactions with a variety of people and constant interruptions. Even the interruptions were interrupted. Martin and Willower also reported that among the principals they studied, "407 interactions were interrupted by 1457 other tasks." Interruptions proliferated to the point where the authors described their principals as doing two things at once.

The argument is sometimes made that teachers are oppressed and that proposed reforms will liberate teachers from administrators. But administrators do not control teachers, nor even really direct them. The popular argument some years ago compared teachers to workers and administrators to their overseers. Teachers, it was argued, had been proletarianized. But it was not true then; it is not true now. Teaching is a respected and reasonably well-paid middle-class profession. The Marxian concept of teachers as oppressed workers is long outdated. Moreover, the notion of administrators telling teachers what to do runs counter to teachers' place in the work and class structure. In their discussion of the modern U. S. class structure, Wright, Hachen, Costello, and Sprague (1982) suggested that teachers, like many others, occupy a contradictory place. Neither owners nor employers nor—as the descriptive studies show— subordinate, they are quite independent and highly self-directed. Teachers supervise not only students, but themselves as well, and the more senior among them are often called on to help train junior colleagues. If teachers were downtrodden and oppressed, then giving them voice, autonomy, and control over their own activities would be a good beginning to reforming the profession. But there is no evidence that they are. Except for a brief period in the late 1960s and early 1970s when they were becoming unionized, teachers have never regarded themselves as a proletariat. Nor do studies of class structure indicate that they are. When teachers were on the bottom of the white-collar pay scale; when teaching was a second job for the family or one of two jobs that someone held; when it was an initial job for more ambitious young people, one they held until they decided what career to pursue; when it was something men did on their way to administration and women did before they had children, then teachers could stay in their room and do what they wanted as long as they maintained order among students and didn't embarrass the school board by their personal behavior. But those conditions began to change 30 to 40 years ago. Teaching is now a respected occupation, aspired to by many ambitious and energetic young men and women.

Returning to our earlier description of the education system and the way individuals—including teachers—exercise discretion, the problem today is not that teachers have too little freedom and autonomy. It is that reformers think they have too much freedom. Teachers are not only free of administrative influence; they are equally free of reformers' influence. Reformers know that teachers use their freedom to sidetrack reform, close the door against innovation, and continue with what is comfortable and familiar. Reformers have gotten over the notion that the problem is oppressive administrators and they are getting over the notion that the problem is the bureaucratic structure. They are beginning to see the problem as the right of individual teachers to do what they want. Reformers are intent on penetrating the classroom and directly affecting teachers' behavior, whether teachers want them to or not.

What Reformers Want

Reformers want classrooms changed. They decry the fact that 12 years after *A Nation At Risk* (National Commission on Excellence in Education 1983) and after ". . . virtually every state had acted to impose the higher standards called for by the commission . . . all of these efforts, however well intentioned, have scarcely touched the classroom. . . . Our schools seem firmly anchored in the old" (Rothman 1993, 3).

The old, as that writer explained, is the teacher-centered classrooms that reformers blame for education's problems. To the author of the article, "a good school is a child-centered school where students take more responsibility for their own learning, where teachers lecture less and coach more" (1993, 4), and where, according to Magdalene Lampert, "understanding and intellect are more highly valued than they typically have been" (Rothman 1993, 10).

Sizer (1984) envisioned a classroom structure flexible enough to allow for intellectual exploration. In his "essential schools," students would be engaged with teachers in the common tasks of learning. Natural discipline would emerge from cooperative involvement. Sizer does not blame the overemphasis on control on teachers but on the bureaucracy that forces teachers into controlling behaviors and away from teaching. To Sizer, teachers' obsession with order is a by-product of the schools' out-of-control bureaucracy.

Similar in thinking is the Holmes Group, which in its first major publication, *Tomorrow's Teachers* (1986), argued for the importance of "teaching and learning for understanding," which the authors defined as situations that encourage "lasting learning—the kind that allows students to go on 'learning for a lifetime' " (8). They believed that "teaching for understanding won't happen in classrooms where students sit silent and passive" (11). In the classrooms these authors envision, students will become "complex meaning makers who learn the deepest kind of literacy" (14). Schools will not be "the grim places that too many are," but communities where skill building is accompanied by understanding, where "students' main work [is] to tackle and explain complexity rather than to complete simple assigned tasks," where "every child makes a contribution to the classroom using his or her own experience" (19).

The Holmes Group authors have read the studies describing student resistance to school and learning. But they argued that it is not learning that students resist; it is teacher-controlled classes. Students would like to learn but are prevented from doing so by the oppressive structure.

Reformers of the education system want schools to be more child-centered. They believe that bureaucratic demands have forced teachers into dominating classrooms with lectures and an insistence on order. They believe that order has replaced learning as the school's major goal.

Tomorrow's Schools (1990), a later report by the Holmes Group, argued that the traditional view of teaching is limited to the presentation of information and the maintenance of order. The authors envision collaborative classrooms where students with less information drive students with more. They also want to "[provide teachers] with opportunities to contribute to the development of knowledge in their profession, to form collegial relationships beyond their immediate working environment, and to grow intellectually as they mature professionally" (Holmes Group 1990, 56).

The authors also want to diminish the power of the education organization relative to teachers. Well-prepared teachers will not simply follow guidelines. They will examine and critically interpret materials in terms of their own understanding of the subject matter and scrutinize the content in light of their own comprehension.

Reformers are almost all multiculturalists. Unlike Cusick (1983), who studied urban schools and suggested that bringing black and white students together created a difficult situation to which the school had to respond with increased emphasis on order, reformers tend to think that order, not racial animosity, is the source of problems. Grant described problems between black and white students but felt that the school's bureaucratic processes prevented the emergence of a common ethos that might serve as an incentive to learn. For Grant, too, diversity is a problem not because it is the source of opposition but because of the schools' attempts to stifle it: "When you take a bureaucratic mode of organization and put on top of it a legalistic mode of accountability, what it does is standardize further, which reduces the professional discretion to personalize for children, which then creates more kids who don't fit. In all our good intentions, we have made matters worse" (1988, 35)

According to reformers, teachers exercise too much control. They stay in the center of the room, they dominate the dialogue, they direct the activity. They behave in ways that indicate they do not believe school learning comes naturally. Rather, they appear to think that students' own inclinations, if unchecked, will emerge in a way that prevents learning. But reformers believe, or talk as if they believe, that students would naturally learn if only teachers would get out of the way and stop dominating everything.

Other reformers call for "systemic reform" of the education system. Smith and O'Day, representing collectivist reformers, advocate a system wherein "teaching and learning rather than control and discipline" (1990, 235) are paramount. Smith and O'Day propose a revised system wherein the state would design and orchestrate the implementation of a "coherent instructional guidance system [consisting of] challenging and progressive curriculum frameworks, a supportive organizational environment, and instructional content directed toward complex thinking and problem solving" (1990, 246). In a more coherent and managed system, a system with more "system" to it, national groups could set standards that would be implemented and tested in classrooms.

Smith and O'Day would no doubt support the National Board for Professional Teaching Standards (NBPTS), which wants schools wherein "student initiative and inventiveness are both stimulated and applauded and expectations are high for all students" (1989, 5). National Board advocates would like to break the one teacher/one classroom syndrome and build a system of teachers with broader responsibilities but a narrower focus, teachers who elevate specialization to a higher level: "Teachers who [are] adept at diagnosing a student misunderstanding in mathematics . . . could review students' work from throughout the school

... and ... work with fellow teachers in formulating a solution to each case" (1989, 11).

My argument is that teachers now enjoy a high degree of professionalism. They are autonomous and self-regulating, they have specialized training, they do their own evaluating and policymaking and develop their own commitments and codes of ethics. But education is now too important to be left to teachers alone. In the past, reformers thought that if they could get administrators out of the way and improve the school climate, teacher behavior would naturally change. They have now come to regard teachers as much too isolated and self-determined. Reformers want teaching to be poetic and exciting, not prosaic and pedestrian as the descriptive studies show that it is. Reformers are now targeting teachers directly and arguing that their stature will be strengthened as they move away from their dominant role in the isolated classroom and into cooperative arrangements, not only with one another but with educators from outside the school, from universities, state education departments, and professional associations. Reformers argue also that isolating teachers in single classrooms has encouraged them in habits that discourage rather than encourage student participation and responsibility for learning. Like Sizer (1984), who advocated the "student as worker and teacher as coach" image, reformers believe that teachers do too much and students do too little. The isolated, specialized, and autonomous classroom that the empirical studies describe has to be penetrated; the teacher who reigns there has to be brought out, engaged, and integrated into a larger community of educators. Teachers need to network with that larger community, join with reform endeavors, and establish links with researchers. Only then, reformers argue, will education be improved. Only then will teachers emerge as true professionals.

How is all of this to be accomplished? The current reform movement contains several elements, including the 1950s emphasis on content, the 1960s belief in the students doing the right thing if allowed the chance, the 1970s efforts to increase equality through integration and reduced tracking, and the 1980s efforts to increase requirements and testing. But despite concerted efforts over four decades, schools are still operating the same way, teachers are still doing the same things, and students are still not learning what they need to know.

Reformers also target teacher education, an endeavor they have always believed was intellectually bankrupt and educationally indefensible. Suggestions for improvement vacillate between giving prospective teachers more expertise and giving them more experience. Among the suggestions to expand experience are linking teacher education programs with professional development schools, running training programs on school sites, creating internships for prospective teachers, having prospective teachers reflect on their own education via process writing, opening programs to mid-life candidates, reducing the methods courses, having more practicing teachers on staff in colleges, and having students keep casebooks. Among the suggestions to increase expertise are requiring more liberal arts in the undergraduate curriculum, raising standards through a national certifying board, requiring more years of service before granting tenure, and adding a fifth year to the undergraduate program.

Then there is the whole restructuring movement. Restructuring means several things—reducing requirements, concentrating on ideas, giving teachers as a group more power relative to their colleagues so that they can monitor one another, creating school councils with real authority, team teaching, teacher decision making, accreditation based on outcomes, reduced emphasis on order and control, and making use of new technology. These reforms are aimed at teachers; more particularly they are aimed at individual teachers. Reformers advocate teacher empowerment, but it is not the empowerment of the individual teacher; it is the empowerment of the collective over the individual. In the schools as envisioned, the isolated teachers will have less power, teachers as members of the collective will have more power.

Will the Proposed Reforms Strengthen Teachers' Professionalism?

We might first ask "Will the proposed reforms take place?" but let us hold that question for the conclusion. For now, let us assume that the reformers have gathered the forces they need to push their programs through the state legislatures, which, like the reformers, believe that education is too important to be left to individual teachers. Let us further assume that teachers will emerge from their classrooms and join with their colleagues and others to work collectively, that students will engage, take responsibility, and become the active learners that reformers envision. What will all of this mean for teachers' professionalism?

Traditionally there has been little collegial policing. Indeed, it would have been considered quite unacceptable for any teacher in Cusick's (1983) Urban High to even suggest that Mr. P was doing nothing in his classes. After all, he was a "good guy." Teachers do not have a common code of ethics to which they hold one another. If one teacher misuses his position, leaves early for his second job, does little or nothing in his classes, or interacts inappropriately with students, other teachers rarely make it their business to intrude. More often they will help the teacher resist the administrator who tries to intrude. There are few commonly determined commitments or ethics.

So what does the new generation of reforms mean for teachers' professionalism? It means that more opportunities are being created in which individual teachers may participate. For those who join Sizer's coalition, the MNPE, the Quality School, or who get on the building or the school improvement team or the North Central Outcome Team, or the local curriculum committee, professionalism will be strengthened. For teachers who join larger efforts such as those sponsored by national associations, many more opportunities for growth, renewal, influence, and prestige will open up. There is great mobility in the education marketplace for teachers who avail themselves of such opportunities. Teachers no longer have to move into administration, or a state education department or a university in order to advance professionally. They can stay in the classroom, and by joining the efforts of those outside the classroom who are pushing for reform and change, exercise a strong voice in a joint effort. Teachers will no longer feel isolated. They will have many more opportunities for recognition, participation, collegiality, growth, responsibility, and influence. The opportunities lost by those who would continue if they could to keep the door closed are offset by the larger opportunities offered to all.

Professionalism for teachers as a collective will be strengthened. But those teachers who choose not to participate in reform will find they have less autonomy and less freedom. There will be heightened scrutiny, more rules and regulations, greater accountability, and higher transaction costs. Individual teachers will be required to spend more time outside the classroom and will be forced to comply with a host of demands that they cannot avoid by closing their doors. If current reform efforts are implemented, power will pass from the individual teacher to the collective, and that collective will include not only teachers but many others who have an interest in education. Teachers are going to be an important part of education reform, but they are not going to control the forces that will be empowered to intrude on their individual classrooms. Thus strengthening collective professionalism will result in a weakening of the individual teacher's freedom and autonomy.

Let us summarize by taking each element that makes up professionalism and estimate whether it will increase or decrease with reform, as shown in Table 1.

Conclusion: Cautionary Notes

There are two matters that reformers never mention but that the education system—as presently constructed—handles nicely. The first is con-

Table 1
Effect of Reform on Teachers' Professionalism

Characteristics	Effect of the Reforms on the Individual Teacher	Effect of the Reforms on All Teachers
Policy-Making Authority	for most, less	less
Self-Regulation	less	less
Special Expertise	more	more
Evaluate Own Performance	less	less
Determine School Policies	for most, less	less
Autonomy	less	less
Hold Monopolies	less	less
Commitment to Service	more	more
Code of Ethics	more	more
State Boards	more	more
Policing and Sanctioning	more	more

trol of students. Reformers assume that acquiring abstract knowledge can be made interesting and exciting if the conditions are right. Experienced teachers are skeptical. There are flashes of interest, flashes of brilliant teaching, flashes of student insight. But the business of keeping a crowd of students on task and mastering logarithms, grammar, geography, or periodic tables is difficult and often frustrating. Learning calculus, writing a decent paragraph, and speaking a foreign language are demanding skills and do not come easily. And because learning is hard work, many students need teachers in the center maintaining control and encouraging dialogue. One teacher in his or her classroom is an efficient way to handle instruction and to control students. It enables teachers to build personal relations that they then can use to keep students, particularly the less interested, on track. Reformers are too casual about the importance of order, the difficulty of learning and of keeping students learning, and of the advantages to teachers offered by the single classroom with the closed door. Experienced teachers who know students, who know how hard learning is, and who know what it takes to teach should be careful of what they may lose in the name of reform. In my opinion, teachers are not being assertive enough about protecting certain rights. Education policymaking has been taken overtaken by those who were never teachers, who have no idea what it takes to manage a classroom, and who believe that the whole business can be readily rationalized. Experienced teachers know better; teaching and learning are not irrational processes, but neither are they as rational as reformers make them sound. When reforms are implemented, and the evidence is that they will be, accommodations will have to be made to the old exigencies that forced schools into the practices that reformers are now trying to change. Whether those accommodations will include a healthy measure of the old practice of leaving teachers alone to work out matters behind closed doors remains to be seen.

The second issue not addressed by the reform movement goes back to education as a private good. Professionalism, as we have explained it, means strengthening the power of the teachers as a collective relative to the individual and to other parties in the system. At present, while teachers run classrooms, nonprofessionals still feel they have a say and that schools and teachers are open to their influence. There is an openness and accessibility to the schools that the public likes.

Reformers do not want to admit it, but most are centrists. They regard the education system that gives teachers the right to refuse reform, students the right to not learn, and parents direct access to classrooms as messy and anarchic. Reformers want more power lodged in the state and more state mandates upon schools. But this might knock the system off balance in favor of professionals and give nonprofessionals less access. Will the public put up with schools where "expert decisions" are made about their children without their participation and approval? If reforms that strengthen teachers' collective professionalism are seen as excluding all those parties who at present have open access to the schools, there will be a backlash. Some balance will have to be reached between the old ways and the new. The autonomy of the individual teacher did not come about because someone planned it. It came about because it made sense. It solved certain problems—of order, of student control, of personal relations. The old exigencies will remain and any reformed system will have to somehow accommodate them. In that synthesis of the old and the new, teachers' professionalism will be strengthened.

References

Aldridge, B. 1992. "Project on Scope, Sequence and Coordination: A New Synthesis for Improving Science Education." *Journal of Science Education and Technology* 1: 13–22.

Benavot, A., Yun Kyung Cha, D. Kamens, J. Meyer, and Suk-Ying Wong. 1991. "Knowledge for the Masses; World Models and National Curricula: 1920–1986." *American Sociological Review* 56: 85–100.

Brinelow, P. and L. Spencer. 1993. "National Extortion Association." *Forbes*, June 7, 1993. 151: 78–84.

Beyer, L., W. Feinberg, J. Pagano, and J. Whitson. 1989. *Preparing Teachers as Professionals.* New York: Teachers College Press.

Cohen, D. 1982. "Policy and Organization: The Impact of State and Federal Educational Policy on School Governance." *Harvard Educational Review* 52: 474–99.

Cusick, P. A. 1973. *Inside High School.* New York: Holt, Rinehart and Winston.

Cusick, P. A. 1983. *The Egalitarian Ideal and the American High School.* New York: Longman.

Cusick, P. A., and C. Wheeler. 1987. "Improving Education Through Organizational Change." Report #400-83-0052. Washington, D. C.: National Institute of Education.

de Tocqueville, A. 1839/1969. *Democracy in America*. Garden City, N. Y.: Doubleday and Company.

DiMaggio, P., and W. Powell. 1983. "The Iron Cage Revisited: Institutional Isomorphism and Collective Rationality in Organizational Fields." *American Sociological Review* 48: 147–160.

Dumas, W., T. Weible, and S. Evans. 1990. "State Standards for Licensure of Secondary Social Studies Teachers." *Theory and Research in Social Education* 18: 27–36.

Education Week. 1993. "Charting a Course for Reform: The Next 10 Years." Special Report, February 10, 3–4.

Everhart, R. 1983. *Reading, Writing and Resistance: Adolescence and Labor in a Junior High School*. Boston: Routledge and Kegan Paul.

Glaser, W. 1992. *The Quality School*. New York: Harper Perennial.

Gold, B. A., and M. Miles. 1981. *Whose School Is This Anyway?* New York: Praeger.

Goodson, I., ed. 1992. *Studying Teachers' Lives*. New York: Teachers College Press.

Grant, G. P. 1988. *The World We Created at Hamilton High*. Cambridge, Mass.: Harvard University Press.

Hammond, L. D., T. Gendler, and A. E. Wise. 1980. *The Teaching Internship: Practical Preparation for a Licensed Profession*. Santa Monica, Calif.: Rand Corporation.

Holmes Group. 1986. *Tomorrow's Teachers: A Report of the Holmes Group*. East Lansing, Mich.: Holmes Group.

Holmes Group. 1990. *Tomorrow's Schools: Principles for the Design of Professional Development Schools*. East Lansing, Mich.: Holmes Group.

Jackson, P. 1968. *Life in Classrooms*. New York: Holt, Rinehart and Winston.

Johnson, N. B. 1985. *Westhaven: Classroom Culture and Society in a Rural Elementary School*. Chapel Hill, N. C.: The University of North Carolina Press.

Kennedy, M. 1987. *Inexact Sciences: Professional Education and the Development of Expertise* (National Center for Research and Teacher Learning Issue Paper 87–2). East Lansing, Mich.: Michigan State University.

Kemetz, J. T., and D. J. Willower. 1982. "Elementary School Principals' Work Behavior." *Educational Administration Quarterly* 18: 62–78.

Kidder, T. 1989. *Among Schoolchildren*. Boston: Houghton Mifflin.

Kon, J. 1993. *A Thud at the Classroom Door*. Unpublished doctoral dissertation. Stanford, Calif.: Stanford University.

Labaree, D. 1992. "Doing Good, Doing Science: The Holmes Group Reports and the Rhetorics of Educational Reform." *Teachers College Record*. 93: 628–40.

Lightfoot, S. L. 1983. *The Good High School*. New York: Basic Books.

Lortie, D. 1975. *Schoolteacher*. Chicago: University of Chicago Press.

Martin, W., and D. Willower. 1981. "The Managerial Behavior of High School Principals." *Educational Administration Quarterly*, 17: 69–90.

McNeil, L. M. 1986. *Contradictions of Control: School Structure and School Knowledge*. New York: Routledge and Kegan Paul.

McLaughlin, M. 1987. "Learning from Experience: Lessons from Policy Implementation." *Educational Evaluation and Policy Analysis* 9: 171–78.

Moore, G. A., Jr. 1967. *Realities of the Urban Classroom*. Garden City, N. Y.: Anchor Books.

Muncey, D., and P. McQuillan. 1993. "Preliminary Findings from a Five-Year Study of the Coalition of Essential Schools." *Phi Delta Kappan* February, 74: 486–89.

Myers, M. 1994. "NCTE's Role in Standards Project." *Journal of English Education*.

National Board for Professional Teaching Standards. 1989. *Toward High and Rigorous Standards for the Teaching Profession: Initial Policies and Perspectives of the National Board for*

Professional Teaching Standards. Washington, D. C.: National Board for Professional Teaching Standards.

National Commission on Excellence in Education. 1983. *A Nation at Risk: The Imperative for Educational Reform*. Washington, D. C.: U. S. Department of Education.

National Council of Teachers of Mathematics. 1989. *Curriculum and Evaluation Standards for School Mathematics*. Reston, Va.: National Council of Teachers of Mathematics.

National Council of Teachers of Mathematics. 1990. *Professional Standards for Teaching Mathematics*. Reston, Va.: National Council of Teachers of Mathematics.

Parsons, T. 1949. *The Structure of Social Action* (Vol. 1). New York: Free Press.

Powell, A., E. Farrar, and D. Cohen. 1985. *The Shopping Mall High School: Winners and Losers in the Educational Marketplace*. Boston: Houghton Mifflin.

Rothman, Robert. 1993. "Obstacle Course: Barriers to Change Thwart Reformers at Every Twist and Turn." *Education Week* (Special Report), February 10, 9–13.

Sizer, T. 1984. *Horace's Compromise*. New York: Houghton Mifflin.

Smith, L. M., and W. Geoffrey. 1968. *Complexities of an Urban Classroom*. New York: Holt, Rinehart and Winston.

Smith, L. M., and P. M. Keith. 1971. *Anatomy of Educational Innovation*. New York: John Wiley and Sons.

Smith, L. M., P. F. Kleine, J. P. Prunty, and D. C. Dwyer. 1986. *Educational Innovators Then and Now*. New York: Falmer Press.

Smith, M. S., and J. O'Day. 1990. "Systemic School Reform." *Politics of Education Association Yearbook* 233–66.

Stinchcombe, A. 1964. *Rebellion in a High School*. Chicago: Quadrangle Books.

Torres, D. 1988. "Professionalism, Variation and Organizational Survival." *American Sociological Review* 53: 380–94.

Waller, W. 1932. *Sociology of Teaching*. New York: Russell and Russell.

Watkins, B. 1993. "1,000 Schoolteachers Sign Up for Evaluation That Would Lead to National Certification." *Chronicle of Higher Education* September 22, 1993. 40: A/9-A/21.

Wolcott, H. 1978. *The Man in the Principal's Office*. New York: Holt, Rinehart and Winston.

Wright, E., D. Hachen, C. Costello, and J. Sprague. 1982. "The American Class Structure." *American Sociological Review* 47: 709–26.

PART
VI

STANDARDS AND THE FUTURE OF SUBJECT MATTER ASSOCIATIONS

12

National Curriculum Content Standards: The Challenges for Subject Matter Associations

Diane Massell

Consortium for Policy Research in Education

We entered the 1990s with intense conversation at all levels of the policy-making system, among the public, and throughout professional education communities about the nature and content of what is to be taught and learned in school. Public debate about curriculum content is not new, of course; what is new is where and with what frequency and broad scope these debates are occurring. These debates and activities portended a reform of major consequence. With the passage of the Goals 2000: Educate America Act on May 16, 1994, the federal government enacted historic legislation that will further fuel these discussions. Goals 2000—plus the wide range of ongoing efforts initiated by national groups, state and local governments, and private organizations—will provide unprecedented opportunities to, and challenges for, subject-matter groups and associations. In this section, I consider some of the central challenges that confront these organizations in the current climate of reform.

The intellectual foundation of this reform movement hinges on the concept of standards-based systemic reform. This pinpoints the lack of clearly articulated and challenging standards, defining what all students should know and be able to do as one of the critical problems in public education. To be sure, the education system in this country has expectations, but they are rarely voiced and for the last 20 years or more, they have been tied to the achievement of low-level competencies and basic skills in key areas of instruction. The assumption is that by establishing more rigorous academic standards for all students, linking related policies to these high standards, and freeing schools and teachers from regulatory strangleholds on innovative practice, education will be improved (Smith and O'Day 1991).

Federal policymakers have assumed a prominent role in the new reform movement, reversing a trend in which these actors largely avoided discussions about curriculum content.[1] In 1989 then-President Bush and the state governors adopted six education goals for the nation, among them one that called for students to demonstrate competence in challenging subject matter in five subjects: English, mathematics, science, history, and geography. Soon afterward they created the National Education Goals Panel (NEGP) to monitor the country's progress toward meeting these goals. In the 1980s, efforts of the National Council of Teachers of Mathematics (NCTM) to set content standards in its field and of states like California to upgrade the content of their curriculum frameworks provided successful, concrete examples of standards-based reform. Soon after the so-called education summit, the U.S. Department of Education let contracts to a number of consortia, including professional subject-matter associations and university centers, to develop their own standards projects. Some groups, whose discipline areas were not included or added[2] to those laid out in the national report, or who seek to provide an alternative to the project, have set out independently to develop their own standards. The bill passed by Congress, the Goals 2000: Educate America Act, creates an entity called the National Education Standards and Improvement Council (NESIC) to certify national and state-level content standards, performance and opportunity-to-learn standards, as well as a system of assessments keyed to these standards.

Several national groups are working to create other essential "software" components for reform, such as alternative forms of assessment, as well as standards in other areas such as teaching, that were not addressed in the initial effort. Finally, the vast majority of states are also engaged in setting new standards for what students ought to know and be able to do as cornerstones for their own versions of systemic reform.

---

[1] Only a decade ago, it was almost unheard-of to use the word curriculum or content standards in the context of federal government and national education policies. In preceding years, bitter social and political battles over large-scale, federally funded curriculum projects ended in sharply diminished congressional support for education research. Looming large over these disputes has been the perennial tension between federal versus state versus local control over education, and the tendency to view federal involvement in school instruction with suspicion.

[2] After some lobbying, the five subjects were expanded to eight; foreign languages, the arts, and civics were added to the list.

This active reform climate poses many challenges for subject-matter organizations that are setting out to develop standards, and here I focus on three: (1) the challenge of developing professional support and consensus around core sets of standards; (2) the challenge of maintaining and honoring intellectual diversity in their respective fields; and (3) the challenge of building an organizational infrastructure to support the development and implementation of standards. This section will explore issues generated by the current political climate as well as by the very structure and purpose of traditional subject-matter organizations. I draw heavily on previous research that examined the standards-setting efforts of the National Council of Teachers of Mathematics and the state of California in the area of history/social science, and on research on four state efforts to develop standards for what students should know and be able to do (Massell 1994a; Massell 1994b; Massell 1994c; Massell and Kirst 1994). In addition, I contacted executive directors and administrators in five subject-matter associations involved in national standards projects, as well as a few local affiliates, to gain an understanding of association structures and explore some key issues in standards setting. The ideas presented in this section are preliminary and attempt to suggest some questions and start a discussion about the role of these associations in standards-based reform.

The Consensus Challenge

Developing professional as well as public consensus around a set of national content standards is a critical, but very thorny, endeavor. Efforts to reform public education have taught us over and over again the importance of building a foundation of understanding and support across a range of actors, beginning with teachers but extending to principals, district specialists and administrators, and parents as well as the business community and other members of the public. The most analogous antecedents to today's national reforms are the large-scale curriculum projects undertaken by the National Science Foundation (NSF) from the 1950s to the 1970s. As was true of most public policy efforts focused on education at that time, they proceeded under the rationalistic assumption that if high-quality products were developed and provided to teachers, implementation would proceed smoothly. But the majority of the NSF projects failed to secure broad implementation, in large part because they failed to build wide support for the undertakings. In fact, the public furor that arose over one of the projects, Man: A Course of Study, led Congress to retreat from forays into curriculum reform (Jackson 1983). In retrospect, one of the major flaws in the NSF projects was the way the developmental process and follow-up were designed, a design that reflected such rationalistic assumptions about how change occurs. First, most of the projects involved only academic elites (Nobel prize winners, university faculty, etc.) in the development process. Teachers, teacher educators, administrators, parents, and community leaders had only limited, if any, involvement, were uninformed about the changes they were expected to make, and were ill-prepared to defend the reforms when challenges arose at the local level (Massell 1994a; Yee and Kirst 1994). Second, and in part as a result of the failure to involve a broad spectrum of actors, the new curriculum standards frequently ignored the social, political, and technical realities of implementing new policies in schools (Yee and Kirst 1994; McLaughlin 1991).

Educational reformers today are keenly aware of the problems that result when concepts of change are not widely shared in the community (Carlson 1992), and, following the lead of the NCTM in this regard, most are engaging professionals with subject-matter expertise as well as those with school and teaching knowledge in their standards-development enterprises. In addition, the U.S. Department of Education is requiring its national standards project grantees to engage in a broad review and feedback process to gather diverse input. The hope is that this process will produce standards that can more easily be implemented in the school context, and that it will yield a shared vision and a foundation of support. This will be vital to maneuvering the content standards through increasingly treacherous political waters at the national, state, and local levels. Over the last two years, a number of citizens' groups have become quite vocal and organized in their opposition to reforms (Harp 1993a, 1993b).

But in addition to political challenges from the lay public, the national standards projects confront a number of additional obstacles to gaining support and consensus within their own subject-matter fields.[3] Some of these obstacles arise from: (1) the nature of the task, which is to articulate a strong point of view that is widely seen as leading to major changes in practice; (2) the nature of particular disciplinary fields, which makes consensus more difficult; and (3) the broader political environment today, which poses questions about professional autonomy.

Nature of the Current Task: Pushing Beyond the Status Quo

One of the overarching goals of the current reform movement is to replace the low-level, basic-skills curricula that have been the de facto

---

[3]Public and professional consensus are related, but they may be distinguished by the kinds of issues that are discussed and the obstacles that are raised to achieving broad support.

standards in this country with more rigorous academic goals. A leading standard, by definition, moves beyond the current curricula. It can do that in a number of ways, including the presentation of a coherent point of view seen as at the leading edge of the field, or of a new synthesis of different professional perspectives. But specifying what students should know in a particular subject—what key concepts, ideas, and topics to cover and when during the elementary/secondary career—can galvanize opposition from many professional, political, and social spectrums. In many areas of U.S. education, strategies for achieving consensus on difficult issues often borrow from a democratic politics of intellectual patchwork and compromise, or use broad language open to multiple interpretations. The long history of textbook publishing provides an obvious example of this approach. To appease the watchful eyes of vocal interest groups, publishers often water down their materials by using vague language, avoiding controversy, and covering as many topics as possible to make sure their publications have broad appeal—and a broad market. State specifications for textbook purchases often reinforces such strategies. But in this equation, consensus and leadership standards clearly are not the same thing.

To achieve the goal of producing leadership standards in a field, it will often be necessary to move ahead and approve standards that not everyone will immediately support. An individual on one of NCTM's professional standards committees noted that if members of the community were ruffled by the standards and communicated this during the review process, the committee members took it as a sign that they were providing leadership on some of the tough issues and not just reflecting the status quo or avoiding the problems (Ball 1992).

But, as the NSF projects of the 1950s to 1970s and other reform efforts demonstrated, such leadership must be balanced with a broad measure of support if meaningful change is to occur. If subject-matter groups develop national content standards that move too far ahead of the field, or too far to one side of controversial professional and public issues, vital interest groups may withdraw support, or the groups targeted for change may refuse to budge. This was the case when California adopted its history/social science curricular framework in 1987. Whether or not we support the intellectual positions laid out in the California document, most would agree that it was successful in setting forth a definitive point of view that was not watered down and did not use vague language. It tackled head-on some of the critical issues in the subject areas that most publishers avoided, such as the topic of religion. But even after the framework was adopted, and even with the enticement of the California book market, most publishers were reluctant to submit texts that they feared would be too controversial.

A critical question for those involved in national standards projects is when they should compromise to ensure the broad consensus necessary to support implementation, and when they should stand their ground. Unfortunately, there is no easy answer to this question. Balancing consensus and leadership is difficult, and trade-offs are involved if an approach leans heavily toward one end of the scale. But research on policy implementation has shown that reforms can have a strong impact over time even if the stakeholders do not universally agree on the goals beforehand (McLaughlin 1991). Only if supportive structures for implementation, as well as on-going efforts to secure understanding and consensus over time, are written into a reform plan before the documents are finalized will curricular reform take hold.

Nature of the Disciplinary Field

The specific characteristics of various subject-matter disciplines vary significantly, and these differences have consequences for constructing consensus around new curriculum standards. In this regard, the important factors that may influence debate are the extent to which the discipline is fragmented across subfields, the degree to which it tends to raise emotional public issues, and historical relationships among associations that represent different specialties in the field or different levels in the education system.

In 1989, the NCTM published its highly touted content standards and two years later its professional standards for mathematics teaching. The NCTM standards have been widely embraced by mathematics organizations and state and national policymakers. Colorado Governor Roy Romer, a prominent player in the education reform movement and former chair of the National Education Goals Panel, and former U.S. Secretary of Education Lamar Alexander, both hold up the NCTM standards as the premier example of what national standards should be—that is, standards widely viewed as being at the cutting edge of their fields, and that have broad public respect and support.

NCTM's success in "pushing the envelope" on mathematics standards and achieving a high degree of legitimacy and support relates in part to the unique nature of mathematics as a discipline and of the mathematics community in the United States. In most countries, mathematics educators and the mathematical sciences do not see eye-to-eye, but in the United States the high level of collaboration has been remarkable (Bishop, 1990). The different professional associations in mathematics work closely together, often undertaking joint projects and programs. The collegiality within the mathematics community results in part from its small size, both in terms of numbers of professionals and of professional organizations. Regular communication is facilitated because organizational memberships often overlap. By contrast, when the "new mathematics" projects were developed in the 1950s and 1960s, the field had few organizations or even publications through which debate and discussion could be aired, and deeper schisms existed in the field at that time.

Consensus is also promoted by the rather unique nature of mathematics as a discipline. It has a small and relatively cohesive set of subfields (geometry, algebra, trigonometry, etc.) that share a common set of conceptual tools and a common language. The latter facilitates discussion and makes certain goals of the current reform effort, such as aiming for curricula that go into depth rather than skimming the surface of many topics, more readily attainable. It is also easier to identify a compact, feasible set of goals. The objectives of depth over breadth and parsimony require trade-offs and compromises concerning what gets taught and what does not.

Contrast mathematics to the sciences or social studies, which are huge by comparison. These fields are fragmented into a broad array of disciplines and subdisciplines with their own autonomous professional societies. They often do not share basic conceptual constructs or a common language; the oceanographer, for example, needs to know little about astronomy. In social studies, not only do the various disciplines lack these commonalities, but educators also fundamentally disagree over whether traditional disciplinary perspectives should structure the precollege curricula (and if so, which ones and with what emphases), or whether social studies has its own content separate and distinct from these disciplines. Furthermore, unlike mathematics, the relationship between academic subject-matter experts and teachers or other education specialists is often more strained in fields such as the sciences. Membership in professional associations can be sharply divided along these lines, and there is often little communication. Achieving consensus concerning what content to include in a single set of standards is made much more complex in these disciplinary environments, and parsimony presents an even more difficult challenge. In other words, to reach agreement, it is tempting to be broadly inclusive, an attitude summed up by one individual involved in a national curriculum project who said, "These standards are OK as long as they represent more of what *I* teach."

Further complicating consensus within professional communities is the extent to which a discipline is linked to highly volatile social, political, or religious issues. We can count on multicultural debates erupting in any discussion about social studies standards, and issues of creationism fostering public discussions about science standards. Although this type of debate is not completely unknown in mathematics, the field does not tend to ignite public opinion in the same way.

The debates and contours of a particular field have implications for the way the subject-matter associations themselves are organized. Finding routes to bridge these institutional divides is essential if consensus is to be achieved.

The Broader Political Environment and Professional Autonomy

The education policy climate today is very different from the one that prevailed when NCTM undertook its effort to define standards for the field of mathematics. NCTM made the decision to embark on this task in the early 1980s, before the current standard-setting fervor had seized the imagination of policymakers and professionals. No Goals 2000 bill was pending in Congress, there were no National Education Goals Panel or really big external stakes (resources or legitimacy) riding on the outcome. In fact, at that time the idea of curricular standards was anathema to federal policymakers and foundation executives, and political interest in standards had not spread much beyond the state of California. So NCTM sought but received very little financial support for its undertaking. This meant that NCTM had to gain the grass roots support of its members first. The relative quiet in the broader policy arena allowed NCTM to take on the challenge of setting content standards without the kind of intense scrutiny that subject-matter groups undertaking this task today undergo, and to establish a very different time line.[4]

In the context of systemic reform, both federal and state governments are redefining their roles in developing curriculum policy[5] and raising the stakes significantly for this activity. One of the greatest concerns held by

[4]NCTM first laid out its agenda in 1980 and took the next nine years to prepare for and develop its content standards. Current projects with U.S. Department of Education funding are operating under a two-year time line, with the added pressure that if they do not complete their work quickly, the systemic reform train in states and districts will leave the station without them.

[5]State governments traditionally have not been as assertive in directly specifying subject-area content as they are becoming today. States sometimes listed courses that students should take, accompanied by a brief description. Curriculum frameworks were frequently laundry lists of behavioral objectives and facts (see Curry and Temple 1992; Archbald 1994). And, as alluded to earlier, the federal government has been wary of this type of involvement since the NSF experiences with large-scale curriculum reform projects, not only because of the emotional battles that erupted over efforts like Man: A Course of Study, but also because they touch the sensitive federal-state authority lines concerning education policy.

many educators is that the new reforms, particularly if national certification by NESIC becomes a reality, will narrow the zone of professional control over content standards. At an even more basic level, some educators are concerned that any national standard, however derived, will reduce their autonomy. Certainly discretion over one's work is highly prized in any field, but it is particularly so in academic communities. Academic freedom has a long tradition in public higher education, but not in public elementary and secondary education. In K through 12 schooling, local boards, state departments of education, state legislators, and national textbook publishers and testing companies have long attempted to guide and control the general nature of subject-matter content in the classroom, though never to the extent that such control is exercised in many European nations.[6] But the overriding feeling among many U.S. teachers is that government is an intrusive entity, that it has steadily eroded their professional autonomy, and that they must diligently protect themselves from it. Subject-matter associations, like teacher unions, have been seen as places of refuge, as protectors against government control. Thus, in some instances, teachers have felt betrayed by the efforts of their organizations to even enter into the national standards debate.

These concerns are exacerbated by the prospect that other stakes may be attached to what are presented as *voluntary, national* standards, giving them a mandatory and federal character. For example, the Goals 2000 act provides for grants and a system of voluntary national assessments. It is possible and likely that certified standards may be required to receive other federal funding. Furthermore, many advocates for the disadvantaged, frustrated by the failure of the past 20 years of school finance reform and desegregation to achieve educational equity, hope that national standards will provide a ballast for a new round of court litigation based on substantive equity[7] (Myers 1994). This could significantly transform the federal courts' role in equity cases and give nationally certified standards an extraordinary power. The higher stakes attached to the standards out-

---

[6]In France, for example, the central ministry dictates precisely which pages in which books teachers must cover, and when they must do so (Cohen and Spillane 1993).

[7]State courts have already begun to set precedents in this regard. The most celebrated of these is the 1989 Kentucky Supreme Court decision in *Rose v. Council for Better Education, Inc.* (Ky., No. 88-SC-804-TG), which wrote into its decision the minimal characteristics of an efficient education system, including goals such as "sufficient grounding in the arts to enable each student to appreciate his or her cultural and historical heritage" and "sufficient oral and written communication skills to enable students to function in a complex and changing civilization." The court specified that the system should be focused on outcomes and student performance, not just on inputs. As Myers pointed out, civil rights groups may claim that national content standards represent a civil right that all students should be entitled to under the guarantee of the Constitution (Myers 1994).

comes may also have the effect of exacerbating intellectual schisms in a field and making consensus-based leadership more difficult to achieve. One long-time observer of California school policy noted how the political dynamics changed and tensions rose when the state frameworks became more than just guides for textbook selection and came rather to represent the foundation for testing, staff development, evaluation of schools, and more.

In response to such concerns, over time some of the broader implications of legislative reform efforts were diluted in an effort to recast the proposed system of standards as a truly national, not federal, enterprise, and as truly voluntary.[8] For example, the original version of the bill introduced by former President Bush called for a single national test coordinated with the standards as a coequal part of the reform plan. But the notion of assessments tied to content standards not only raised issues about federal/state control, but also generated volatile debates over what came to be called opportunity-to-learn standards.[9] The idea of a single national test was later modified and became a voluntary *system* of national assessments certified by NESIC. The new legislation will allow states to submit their own assessments for certification by NESIC. The diminished likelihood of national tests has been evidenced by the steadily less vocal presence of lobbyists from testing companies.

Yet the standards do have substantial consequences that are probably necessary to make the reform effort worthwhile to undertake and that may make the standards more meaningful instruments of reform. In the final analysis, what can we say about the balance of power between government and the professions over subject-matter content under the proposed reforms? I think it is clear that the curricular reform is not a zero-sum game in which one faction gains power at the expense of others; instead, all sides tend to gain greater authority over curricula in a sort of corporatist arrangement.[10] The increased interests and resources currently or soon to become available in the broader policy environment have motivated many subject-matter associations to tread into standards development waters that they (arguably) would not have otherwise entered. The new impetus gives teachers and other educators the respon-

---

[8]The autonomy issues and the stakes exposed by Goals 2000 not only concerned subject-matter professionals but also states, and the act has exacerbated the classic tensions between federal and state authority in education.

[9]The concept underlying opportunity-to-learn standards is that it is unfair to hold students accountable to high standards if their school does not provide them with sound, and equal, opportunities to achieve those standards.

[10]In corporatist arrangements, governments work in close association with the private sector to develop policy and to govern.

sibility for developing their own content standards to serve as guidelines for public policy decisions, and thus puts them in a position of gaining substantial professional authority over the fundamental conditions of their work. Leaders of several subject-matter associations believe that the standards-setting efforts will have a positive effect on the professional identity of their members and their organizations as a whole. Furthermore, reform activities have the potential to generate new resources for professional subject-matter associations, to give them new salience and authority among their members, and to expand their power and authority in other national, state, and local policy spheres. The stakes attached to the reforms can enhance professional authority substantially beyond the more temporary, nonsystematic influence subject-matter professionals have had on education policy in the past.

In this new environment, the federal government will also gain substantial influence over content through certification and through the various mechanisms it controls for influencing the implementation of the standards (grants, Chapter 1 legislation, etc.). Maintaining the diversity of professional points of view and making certain that one version of "official" knowledge is not forced on the system, are critical challenges that are intimately linked to the issue of autonomy.

Maintaining Diversity

There are several strategies for maintaining professional diversity in the development of national content standards, and here I explore three: (1) certifying multiple standards; (2) setting up an alternative certification procedure outside NESIC; and (3) flexibility.

Certifying Multiple Standards

Some players, including senior officials from the U.S. Department of Education, have advocated that NESIC should certify more than one set of national content standards in a particular subject area. The argument is that approval of multiple standards would allow for greater professional (and cultural) diversity, a strategy that would strengthen the academic autonomy side of the scale and calm some professional fears about national/federal "thought patrols" regulating subject-matter content. Furthermore, advocates of multiple standards say that an array of well-developed, alternative viewpoints could help stimulate critical discussions among teachers and local communities, which is one of the central objectives of the reform efforts.

However, the arguments against multiple standards are compelling.[11] Many feel that multiple standards would undermine the central purpose of the current reform movement—presenting a unified and coherent set of subject-area standards that can leverage sympathetic, systemic change throughout the education system. Although the specific criteria by which the content standards will be certified have not yet been developed, the National Education Goals Panel did establish a Goals 3 and 4 Technical Planning Group chaired by Shirley Malcom to prepare for the task ahead. In late November 1993, the group issued an advisory report called "Promises to Keep: Creating High Standards for American Students." On the subject of multiple standards, it said:

> The Technical Planning Group concluded that to reach the purposes of standards-driven reform, there can logically be only one set of national education standards per subject area. Certifying more than one set of standards in a subject implies that no set represents the core to which students, teachers, schools, and communities should commit themselves. Even if states exercise their authority to develop content standards that vary from those in other states, within a state only one set of standards per subject should operate." (1993, 11)

Underlying this argument is a concern that multiple standards would simply exacerbate fragmentation and add to the confusion of purpose in which schools are currently mired. In addition, multiple standards might ultimately weaken the external incentive that certification provides to a subject-matter field, that is, the incentive for diverse groups to participate, compromise, and reach consensus. The prospect of multiple standards may also reduce the potential of a reform project to produce the kind of leadership that yields a new synthesis in a field.

An Alternative Certification Procedure

The idea of an alternative certification procedure has been floated more than once as a remedy for the diversity and autonomy problems that are raised by the NESIC certification system. It seems, however, that if a competing certification procedure were set up outside NESIC, problems concerning compromise and consensus, similar to those that might result from the certification of multiple standards, might arise. What would compel professional groups with diverse perspectives on a field to participate in a unified standards project when they could devise their own standards

---

[11] The few representatives of national subject-matter associations with whom I spoke were divided on this issue.

and seek certification elsewhere? Similarly, standards certified by an alternative body could be challenged in the federal courts, which might be more likely to affirm those standards developed under the ambit of national authorities.

For these reasons, setting up an alternative certification procedure may not be a good idea; it might not restore the sense of professional autonomy and control that many groups feel is threatened by national certification, or leverage education policy in significant ways. And it might decrease the incentive to participate that a single certification process offers.

To enhance a sense of professional discretion and control and to maintain diversity, the currently proposed national certification structure may be a stronger incentive for participation and professional growth. National organizations may find it more constructive to provide the support for their affiliates to work within their respective states or local districts to produce companion standards documents. Because Goals 2000 provides avenues for states to have their own standards certified, even those subjects currently left out of the national goals[12] effort would have access to national certification. The fact that both Goals 2000 and the Elementary and Secondary Education Act will likely reaffirm the traditional power and authority of states with respect to education makes it important that affiliate organizations establish and maintain good working relationships with state education agencies. Given that states demand a sense of ownership over education policy in the U.S. system of government—and given the proliferation of standards activities in many states—professional subject-matter associations will have ample opportunity to become involved in education policy at the state level.

Flexibility

Another way to introduce diversity into a single set of standards for a subject-matter field is to create standards that are flexible. Standards could be devised in such a way that they stimulate public and professional discussion, and allow for significant local discretion. Advocates of reform are quick to point out that content standards are not meant to be a curriculum, but rather (to use NCTM's phrasing) a "flag" that reflects the valued goals around which a team or group can rally (Romberg 1988).

One way to ensure flexible standards is to develop them at a relatively high level of abstraction that will permit diverse interpretations and a broad array of curricular approaches. But when do content standards become so general that they fail to express the leading thinking in the field

---

[12]The Malcom report recommends that NESIC review and comment on but not certify standards that are outside the ambit of the national education goals.

and are unable to address the contentious debates? Another concern is that the content standards might become so flexible that they will not provide sufficient guidance for the reform of other elements of education policy. Another way to meet demands of diversity is to develop several strands of alternative standards at a higher level of specificity. A variation on this approach is to publish dissenting views within the body of the national standards document itself, an alternative under consideration by the English Language Arts project (Myers 1994).

Affiliate Organizations and Their Role in Standards Reform

Affiliates of the national subject-matter associations can be important contributors to consensus and leadership for three related reasons. One is their critical role in helping to develop a sense of ownership over and support for the national standards documents across association memberships. A second is their potential for contributing to the many standards-development projects underway at the state and local levels, thereby supporting professional independence and growth as well as providing alternative access to NESIC certification. A third reason is that affiliate organizations can bridge gaps in understanding and encourage teachers and other educators to support and enact the standards, particularly if the affiliates are mobilized to facilitate ongoing networks for discussion. Studies of the predominant "one-shot workshop" approach to staff development shows such efforts to be of minimal value in improving teachers' practice (Little 1993) because they treat teachers as passive consumers of fragmented knowledge (Moore and Hyde 1981; Little 1989). Ongoing discussion and exploration present a more fruitful approach to understanding and learning how to use the more constructivist pedagogy that underlies most current reform efforts. Furthermore, affiliate networks can help empower teachers by introducing them to diverse points of view.

What are some of the characteristics of affiliate organizations and their broader environment that can help or hinder reform goals?[13] It is useful to review the findings of a study that looked at the organizational characteristics supporting the active involvement of statewide teacher, administrator, parent, and community education associations in collaborative school improvement projects. Some of the features associated with

---

[13] The following discussion does not pretend to represent the population of affiliate organizations or members, a task that would require considerable research. Rather, it is meant solely to raise questions and provoke discussion.

positive levels of involvement included a *statewide orientation* with an understanding of common needs; *good communication systems* including publications, conferences, and local networks; and *high credibility* with their membership. *Larger associations with more adequate resources and power* tend to be more capable of initiating and sustaining programs, particularly when raw political power is required. *Stable leadership* is important for high levels of involvement, as is an environment encouraging *collaborative relationships* with other associations and government agencies. Finally, associations in which *membership is voluntary* encourage involvement because such groups tend to invest more heavily in information and in-service programs than do those in which membership is mandatory (Corcoran and Rouk 1985).

Certainly the national offices of subject-matter associations have many of these features. They have a wide variety of publication and communication vehicles, including conferences and meetings, and they tend to have stable executive leadership and a cadre of staff (although the size of staff in different national offices varies considerably). The national offices frequently collaborate with other similar organizations, both within and across disciplinary lines. They also form proactive networks; for example, in 1980, 44 foreign language organizations joined together to form the Joint National Committee for Languages. This committee was responsible for expanding the national education goals to include foreign languages.

On the whole, the picture is quite different at the regional, state, and local affiliate levels of these organizations. Of course, members in the affiliates receive national publications and participate in statewide as well as national meetings. But the majority of affiliates lack any staff, and in the few that do have them, the staff is often part time. Without a strong infrastructure, it is difficult to sustain affiliate involvement in the national standards-setting process or in the reform of state policy. One affiliate member reported that the request by the national office to set up task forces to review drafts of national standards documents was difficult to organize and that the task forces met only infrequently.

The leadership of affiliate organizations tends to be dominated by college/university faculty or career teachers, whose flexible schedules permit participation and who receive external rewards and support for such activities. One local affiliate member said rank-and-file teachers felt that the organization was a "club" for these few, and that they had little desire to participate. A serious challenge for subject-matter associations is to expand local participation and provide professional rewards for "regular" teachers who become involved in association affairs.

When asked to identify their most active affiliates, national organization representatives often pointed to groups in very large states like California, Texas, and New York. The size and scale of the membership provides these organizations with the resources to construct an infrastructure. These affiliates, in contrast to the majority, tend to have if not full time, at least part time staff. Furthermore, they tend to have stable leadership. As one respondent noted, these states have highly staffed education agencies with career curriculum specialists; it was these specialists who provided leadership for the affiliate associations. With state agencies around the country experiencing severe cutbacks,[14] affiliates may need to look elsewhere for a cadre of stable leaders.

In some cases, however, the absence of state curriculum personnel may force the states to rely *more* heavily on subject-matter associations for support than they did before, so reductions in state agency staff do not necessarily produce negative results if the affiliates can find institutional support and leadership elsewhere. But it is interesting to consider whether and to what extent weak state departments of education—e.g., those that have few subject-matter specialists—are more open to collaboration with state and local affiliate associations.

Although there are notable exceptions, many affiliates are isolated entities that communicate little with one another and infrequently act in concert on any issues. One of the factors that contributes to this absence of professional networking is limited staff and resources. In addition, the way affiliates are organized can reinforce traditional schisms within a discipline and restrict networking; in other words, some affiliates are organized by topics or subfields within the discipline, or by "jobalikes," that is, common roles such as curriculum supervisors, teacher educators, etc. Finally, some subject-matter organizations have few local affiliates at all, or few in particular areas of the country. This, of course, also limits their ability to develop teacher networks and engage in a consensus-building process.

The strength of affiliate organizations would be enhanced if they were to enter collaborations with other professional associations active at the state level in developing or responding to policy initiatives. This is easier said than done, however, because of the long-held mistrust of government and government policy mentioned earlier. Classroom teachers often feel threatened by the endless flow of state policy edicts; one respondent said that she felt the people most active in her affiliate were those who were

[14]In the early 1980s and early 1990s, the Consortium for Policy Research in Education (CPRE) reported reductions in staff of approximately 25 percent in a number of state departments of education (Massell and Fuhrman 1994). In the last four years, the New Jersey agency has lost 363 positions, or 25 percent of its total staff. In Georgia, the state education department lost 89 of its 450 positions in 1992. This is not an unfamiliar story across the country.

the most outspoken against state dominance in education matters. The Michigan Council of Teachers of English (MCTE) agonized over whether to get involved with a state project to develop a testing framework for a proficiency examination in communicative skills. It decided, however, that if it did not participate, the state agency would proceed without it and turn to national testing companies. Involvement in the project appears to have produced a number of positive side effects for MCTE as an organization. With a $40,000 contract from the state, MCTE was able to control how the money would be spent, who would be involved, and how the project would be carried out. This project enabled the affiliate to hold regional meetings around the state to open up dialogue with teachers about what students should know and be able to do. Through strategy sessions and other cross-disciplinary meetings, they were able to develop and strengthen relationships with other subject-matter organizations. Furthermore, it enabled them to form links with other powerful interest groups that influence state and local education policy (Brinkley 1993). By helping to shape reform and not merely reacting to it, the association gained new authority and leverage. The important message for subject-matter affiliates is that through greater involvement in state and national policymaking they can more strongly influence education reform and that cooperation with government does not necessarily mean intellectual compromise. Again, engaging in standards setting or other forms of policymaking is not a zero-sum game in terms of professional autonomy.

These are some of the major challenges faced by affiliates that want to develop a structure that is responsive to the critical needs of standards-based reform. Of course there are no simple solutions, and I am sure that the questions I have posed are often confronted by the executive directors of these associations. Standards reforms may provide new opportunities for addressing these challenges. The associations might want to consider asking local districts to sponsor meetings on drafts of standards documents; these meetings could become the seeds of teacher networks constructed to implement national or state standards frameworks. The term "implementing" here means discussing, building curriculum around, and developing pedagogical strategies for the standards. Given the lack of full-time staff in most affiliates, it is imperative that the national offices help to set up and structure the agenda for reviewing national documents. Perhaps the national organization can also encourage dialogues between local affiliates and state policymakers through special meetings to discuss the national drafts and their potentials for state efforts.

Conclusion

In this paper, I have discussed the challenges faced by current national standards projects, particularly as these projects seek to develop consensus around leading ideas in the various curricular areas, and as they try to create a new sense of professional responsibility and community. Current efforts confront a much different education policy environment than did the National Council of Teachers of Mathematics. Furthermore, the nature of some disciplines makes achieving consensus and leadership a greater challenge. But by working through their local and state affiliates, and engaging a wider array of members, as well as state and local policymakers in the review and feedback process, subject-matter associations can contribute to, and benefit from, the development of national content standards.

References

Archbald, D. A. 1994. "On the Design and Purposes of State Curriculum Guides: A Comparison of Mathematics and Social Studies Guides from Four States." New Brunswick, N.J.: Consortium for Policy Research in Education.

Ball, D. L. 1992. "Implementing the NCTM Standards: Hopes and Hurdles." East Lansing, Mich.: National Center for Research on Teacher Learning. Issue paper 92–2.

Bishop, A. J. 1990. "Mathematical Power to the People." *Harvard Educational Review* 60:357–69.

Brinkley, E. 1993. "Michigan Group Designs Assessment Frameworks and Is Paid for Its Effort." National Council of Teachers of English Council-Grams LVI(3): August/September, 1–4.

Carlson, C. G. 1992. *Metamorphosis of Mathematics Education*. Princeton, N.J.: Educational Testing Service.

Cohen, D., and J. Spillane. 1993. "Policy and Practice: The Relations Between Governance and Instruction." In S. Fuhrman, ed., *Designing Coherent Education Policy: Improving the System*. San Francisco: Jossey-Bass.

Corcoran, T. B., and U. Rouk. 1985. "Using Natural Channels for School Improvement: A Report on Four Years of the Urban Development Program." Philadelphia: Research for Better Schools.

Curry, B., and T. Temple. 1992. *Using Curriculum Frameworks for Systemic Reform*. Alexandria, Va.: Association for Supervision and Curriculum Development.

Goals 3 and 4 Technical Planning Group. 1993. "Promises to Keep: Creating High Standards for American Students." A Report to the National Education Goals Panel. Washington, D.C.: National Education Goals Panel.

Jackson, P. W. 1983. "The Reform of Science Education: A Cautionary Tale." *Daedalus* 112:143–66.

Little, J. W. 1989. "District Policy Choices and Teachers' Professional Development Opportunities." *Educational Evaluation and Policy Analysis* 11:165–79.

Little, J. W. 1993. "Teacher Professional Development in a Climate of Educational Reform." *Educational Evaluation and Policy Analysis* 15:129–51.

Massell, D. 1994a. "Setting Standards in Mathematics and Social Studies." *Education and Urban Society* 20:118–41.

Massell, D. 1994b. "Three Challenges for National Content Standards." *Education and Urban Society* 20:185–95.

Massell, D. 1994c. "Achieving Consensus: Setting the Agenda for State Curriculum Reform." In S. Fuhrman and R. Elmore, eds., *Governing Curriculum*. Arlington, Va.: Association for Supervision and Curriculum Development.

Massell, D., and S. H. Fuhrman. 1994. "Ten Years of State Education Reform, 1983–1993: Overview with Four Case Studies." New Brunswick, N.J.: Consortium for Policy Research in Education.

Massell, D., and M. Kirst. 1994. "Determining National Content Standards: An Introduction." *Education and Urban Society* 20:107–18.

McLaughlin, M. W. 1991. "The Rand Change Agent Study: Ten Years Later." In A. R. Odden, ed., *Education Policy Implementation*, 143–55. Albany, N.Y.: State University of New York.

Moore, D., and A. Hyde. 1981. "Making Sense of Staff Development: An Analysis of Staff Development Programs and their Costs in Urban School Districts." Chicago: Designs for Change.

Myers, M. 1994. "Problems and Issues Facing the National Standards Project in English." *Education and Urban Society* 20:141–57.

National Council on Education Standards and Testing. 1992. "Raising Standards for American Education." Washington, D.C.: U.S. Government Printing Office.

National Council of Teachers of Mathematics. 1980. *An Agenda for Action: Recommendations for School Mathematics of the 1980s.* Reston, Va.: National Council of Teachers of Mathematics.

National Council of Teachers of Mathematics. 1989. *Curriculum and Evaluation Standards for School Mathematics.* Reston, Va.: National Council of Teachers of Mathematics.

National Council of Teachers of Mathematics. 1991. *Professional Standards for Teaching Mathematics.* Reston, Va.: National Council of Teachers of Mathematics.

Romberg, T. A. 1988. "NCTM's Standards: A Rallying Flag for Mathematics Teachers." *Educational Leadership* 50:36.

Smith, M. and J. O'Day. 1991. "Systemic School Reform." In S. Fuhrman and B. Malen, eds., *The Politics of Curriculum and Testing.* Bristol, Pa.: Falmer.

Walker, D. 1990. *Fundamentals of Curriculum.* N.Y.: Harcourt, Brace Jovanovich.

Yee, G., and M. Kirst. 1994. "The New Science Curriculum of the 1950s and 1960s." *Education and Urban Society* 20:158–71.

13

Problems and Issues Facing the National Standards Project in English

MILES MYERS

Miles Myers is executive director,
National Council of Teachers of English

Introduction

Since the late 1800s, at least four national commissions have proposed a
set of national standards for the content of English studies and English
language arts, and each has left unresolved a problem with which future
English teachers have had to struggle. The first commission was the National Education Association's (NEA) Committee of Ten, which in 1892
appointed 10 subject-matter conferences to describe the core content of
the secondary curriculum. The Committee named English as 1 of the 10
subject conferences, thereby providing the first national endorsement for
English as a school subject, and named English literature and language
as the core of an English course, thereby giving English literature for the
first time a nationally recognized status in the public schools (Berlin 1987).
Literature, to a large degree, dominated the 1894 curriculum because
selected moral touchstones from literature were thought to knit together
a cohesive cultural heritage and to build character and civility. The teaching of writing and much of traditional language study were assigned a
secondary role.

Prior to the 1894 report, English was often regarded as a combination
of language history, grammar study, and the reading of Homer and various
Greek myths in translation. The 1894 report gave English "the necessary
unification of disparate studies" (Applebee 1974, 33) by putting English

literature at the center. The report also addressed the tension between goals for all students and goals for the college preparatory student by putting the college preparatory student at the top of the secondary school agenda (Applebee 1974; National Education Association 1894). This view of English left unresolved, of course, the problem of English for all students and the social need to use English for communication in business and government.

Within 25 years, a second national commission had decided to reject the 1894 report's emphasis on the college preparatory students in secondary English, to give the content of elementary schools some serious attention, to include all students in K through 12 schools, and to track secondary students into two types of English, one focusing on college preparatory English and the other focusing on vocational and citizenship needs. College preparatory English in this second national report was quite similar to the English of the 1894 report, structuring English as literary periods and as moral touchstones. But vocational English was different. It structured English as writing for everyday communication, reading drills, basic word lists, and reading selections with the "power to arouse interest" but not necessarily with any "excellence of style" (National Education Association 1917).

This second commission and its supplemental committees published the *Cardinal Principles of Secondary Education* in 1916, the *Reorganization of English in Secondary Schools* in 1917, and between 1915 and 1919 several papers from the NEA's committee on Economy of Time in Education. The National Council of Teachers of English (NCTE), organized in 1911, helped initiate this second national commission as part of a revolt of high school teachers against the Uniform Book List and control of high school content standards by college faculty. Remember that college faculty at the time were simply following the 1894 mandate to organize secondary school English around the needs of the college preparatory student.

But by 1916 secondary teachers were insisting that secondary schools had a role different from that of colleges, a role in which teaching and pedagogy had a much higher status and in which English was taught to *all* students, not just the few. The 1917 *Reorganization of English* said that English was to be "social in content and social in methods of acquirement" (46) and was to be organized around "expressional and interpretive experiences of the greatest possible social value to a given class" (27). Some observers thought the 1916 and 1917 reports left unresolved a number of issues raised by, among others, John Dewey and Fred Newton Scott. For one thing, Dewey and Scott wanted the curriculum to emphasize personal growth and participation in democratic forums, but the two-track system of the reports of 1916 and 1917 focused instead on vocational and college requirements. Other observers have argued that these 1917 standards did not change content very much (Applebee 1974). The 1917 college preparatory courses, for example, continued the 1894 emphasis on cultural heritage and moral touchstones. But others have argued that these standards of 1916 and 1917 shifted English to a vocational emphasis on skills and processes and a deemphasis of content (Hirsch 1988).

The report of the second national commission was one part of an overall effort to centralize schooling through testing, management, and sequenced learning. The 1917 report's emphasis on processes for the general student was generally consistent with Edward Thorndike's machine-scored tests, Elwood P. Cubberly's centralized, business structures for schools, and B. F. Skinner's behaviorist theory of learning. As a result of these trends, many English classes for the general student began to be turned into a series of graded, sequenced, machine-scored drills, almost devoid of cultural content. In fact, by the 1950s English for the college preparatory student had become about one-third of the high school English curriculum, and this college preparatory area had become the only area in secondary English where students actually wrote whole essays. Throughout this period, textbooks and machine-scored tests, driven by state, local, and school site adoption processes, became the major instruments for standards setting.

The 1916 reform effort, unlike the 1894 effort, did not ignore elementary schools. Between 1915 and 1919 the NEA's Committee on the Economy of Time in Education produced papers on minimum reading rates by S. A. Courtis, on graded texts by J. H. Hoshinson, and on principles of teaching reading by William S. Gray. Between 1915 and 1919 these reports and the others reorganized elementary reading instruction around basal readers, sequenced instruction (Goodman, Shannon, Freeman, and Murphy 1988), and a "machine-like system of interrelated communication skills possessing a hierarchical structure" (McEwan 1992, 101). In reading, the parts became letters, syllables, words, and communication skills, and in literature the parts became character, plot, foreshadowing, contrast, figures of speech, rhyme, and so forth. The reading parts came from the new technicians of reading who defined texts as a form of behaviorism, and the literature parts came from new critics like I. A. Richards (1924), who argued that literary language was a poetic subject quite different from the language of communication and information. In other words, the two-track system of *The Cardinal Principles* was from the beginning built into the assumptions of English as subject. English became something called reading *and* literature, and English in elementary schools largely became reading.

In summary then, the Committee of Ten's Report of 1894 and the *Reorganization of English* report of 1917 had distinctly different approaches to the English curriculum. The 1894 report, emphasizing the college preparatory student, seemed to capture what Berlin (1987) called the rhetoric of the liberal culture. In this view, young men could write because literature made "young men more sensitive, more observant, more just, more consistent," an approach that was said to be "peculiarly adapted to the training of better men" (Osgood 1915, 234–35).

The 1917 report, however, aimed for a scientific view of writing in which composition courses focused on techniques for organization, clarity, and efficiency. The primary purpose of vocational and general English courses was to teach people practical writing—to teach them to write, for example, for business and professional purposes. The 1917 report had within it the possibilities of another view of writing—that is, the view of Dewey and Scott that writing should be a balance of the political and the personal, one's social participation in a democracy and one's exploration of one's own development (Berlin, 1987, pp. 46–47). But the emphasis of the curriculum reform reports between 1915 and 1919 was on thinking processes as defined by the behaviorism of the day and on communication skills for the vocational or general student, not on participation in democracy and personal growth. The issue of English for personal growth was left unresolved as was the question of whether tracking served *all* students well.

Forty years after the publication of *Reorganization of English* (1917), the nation was jolted by *Sputnik* (fall of 1957) and an emerging fear that the nation was about to be overrun by the Soviet Union. As a result, the United States turned once again to its schools and especially to the content of K through 12 curriculum for solutions to a national crisis. Education and the English teaching profession responded first with the Basic Issues conferences funded by the Ford Foundation in 1958, second with the Commission on English appointed by the College Board in 1959, and third with Project English from the National Defense Education Act (NDEA) of the 1960s. From these projects came a reconstruction of English as a disciplinary tripod of language, literature, and composition. The new English of this disciplinary tripod was organized around the findings of a new cognitive science emphasizing schema, structures in the mind, and information processing.

At first, Congress and the federal government ignored English and its contribution to the nation's agenda, passing the National Defense Education Act in 1958 without any funding for English. But after the NCTE Executive Committee in 1961 sent a copy of the *National Interest and the Teaching of English* (Committee on the National Interest 1961) to every member of the House and Senate, Congress in late 1961 passed Project English, putting English onto the list of the nation's top priorities in education. As a result, the federal government funded three types of staff development and standards activities for English teachers—research projects, curriculum centers to write curriculum guides, and professional activities for developing a consensus around these guides. These curriculum guides, shaped by the research findings of college faculty, were the primary method of standards setting. These guides differed from the present approach in two significant ways. First, the guides were developed at several regional centers. Thus there were several guides, not one. This approach had several attractive advantages, as I will note later. One advantage is the multiplicity of approaches. Second, these guides were accepted as the way to reform schools. There was no apparent awareness that curriculum guides could not change schooling without changes in testing and school organization.

These various standards-setting projects of the 1960s did have a kind of consensus. Project English publications from 1961 on, the two publications of the Basic Issues conferences (*The Basic Issues in the Teaching of English* [Stone 1964], and *An Articulated English Program: An Hypothesis to Test* 1959), and the publication of the College Board's Commission on English, *Freedom and Discipline in English* (1965), agreed that each part of the disciplinary tripod of language, literature, and composition had its own classification system of structure and processes. From the linguists came the cognitive structure of language (e.g., Chomsky's transformational grammar), from the New Critics came universal structures for literature (e.g., Northrup Frye's modes), and from rhetoric and sometimes linguistics came structures for composition (e.g., Christensen's sentences). These structures described English in a way quite different from the behaviorist models of the liberal tradition dominant between 1916 and 1959. In addition, there was a new verbal commitment to *all* students. The Basic Issues documents, arguing against the 1916 tracking of vocational and college preparatory students, suggested that all students be taught the tripod: "What can we do with the best students? If such an approach is good for them, it must be good for everyone" (Applebee 1974).

This commitment to all seemed to arise from the fear that English for the general student was taking over English departments as mass education grew. The solution: Teach all students college preparatory English. The Basic Issues conference warned that as a result of the 1917 emphasis on everyday skills, "the fundamental liberal discipline of English" had been replaced "at some levels of schooling, by ad hoc training in how to write a letter, how to give a radio speech, manners, dating, telephoning, vocational guidance" (Stone 1964, p. 6). A similar warning appeared in the College

Board's twelfth recommendation urging "that the core of the English program be defined as the study of language, literature, and composition, written and oral, and that matters not clearly related to such study be excluded from it" (College Board's Commission on English 1965, 2). Michael Shugrue (1968), executive director of the Modern Language Association, concluded that these documents "made it possible for English teachers to develop an English curriculum with clearer goals" (27). But the more accurate assessment could be that these documents outlined the shift from the standards of the early 1900s to the new standards for the 1960s.

The ink was hardly dry on the documents from Project English, the College Board, and the Basic Issues conferences before tensions erupted in the English teaching community around issues raised by the Dartmouth conference of August–September 1966, by the Chapter I English/reading programs of 1965, and by the political activists trained in the free speech and civil rights movements of the 1960s. During the Dartmouth conference, English teachers from the United States found that their colleagues from the United Kingdom were critical and sometimes even hostile toward the Basic Issues definition of English as a tripod of language, literature, and composition. According to the United Kingdom's John Dixon, English teachers faced a choice among three models of mind and literacy—the first the *skills* model based on a nation's needs in initial literacy, the second the *cultural heritage* model based on a nation's needs for "civilizing and socially unifying content," and third the *personal growth* model focusing on the individual's effort to find significance in his or her life (Dixon, 1969). Dartmouth did not distinguish between the cultural heritage model of 1894 (English as cultural history and moral touchstones) and the tripod model of 1959 (English as an object of study) because both represented to Dartmouth an academic approach that ignored the needs of individuals in K through 12 schools. In place of the genres, fictional modes, and archetypal characters of the tripod model of 1959–1965, Dartmouth proposed the personal growth model in which "the English lesson is . . . a time in which order may be brought to some of the bewildering elements [of the adolescent situation] and the individual encouraged to make sense of his personal world" (Medway 1989, 14).

Whereas Dartmouth was reconstructing English as "personal growth" for individual development, the Chapter I programs of 1966 were reconstructing English as skills for employment and political participation. (See Chapter 1, formerly Title 1, of the Elementary and Secondary Education Act.) The differences between Dartmouth and Chapter I were often extreme. Dartmouth's personal growth model of English emphasized literature, and Chapter I programs often emphasized reading for information.

Dartmouth models emphasized processes for personal growth, but Chapter I emphasized writing and reading skills for employment and citizenship. However, both Dartmouth and Chapter I advocates agreed on the necessity to broaden the list of books typically assigned in English and English language arts. To meet the needs of individuals and different groups of students, high school and college English teachers from both Chapter I and Dartmouth models created courses on Asian literature, African American literature, Latino literature, and different registers of language.

This trend was consistent with the position of political activists such as Stanford English Professor Bruce Franklin, who argued that the New Criticism of I. A. Richards, Northrup Frye, and Kenneth Brooks had created the rule of interpretive "objectivity" to ignore the politics of time, place, gender, ethnicity, and so on. Franklin (1970) and others argued that literary theories like the "affective" fallacy (the fallacy of heeding one's feelings while reading a work) and the "intentional fallacy" (the fallacy of using author intent to explain a work's meaning) were simply devices to train students to ignore the political world in which they lived. By the end of the 1970s, "objectivity of meaning" was being attacked as a retreat from the "politics of meaning," the "curriculum of diversity" was being attacked as "a shopping mall" without any coherent direction (Powell, Farrar, and Cohen 1985), the "curriculum of skills and processes" was being attacked as empty of content (Hirsch 1988), and the emphasis on the personal was being attacked as lacking history and the social contingencies of race and gender (Eagleton 1983).

Instead of finding a consensus, the field of English found new differences to divide the field. In the United Kingdom, Terry Eagleton in his 1985 keynote to the National Association of Teachers of English charged that the personal growth model ignored politics:

> Why does it [the personal growth model] insist so dogmatically on abstracting personal values and qualities from the whole concrete context—political society—in which they are embedded? Why does it continually offer us the cerebral abstraction of something called interpersonal relationships or personal growth or immediate experience, when a moment's thought is enough to reveal that such things gain their fully concrete significance *only* in the whole political and historical context which shapes them?

Eagleton's views constituted a critical theory/problem critique model of English, one quite different from personal growth, cultural heritage, or basic skills traditions. By the 1980s, most teachers and researchers in the English language arts community knew that the tensions among the tripod model of the early 1960s, the New Criticism of the 1950s and 1960s, the

Dartmouth model of the mid-1960s, and the Chapter I models of the late 1960s had not been satisfactorily resolved. Everyone knew there was a new commitment to English for all, but almost everyone was uncertain about what direction to take to change the 75-year tradition of *The Cardinal Principles*. For a time, there was an emerging consensus around the reinstatement of writing as a central part of the English curriculum and a new emphasis on writing and reading as meaning-making processes, but the public seemed uncertain about its goals for schools, calling for basic skills one moment and high-order skills the next.

At about this time, the Secretary's Commission on Achieving Necessary Skills' *A Nation at Risk* (1983) entered the debate and proposed to answer the question "Why do we need schools? Why do we need English?" The answer was that U.S. schools should be teaching to solve national problems of citizenship and economics. This approach did not apologize for the fact that English was a cultural invention to meet social needs. In a dozen school reform books and legislation following *A Nation at Risk*, the public seemed to abandon its call for back-to-the-basics and instead called for problem-solving strategies at "higher" levels of literacy and numeracy, an understanding and appreciation of pluralism at various levels of cultural practice, and a caretaking sensibility developed in new forms of social capital for socializing the young. The need for literacy/numeracy referred to new standards of reading, writing, oracy (speaking and listening), numeracy (mathematics), and critical analysis (problem solving). The public had begun to expect students to be able to do inferential and critical reading of whole pieces, to write whole pieces, to use computers, and to translate a problem from one sign system to another—for example, from numbers to visuals or from school books to a situation in daily life. This higher standard of literacy was to be available to all students, largely in untracked settings.

Pluralism referred to the need for new standards of multicultural understanding in which citizens democratically interact with the diversity within their communities and within the world, a diversity increasingly connected by new networks of communication but always differentiated by history and values. To achieve multicultural understanding, each citizen was expected to have experience with cross-cultural exchanges, not just local field trips; with collaborative work, not just individual efforts; with texts as negotiated meanings, not just as delivered opinions; and with language as value laden, not just as a neutral container. The key challenge in pluralism was to maintain respect for differences and at the same time commit to fundamental tenets of democratic cohesion.

The third need for a caretaking sensibility, a kind of social capital, evolved from a series of problems involving the care of children and youth—latchkey children, drug abuse, teenage pregnancy, lack of food and shelter for the increasing numbers of children living in poverty, and the decline of adult volunteers in youth activities, to name a few. Senator Daniel Moynihan charged that our nation might be the first to forget how to care for children and youth. The problem was especially acute for disadvantaged youth because for them the interactive support of a caring adult or older mentor (even an older child) appeared to be the single most potent predictor of success. This need for social capital required a new standard of community service for all students—for example, redefining the school-community boundary first by institutionalizing the use of our students as tutors and as assistants-to-adults in the schools and in the community and second by initiating community service as a prerequisite for all youth attending high schools and colleges. Since 1983, we have learned that these three social needs are not likely to be met or to generate healthy environments for learning unless we radically change our mainstream conceptions of curriculum, school structure, testing, accountability, and, of course, English.

In 1987, a half-dozen organizations of English teachers came together as the English Coalition to review how English studies and English language arts could or should respond to these various demands for change. The English Coalition asserted its (and Dartmouth's) view of the learner as an active maker of meaning who is seeking personal growth through language (Peter Elbow's *What Is English?*; Julie Jensen's *Stories to Grow On*; and *The English Coalition Conference: Democracy Through Language* from NCTE). But some participants at the coalition felt that the coalition's emphasis on "'making meaning' and 'active learning' as individuals implied that we are free autonomous subjects" (Elbow 1990 19). Alas, the problem of social and historical contingency emerged again. The coalition seemed to agree generally with Gerald Graff that we have kept issues of theory and ideology far too hidden in our descriptions of knowledge in English (Graff 1992).

Most agreed with Shirley Brice Heath who suggested that English be defined as (a) *using* language actively in a diversity of ways and settings and as (b) *reflecting on* our use of language and the use of others (Elbow 1990). The English Coalition spent considerable time attempting to define "reflecting on" and finally concluded that the English curriculum must include "theorizing about language" (xxii), including the different perspectives of gender, age, cultural/ethnic differences, and so forth. In general, then, the coalition attempted to add history and politics to the personal growth model of Dartmouth by asserting the importance of historical and social premises and stipulating that democratic principles governed

language interactions in the English classrooms of the United States (Elbow 1990).

These democratic principles included an emphasis in English courses
on the use of English for political purposes, on the development of con-
versational habits recognizing our democratic obligations to both groups
and individuals, and on social and historical negotiations of our definitions of excellence. In addition, Heath urged the coalition to examine the
conditions of teaching and learning in English classrooms, and as a result
of this examination, the coalition adopted a statement of rights and conditions for both students and teachers (Lloyd-Jones and Lunsford 1989).

The English Coalition in this last act took a direction quite different
from Dartmouth, from the Basic Issues conferences, and from the 1917
report, *The Reorganization of English*. That is, English teachers took the
ultimate step and declared that their method of teaching and the student's
method of learning could not be separated as an issue from the way schools
were organized. The English Coalition asked the following questions: Do
teachers have phones, do they have office space, and, in other words, do
they have the space to be learners in schools? The coalition also asked
about students: Do they have libraries in their schools, do they have choices
of materials, do they have the space to be learners in schools? These
institutional questions in the English Coalition reports are among its best
kept secrets and its most revolutionary statements.

The coalition had hardly issued its last publication (Elbow 1990) when
the nation's discussion of curriculum in K through 12 schools began to
have a federal and national character quite different from curriculum reform discussions in 1894, 1916, the 1960s, and 1983. Even in the early
1980s, the traditions of local and state control assured everyone that national and federal curriculum and assessment would not dominate K through
12 schools. Of course, Chapter I programs had nationalized parts of the
English curriculum, and the decision by states to use scores from the
National Assessment of Educational Progress (NAEP) to compare themselves with other states had been a step toward national assessment. But
by the 1990s, the National Board of Professional Teaching Standards was
creating national standards for expertise in English teaching, the New
Standards Project was attempting to create among districts and states a
national movement toward portfolio assessment in English, and finally the
federal government was preparing to fund projects to describe standards
of curriculum content in various subjects, including a project to describe
K through 12 curriculum content in English. In October 1992, the U.S.
Office of Education funded the Center for the Study of Reading at the
University of Illinois, the International Reading Association, and the National Council of Teachers of English to develop standards in the English
language arts.

What is the difference between federal and national standards? First, federally certified standards may be voluntary in some instances, but, in other instances, they may become a requirement for federal funding. National standards are a national consensus, not a federal mandate. The move toward federalization of education standards may result from the claims of civil rights groups that curriculum content standards represent a civil right, an opportunity to learn, which all students should have under the guarantees of the Constitution. Recently an Alabama state court ruled that the Alabama K through 12 school system was unconstitutional because the school system did not provide an adequate opportunity for students to learn to communicate as citizens of the world and to attain a sufficient understanding of the arts to enable each student to appreciate his or her cultural heritage and the cultural heritage of others (*Alabama Coalition for Equity, et al. v. Governor Guy Hunt, et al.* 1993, 122). In June, The *Wall Street Journal* editorialized that this case was proposing a new standard of educational equity.

Indeed, it was. The decision is at the root of the support of many civil rights organizations for the national standards movement. Many leaders of the civil rights movement have been disappointed by the access theories of equity in *Brown v. Topeka* because access did not mean equality. For one thing, some schools spent twice as much or more on the education of each student. But equalization of money in California's *Serrano vs. Priest* did not produce equity either. First, many districts created their own foundations and sources of outside support to get around the equalization of public money.

Next, even those schools with equal money sometimes tracked ethnic minorities into inadequate, basic skills programs, denying those students the opportunity to read whole books, to write whole pieces. In the view of many civil rights leaders, the standards movement provides a possible new foundation for civil rights in which an opportunity to experience an adequate content in English language arts is a civil right. But what is adequate content? Many civil rights leaders look to the English standards projects to negotiate an agreement between the public and educators on what adequate curriculum content is in English. In summary, then, standards documents may be used to launch a new kind of civil rights movement focused on educational opportunity, and, as a result, the present standards movement may begin to have a federal and national character quite different from past standards movements.

The national and federal character of the present standards movement is also related to changes in industry and business. The business community has begun to put pressure on schools to teach a different form of literacy, calling for transformative "readings" or interpretations (e.g., developing translations from one group to another), distributed problem solving (e.g., using computers and engaging in collaborative work), and situated thinking (e.g., shifting sign systems, settings, and modes). The Secretary's Commission on Achieving Necessary Skills (SCANS) Report for America 2000 (SCANS 1992) is one example. This report proposed restructuring both factories and schools to use these skills and to teach them. As a result, at the same time that the federal government funded the English Standards Project, the Clinton administration also introduced a federal standards project providing incentives for business and industry to upgrade skills in the workplace. The response of businesses was not unlike that of subject-matter organizations. Many business leaders said, "We think it should be industry-led, not one-third industry."

Not one of the previous curriculum standards movements, it seems to me, had before them the complexity now facing the English Standards Project. Consider the many models of English that we can find in the classroom:

- English as our cultural heritage and/or moral touchstones—the 1894 report;
- English as a hierarchy of communication skills and/or a communication machine with parts—the 1917 report;
- English as a discipline with a structural tripod of language, literature, and composition—the 1959 Basic Issues report, the College Board 1965 report;
- English as a language process for personal growth—the Dartmouth conference, 1966;
- English as language processes for skills and strategies to get employed—Chapter I programs, 1965; and
- English as the use of language for problem solving, both personal and social—the English Coalition, 1987.

Each of these perspectives has advocates within the community of English teachers, some proposing that English be viewed as communications skills and others insisting that English be viewed as a form of culture practice embedded in individual life and in social history. In other words, the task of describing content in English is happening at the very moment that the foundations of the discipline are a matter of professional and public debate. We are not describing a target that is standing still.

The basic differences between the past standards movements of 1894, 1916, and the 1960s and the present standards movement are first that the learner is active, not passive; second, that meaning is socially and historically contingent, not universal for all times; and third, that the purpose of English is the development of language for political power and the creation and appreciation of connections—intertextual, interpersonal, and intergroup. These aims are commitments for all students. In other words, "higher-order thinking skills" will no longer be reserved for the few. The primary purpose of English is not the learning of decoding skills, although that can be a means to the larger end, or the memorizing of moral touchstones, although this can be helpful in some situations. In summary, the present standards movement is making fundamental revisions in our views of the learning and teaching of English.

The present standards movement also presents a serious challenge to the traditional public policy role of organizations like NCTE. A profession is created as a result of a compact between the profession and the public in which the public agrees to cede to the profession some prerogatives in exchange for a high level of professional service. The public has ceded to individual teachers two areas of privilege. First, the public limits the role of the public school teacher to those with credentials. This makes the professional preparation of teachers a matter of public interest and constitutes a public acknowledgment that there is something called teacher knowledge.

Second, the public allows public school teachers to "talk with" or to negotiate with local boards on policy matters related to the employee status of teachers, matters such as salary, benefits, and working days. But, the public has not ceded to the teaching profession the responsibility for establishing standards of teaching practice or standards of curriculum content. These two areas have been designated as matters of public policy, not professional choice.

For example, the courts and many other public agencies have ruled that K through 12 teachers do not have the academic freedom to determine their own curriculum—for example, assign any book they want—and do not have the academic freedom to select their own pedagogy. These decisions are a public responsibility and are decided in the forums of local boards and government commissions. When teachers are brought before courts to be dismissed for their pedagogy or selection of books, then public representatives appear before the court to explain why the pedagogy or books were contrary to public policy. At that point, the teacher can introduce expert witnesses who can testify why the pedagogy or books could, in fact, be regarded as consistent with public policy. The expert witnesses will get nowhere if they testify that the public policy was wrong.

In the future, teachers and their witnesses will point to standards statements as a rationale for selecting particular materials or methods, possibly for school change. The interesting turn of events is that national standards documents, which are largely shaped in the professional forums of subject-matter organizations, will begin to shape public policy at the board level. The point is that the documents of the standards movement may become a powerful political lever for shaping public policy in curriculum, far more powerful than any curriculum document from the past. In the last six months, I have heard more than one public official justify public policy in mathematics curriculum on the grounds that the policy was consistent with the standards documents of the National Council of Teachers of Mathematics (NCTM). This trend, I think, constitutes a major change in the direction of curriculum influence. The subject-matter professions are being given a much larger role.

The federalizing of standards in the K through 12 curriculum challenges some key professional traditions of disciplinary discussion. Within NCTE, standards are developed by task forces and committees through a process of consensus. By and large, the assumption is that people can be persuaded to regulate their practices by some shared norms as long as people have the opportunity to freely participate in the discussion. This approach works for professional groups because disciplinary norms are not the result of coercion and are not the result of norms mandated or imposed by government agencies. In other words, the standards-setting process in groups like NCTE evolves through a professional consensus, which develops solidarity without violating autonomy.

This consensus process is useful to all parties within the political system because it helps clarify what people support and what they oppose and, at the same time, helps build a common vocabulary for maintaining some group cohesion. This process is very similar to Gramsci's concept of hegemony, which, says Harvey Graff (1987), permits us to escape the "crudities of social control theories, modernization and enlightenment notions, ideas of overt coercion and excessively voluntaristic interpretations" (11). This approach has worked quite well within the traditional forums of subject-matter organizations and within many states. But the current standards movement threatens all of this.

The federal government proposes to claim sovereignty over standards by establishing a panel to put a seal of approval on some standards and not on others; thus the traditional consensus process within subject-matter organizations is bypassed. To maintain its commitment to consensus within a professional forum, NCTE may find it necessary to assert that the English standards document should *not* be submitted for certification to the federal government by any of the parties developing the document. The very size, centrality, funding, and pervasiveness of the federal government gives it a special ideological position in any education discussion. The feds have the well-known elephant effect: Never ask an elephant, "Have you been invited"; always ask, "Where do you want to sit?"

What can be done to prevent the national standards document from stifling discussion by exerting its own ideological dominance through the elephant effect of the feds? First, NCTE must give considerable attention to the care and feeding of critique. This means that the standards document itself must include some of the voices of difference and dissent, must include within the document the critique of the document itself. In addition, NCTE must continue to publish voices of dissent in its publications (see NCTE 1993), and should consider commissioning an NCTE book committed to a critique of the standards documents. Finally, NCTE must ensure that the reviewers of various drafts of the standards document include those who are opposed to the standards-setting project. The key problem is not just protecting the openness of forums within NCTE. An important problem is the immense challenge of protecting some local knowledge and insight from domination and even elimination in federal mandates and curriculum policies.

To avoid ideological dominance, to offset federal sovereignty over standards, and to protect the local integrity of the school site community, the standards document must represent the shaping of English as a face-to-face process at school sites. One approach to this problem is the decision of the various task forces of the English standards project to describe a standard through a combination of *statements* about what students should be able to do, *elaborations* of these statements through a listing of the beliefs underlying the standard, *vignettes* showing various realizations of the standard in the classroom, samples of student interactions between teachers and students, various *accomplishments* associated with the standard, and research to references illuminating the standard. The standards statement, its elaboration, and the vignettes, the accomplishments, and the research are intended to communicate to public policymakers the many ways a standard can be realized at school sites. Samples of student accomplishments are intended to show the variety of ways students can exhibit what they know and can do, and finally the citations in the document are intended to direct teachers and others to the variety of approaches used by various school sites and communities.

Throughout the document, the classroom and the school site are the primary audience. In fact, one goal of the Standards Project in English Language Arts is to help each site develop a description of its own language policy. Without participation at the local site, there will obviously be no ownership. The national standards document must be anchored in school site discussions, involving parents and students, as well as teachers, and must not depend on the standards bureaucracy of the federal government. Thus the documents of the various standards projects should be positioned as a foundation, support, and supplement to local, school site decision making. To assure that this local process happens, NCTE and other groups must work with district language arts coordinators, state superintendents, and others to position the English standards document within a program of school site activities and local staff development. One proposal might be a request that each school provide several hours of staff development to write a standards statement describing the curriculum at the school site and that NCTE commit to publish various examples of these school site documents, offering these documents as guides to the national standards document.

Finally, the standards document in curriculum content will not be able to avoid the very controversial issue of English delivery standards. Once we have a picture of what the English curriculum should aim for, the next question is "What does it take to get there?" In English this inevitably leads, for example, to the need for an extensive library of trade books for classrooms and schools and to the need for paper, copying machines, and ways to publish and distribute samples of student work. In the English Coalition, the question also led to the need for office space and phones for each teacher. These delivery standards, as one might suspect, have already been characterized as "too expensive" and an "intrusion on local control." For NCTE and other subject-matter groups the issue clearly calls for a response, but the direction this response will take is, at this time, uncertain.

In summary, then, the various standards movements over the last 100 years in the United States have:

1. Shifted English from a course for a few to a course for the many.
2. Shifted the definition of the learner from passive receiver of the cultural tradition to an active constructor of meaning
3. Shifted the role of literary studies from delivering readings of moral touchstones to constructing readings within diverse cultural settings
4. Moved education from strictly local agencies to an interaction of school sites with federal and state agencies
5. Shifted the public policy role of national subject-matter organizations from a minimal role to a major role.

Each of these changes will have an impact on the way subject-matter organizations function. As noted earlier, NCTE, unlike most of the other subject-matter organizations, may not move to Washington, D.C., but some part of it may have to take up residence within the Potomac circle.

References

Alabama Coalition for Equity, et al. v. Governor Guy Hunt, et al. June 9, 1993. Decision by Circuit Judge Eugene W. Reese.

Applebee, A. N. 1974. *Tradition and Reform in the Teaching of English: A History*. Urbana, Ill.: National Council of Teachers of English.

Berlin, J. A. 1987. *Rhetoric and Reality: Writing Instruction in American Colleges, 1900–1985*. Carbondale and Edwardsville, Ill.: Southern Illinois University Press.

College Board's Commission on English. 1965. *Freedom and Discipline in English*. New York.

Committee on the National Interest. 1961. *The National Interest and the Teaching of English: A Report on the Status of the Profession*. Urbana, Ill.: National Council of Teachers of English.

Committee on the Reorganization of Secondary Education of the NEA. 1917. *Cardinal Principles of Secondary Education*. (U.S. Bureau of Education Bulletin, No. 5). Washington, D.C.: U.S. Government Printing Office.

Dixon, J. 1969. *Growth Through English* (3rd ed.). Oxford: Oxford University Press.

Eagleton, J. 1983. *Literary Theory: An Introduction*. Minneapolis: University of Minnesota Press.

Elbow, P. 1990. *What Is English?* New York: Modern Language Association of America, and Urbana, Ill.: National Council of Teachers of English.

Franklin, B. 1970. "The Teaching of Literature in the Highest Academies of the Empire." *College English*, 31, 6.

Goodman, K., P. Shannon, Y. Freeman, and S. Murphy. 1988. *Report Card on Basal Readers*. New York: Richard C. Owen.

Graff, G. 1992. *Beyond the Culture Wars*. New York: W. W. Norton.

Graff, H. 1987. *The Legacies of Literacy*. Bloomington and Indianapolis: Indiana University Press.

Hirsch, E. D., Jr. 1988. *Cultural Literacy: What Every American Needs to Know*. New York: Vintage Books.

Jensen, J. 1989. *Stories to Grow On: Demonstrations of Language Learning in K–8 Classrooms*. Portsmouth, N.H.: Heinemann.

Lloyd-Jones, R., and A. Lunsford. 1989. *The English Coalition Conference: Democracy through Language*. Urbana, Ill.: National Council of Teachers of English, and New York: Modern Language Association.

McEwan, H. 1992. "Five Metaphors for English." *English Education*, 24: 101–128.

Medway, P. 1989. "Into the Sixties: English and English Society at a Time of Change." In I. Goodson and P. Medway (eds.), *Bringing English to Order*. New York: Falmer.

National Commission on Excellence in Education. 1983. *A Nation at Risk: The Imperative for Educational Reform*. Washington, D.C.: U.S. Government Printing Office.

National Council of Teachers of English. 1993. *The Council Chronicle*. Urbana, Ill.

National Education Association. 1894. *Report of the Committee of Ten on Secondary School Studies*. New York: American Book Company for the National Education Association.

National Education Association. 1917. *Reorganization of English in Secondary Schools*. Washington, D.C.: National Education Association.

Osgood, C. 1915. "No Set Requirement of English Composition in the Freshman Year." *English Journal*. 14: 1.

Powell, A. G., E. Farrar, & D. K. Cohen. 1985. *The Shopping Mall High School*. Boston: Houghton-Mifflin.

Richards, I. A. 1924. *Principles of Literary Criticism*. New York: Harcourt, Brace and World.

Secretary's Commission on Achieving Necessary Skills, U.S. Department of Labor. 1992. *Learning a Living: A Blueprint for High Performance*. Washington, D.C.: U.S. Government Printing Office.

Shugrue, M. 1968. *English in a Decade of Change.* New York: Pegasus.

Stone, G. W., Jr. 1964. "The Basic Issues in Teaching of English." In *Issues, Problems and Approaches in the Teaching of English.* New York: Holt, Rinehart & Winston. (Original work published 1959.)

Wall Street Journal. 1991. Editorial, June 22. p. A16.

INDEX